The International Politics of Democratization

This book examines the international dimensions of democratization processes, showing the degree to which international actors, ranging from states to non-governmental players, have an influence on what were once thought of as exclusively domestic processes of political change.

The contributors to the volume look at changes in foreign policy resulting from transitions to democracy in a number of countries and regions. Some of the areas covered include:

- Portugal and Spain in Europe in the 1970s
- Brazil and Argentina in Latin America from the early 1980s
- Eastern and Central Europe in the 1990s
- Various countries in the Arab world.

The chapters adopt a theoretical and empirical perspective: while the two introductory chapters of the book place a special emphasis on interpretation and quantitative analysis of regime change and the role of international actors in such processes, the remaining chapters examine specific case studies.

The International Politics of Democratization will be of interest to students and researchers of International Relations, Politics and Democracy.

Nuno Severiano Teixeira is Professor of International Relations at the New University of Lisbon, Portugal. He has published extensively on Portuguese foreign policy and the history of European integration. He is currently Minister of National Defence of the Portuguese Government.

Routledge research in comparative politics

The International Politics of Democratization

Comparative perspectives

Edited by Nuno Severiano Teixeira

Routledge
Taylor & Francis Group

LONDON AND NEW YORK

First published 2008
by Routledge
2 Park Square, Milton Park, Abingdon, Oxon OX14 4RN

Simultaneously published in the USA and Canada
by Routledge
711 Third Avenue, New York, NY 10017

Routledge is an imprint of the Taylor & Francis Group, an informa business

First issued in paperback 2011

Typeset in Times by Wearset Ltd, Boldon, Tyne and Wear

British Library Cataloguing in Publication Data
A catalogue record for this book is available from the British Library

Library of Congress Cataloging in Publication Data
The international politics of democratization: comparative
perspectives/edited by Nuno Severiano Teixeira.
p. cm. – (Routledge Research in comparative politics; 21)
Includes bibliographical references and index.
1. International relations. 2. Democratization. 3. Comparative government.
I. Teixeira, Nuno Severiano.
JZ1242.I575 2008
327.1'1–dc22   2008002091

ISBN10: 0-415-45303-8 (hbk)
ISBN10: 0-415-66404-7 (pbk)
ISBN10: 0-203-93877-1 (ebk)

ISBN13: 978-0-415-45303-5 (hbk)
ISBN13: 978-0-415-66404-2 (pbk)
ISBN13: 978-0-203-93877-5 (ebk)

Contents

Tables

Contributors

Nuno Severiano Teixeira is Professor of International Relations at the New University of Lisbon. He was a Visiting Professor at Georgetown University (2000) and a Visiting Scholar at the Institute for European Studies, University of California, Berkeley (2004). He has published extensively on Portuguese foreign policy and the history of European integration. He is currently serving as Minister of National Defence of the Portuguese Government.

Laurence Whitehead is an Official Fellow in Politics at Nuffield College, University of Oxford, a Senior Fellow of the College, and Director of the University of Oxford Mexican Studies Centre, and served as Acting Warden of the College (2005–6). He has published extensively on various topics related to Latin American politics, democratization processes, and US and EU relations with Latin America. He is editor of an Oxford University Press series Studies in Democratization, for which series he published the first book. He currently chairs Research Committee 13 of the International Political Science Association (Comparative Democratization); and the section on Europe and Latin America of the Latin American Studies Association; is a member of the steering committee of the Euro-Latin American Network for Governability and Development (REDGOB); and has served as a Region Head for Latin America at *Oxford Analytica*.

Philippe C. Schmitter graduated from the University of Geneva, and obtained his doctorate from the University of California at Berkeley. He was a Professor at the University of Chicago (from 1967), at Stanford (1986–96), and at the European University Institute in Florence (1982–2004). He was a Visiting Professor at the Universities of Paris-I, Geneva, Mannheim and Zürich, and a Fellow of the Humboldt and Guggenheim foundations, and the Palo Alto Centre for Advanced Studies in the Behavioural Sciences. He has published books and articles on comparative politics, on regional integration, and on the transition from authoritarian rule, among other subjects. He is currently working on an emerging Euro-polity, democratization in Southern and Eastern Europe, and "post-liberal" democracy in Western Europe and North America. He is currently a Professorial Fellow at the EUI.

Geoffrey Pridham is Emeritus Professor and Senior Research Fellow at the University of Bristol, UK; and currently ESRC (Economic and Social Research Council, UK) Fellow working on *Europeanising Democratisation? EU Accession and Post-Communist Politics in Slovakia, Latvia and Romania*. He has published extensively on comparative democratization processes, democracy promotion and EU enlargement, among other topics. He was Research Associate at the Department of the Foreign Office, 1965–7; Research Associate at the Institute of Contemporary History, 1967–9; Lecturer at Bristol from 1969, Reader from 1982, Professor from 1993; Former Reviews Editor of *West European Politics*; Associate Editor of *South European Society and Politics* 1995–2003; and Director of the Centre for Mediterranean Studies 1987–2002.

Juan Carlos Pereira is Professor of Contemporary History and History of International Relations at the Geography and History Faculty of the Complutense University of Madrid. He is a Professor of Spanish Foreign Policy at the Diplomatic School of the Spanish Ministry of Foreign Affairs. He was the Director of the Department of Contemporary History at the Complutense University (1996–2004), and he is the President of the Spanish Commission of History of International Relations (1994–present). He has published many books and articles on the history of international relations, the history of European integration, and Spanish foreign policy in the twentieth century. He is currently working on the Spanish transition to democracy and its international dimensions.

Andrés Malamud is a graduate in Political Science of the University of Buenos Aires (1992). He earned his PhD in Political and Social Sciences from the European University Institute, Florence (2003). He is currently an Assistant Researcher at the Institute of Social Sciences of the University of Lisbon. He has lectured at universities in Argentina, Mexico, Portugal and Spain and has published articles in books and a great variety of scholarly journals. His research interests focus on regional integration, comparative political institutions, party politics, and European and Latin American politics.

Alexandra Barahona de Brito has a First Class degree from the University of Manchester (1983), and an M. Phil. (1990) and a D. Phil. in Politics (1993) from the University of Oxford. She works on and has published about Latin American politics, democratization, and human rights, including "transitional justice." She currently works as a freelance editorial consultant and researcher. Previous positions include: Senior Associate Researcher, IEEI (1994–2005, Lisbon) and IRELA (1997–8, Madrid); Professor of Political Theory, Modern University (2000–2003); research fellow at ICS (2005); and visiting fellow at Princeton (1999), and Yale (1991) Universities. She has two children, Carlotta and Afonso, and lives in Cascais, Portugal.

Lawrence S. Graham was Emeritus Professor of Government at the University of Texas at Austin. A specialist in public policy and comparative politics, he has had a faculty appointment at the University of Texas since 1965. Throughout his career, he has combined teaching and research with hands-on experience as a consultant with a variety of national and international organizations. This work has taken him throughout Latin America, Eastern and Southern Europe, and Africa. His publications – fourteen books and over 100 articles – have focused on development policy and administration in Latin America, principally Brazil and Mexico, and in Southern Europe, especially Portugal and Romania.

Richard Youngs is Coordinator of the Democratisation programme at FRIDE. He also lectures at the University of Warwick in the UK. Prior to joining FRIDE, he was EU Marie Curie Research Fellow from 2001 to 2004. He studied at the Universities of Cambridge (BA Hons) and Warwick (MA, PhD), and previously worked as Analyst at the Foreign and Commonwealth Office, United Kingdom.

George Joffé is a lecturer at the Centre of International Studies at the University of Cambridge and Visiting Professor of Geography at Kings College, the University of London. He specialises in the Middle East and North Africa and is currently engaged in a project studying connections between migrant communities and trans-national violence in Europe.

Acknowledgements

This book is the result of the Summer School organized by the Portuguese Institute of International Relations (*Instituto Português de Relações Internacionais*), of the New University of Lisbon (IPRI-UNL), which was held in July 2004, under the title, *The International Dimension of Democratization: Comparative Perspectives*. The aim of this project was to provide a state-of-the-art analysis of the international dimensions of democratization in light of recent theoretical developments in the field, and to compile and publish studies so as to contribute to future research projects on this topic.

The editor would like to thank the IPRI-UNL and the Óbidos local authority as organizers of the Summer School. This project would not have been possible without their generous assistance. The editor is also grateful to all those who participated in the various seminars, speakers and students alike, for engaging in such a fruitful dialogue on the international dimensions of democratization. Their contribution was vital for the success of the work presented in this book. Special thanks are due to Laurence Whitehead, who accepted our invitation to write the conclusion to this book, and George Joffé, who gave his support for publication. The editor would like to thank Alexandra Barahona de Brito who, aside from her own chapter, put the book together, translating and editing the various chapters therein, and Ana Santos Pinto, who accompanied the project from start to finish.

Acronyms

ACHR	Arab Charter of Human Rights
ACP	African, Caribbean and Pacific
AI	Amnesty International
AKP	Justice and Development Party (*Adalet ve Kalkynma Partisi*) – Turkey
AN	*An-Nahda* – Tunisia
ARENA	National Renovating Alliance (*Aliança Renovadora Nacional*) – Brazil
BAT	Air-Transported Brigade (*Brigada Aero-Transportada*) – Portugal
BMI	Independent Mixed Brigade (*Brigada Mista Independente*) – Portugal
CBI	Caribbean Basin Initiative
CDR	Democratic Convention Alliance (*Convenţia Democrată Română*) – Romania
CEEC	Central and Eastern European countries
CIA	Central Intelligence Agency
CNDH	National Human Rights Commission (*Comissão Nacional de Direitos Humanos*) – Brazil
CoE	Council of Europe
DC	Democratic Conditionality
DDR	German Democratic Republic (*Deutsches Demokratische Republik*)
EBRD	European Bank for Reconstruction and Development
ECHR	European Charter of Human Rights
ECSC	European Coal and Steel Community
EDF	European Defence Force
EEC	European Economic Community
EFTA	European Free Trade Agreement
EP	European Parliament
EU	European Union
FIS	Islamic Salvation Front (*Front Islamique du Salut*) – Algeria
FTAA	Free Trade Area of the Americas

GATT	General Agreement on Trade and Tariffs
GPC	General Popular Congress – Yemen
IACHR	Inter-American Commission of Human Rights
IAEA	International Atomic Energy Agency
ICC	International Criminal Court
ICTFY	International Criminal Tribunal for the Former Yugoslavia
ICTR	International Criminal Tribunal for Rwanda
IFI	International Financial Institution
IMF	International Monetary Fund
IO	International Organization
IPU	International Parliamentary Union
ISAF	International Stabilization Force
ISI	Import-Substitution Industrialization
JAI	Islamic Action Front (*Jabhat al-'Amal al-Islami*) – Jordan
JI	Jama's Islamic Group (*Jama'a al-Islamiyya*) – Egypt
MENA	Middle East and North Africa
MEPI	Middle East Partnership Initiative – USA
MERCOSUR	Southern Common Market
MFA	Armed Forces Movement (*Movimento Forças Armadas*) – Portugal
MINUGUA	United Nations Mission in Guatemala
NAFTA	North American Free Trade Association
NATO	North Atlantic Treaty Alliance
NGO	Non-Governmental Organization
NSC	National Security Council – Turkey
NSS	National Security Strategy – USA
OAS	Organization of American States
ONUSAL	United Nations Mission in El Salvador
OSCE	Organization for Security and Cooperation in Europe
PA	Palestinian Authority
PALOP	Officially Portuguese Speaking Countries (*Países de Língua Oficial Portuguesa*)
PICAB	Argentina–Brazil Integration and Cooperation Programme (*Programa de Integração e Cooperação Argentina–Brasil*)
PJ	Justicialist Party (*Partido Justicialista*) – Argentina
PJD	Justice and Development Party (*Parti de la Justice et du Développement*) – Morocco
PLC	Palestinian Legislative Council
PNDR	National Human Rights Programme (*Programa Nacional de Direitos Humanos*) – Brazil
PSOE	Spanish Socialist Workers Party (*Partido Socialista Obrero Español*)
PT	Workers Party (*Partidos dos Trabalhadores*) – Brazil
SAFTA	South American Free Trade Area
SIP	*Sociedad Inter-Americana de Prensa* (Inter-American Press Society)

SMK	Party of the Hungarian Coalition (*Slovakia Strana Maïarskej Koalície*) – Slovakia
UCD	Union of the Democratic Centre (*Unión de Centro Democrático*) – Spain
UCR	Radical Civic Union (*Unión Cívica Radical*) – Argentina
UN	United Nations
UNCED	United Nations Conference on Environment and Development
UNCHR	United Nations Charter of Human Rights
UNDP	United Nations Development Programme
UNEP	United Nations Environmental Programme
UNHRC	United Nations Human Rights Commission
UNITA	National Union for the Total Independence of Angola (*União Nacional para a Independência Total de Angola*)
UNSC	United Nations Security Council
UPD	Unit for the Promotion of Democracy
USSR	Union of Soviet Socialist Republics
WB	World Bank
WEU	Western European Union
WMD	Weapons of Mass Destruction
WTO	World Trade Organization

Introduction

The changing context for democracy promotion

Nuno Severiano Teixeira

When this book was first conceived, the world looked very different. Even though the invasion of Iraq caused grave anxieties, the general view was that good governance and democracy to ensure popular participation and legitimization was the solution to the problems facing the developing world, and that international actors could encourage such processes. As points of reference, there was the experience of Latin America's emergence from dictatorship in the 1980s and 1990s and, of course, the European experience, be it that of Spain and Portugal in the 1970s or the more recent post-Cold War experiences of the Eastern European countries. It is now more than apparent that the issues involved are far more complex than was generally thought to be the case.

Not only has the United States had to take a long, hard look at its assumptions about "democratic peace" and the utility of pre-emptive intervention as a means of imposing such a "peace," but Europe, too, is being forced to reconsider its own assumptions as expressed through the Euro-Mediterranean Partnership (EMP) and, more recently, the European Neighbourhood Policy (ENP).

Why has Europe been so uncomfortable with the democratic success of the AKP government in Turkey, despite its willingness to meet the requirements of the European Union for political reform in accordance with the Copenhagen criteria for accession and eventual membership? How will Brussels deal with the growing setbacks to the Orange and Rose Revolutions in the Ukraine and Georgia, not to speak of the difficulties now facing the Cedar Revolution in Lebanon? And how, finally, will it respond to the massive popular disaffection displayed by recent elections in Algeria and Morocco? One seemingly inescapable conclusion is that the European Union as an "external actor" must try to work out how to promote a democratic culture as an essential component of any process leading to genuine democratization; equally, uncomfortably, it must tackle the knotty problem of the relationship between political Islam and democracy.

In other words, for external actors, it is not "façade democracy" – the external manifestation of the trappings of democracy such as parliamentary institutions and electoral practices – that matters but rather the internalization of the "habits of heart and mind" to which de Tocqueville referred in discussing American democracy in the nineteenth century. Quite how this can be achieved within the short time-spans that the political process normally allows is the quandary that European and American policy-makers find themselves facing increasingly when they work to influence domestic policy to encourage transitions to democracy in other parts of the world.

Past experience, whether it is recent experiences in the Middle East or the longer-term initiatives undertaken as part of the Barcelona Process, or the Free Trade Area of the Americas (FTAA) and the Miami Summit, may no longer be adequate. Instead, a new and more profound re-evaluation of past experience and a more acute awareness of the contemporary political environment may prove to be the way forward.

It is for this reason that this book is so apposite. Written by some of the leading scholars of democratization and based on examples drawn from around the world, it seeks to identify those principles on which genuine democratic transition can be based. It shows the degree to which international actors, ranging from states to non-governmental players, have an influence on what were once thought of as exclusively domestic processes of political change. The book also looks at changes in foreign policy that have emerged from transitions to democracy. The contributors cover a selection of countries and regions relevant to the contemporary experience: Portugal and Spain in the 1970s and Eastern and Central Europe in the 1990s, Brazil and Argentina in Latin America from the early 1980s onwards, and various countries in the Arab world.

In the early literature on democratization, transition theories and models initially focused on domestic politics. The view was that endogenous factors were the fundamental drivers of political change, while the international dimension and the role of exogenous factors to the domestic scene were considered secondary or marginal. Such early theories were partially a reflection of the democratization experiences of the early democratizations of the "Third Wave" in Southern Europe and Latin America. These experiences were undertaken in the thick of the Cold War, and were thus dominated by the rigid logic imposed by two competing power blocs.

Furthermore, such experiments with democratization were highly risky in terms of security because they had the power to generate international instability. For that reason, they were rare, and their fate uncertain. Success depended more on domestic political capabilities than on international factors. It is hardly surprising, then, that the focus of analysis was initially on national states and that theoretical explanations centred on domestic forces and their political and institutional autonomy from international factors.

All this changed dramatically with the 1989 revolution and the post-communist transitions in Eastern and Central Europe. These new experiences drew attention to the impact of international factors on processes of democratization. This shift in practical reality corresponded to a theoretical shift as well, as traditional transition theories were broadened and reconfigured. Thus, in the more recent literature on democratization, the international dimension has become a central focus, and explanatory models are built around the central role of exogenous factors. With the end of the Cold War and the triumph of the

"Western model," democracy appeared to become a universal norm: thus, while an exception thirty years ago, today democratization appears to be the rule. Indeed, the failure of democracy is regarded as a precarious and transient state of affairs, seen as a threat to international security and stability. Policies to "promote democracy" have become common international practice.

In short, the international dimension has become a decisive component of any theoretical explanation. It is hardly surprising, then, that analytical models have changed so radically, focusing on the international components of democratization instead. The contributions of scholars such as Philippe Schmitter and Geoffrey Pridham are essential texts in this respect, but the most central point reference is the work by Laurence Whitehead. From his original pioneering studies until the present work, he has not just developed a general model of democratization but also followed its historical evolution, integrating the multi-dimensional nature of the phenomenon in a global and systematic fashion.

This book, which is based on the proceedings of a Summer School organized by the Portuguese Institute of International Relations of the New University of Lisbon (IPRI-UNL) held in Óbidos, in Portugal, in 2003, opens with Laurence Whitehead's examination of the evolution of the international politics of democratization from Portugal's democratic transition in 1974 until the invasion of Iraq in 2003. It highlights three comparative and theoretical issues that have so far received inadequate attention. With the benefit of thirty years of hindsight, it reassesses prevailing interpretations of many key democratic transitions from an international politics perspective. It concludes by proposing a research agenda on these topics for the future and drawing some provisional conclusions.

More specifically, the chapter proposes three approaches for a comparative historical analysis of this evolution. The first lays increasing emphasis on the links between democracy and security, in contrast to earlier perceptions of democratization as liberation. The second considers the decline in the "counter-hegemonic potential" of democratization during the unipolarity of the 1990s as opposed to an ascendant vision of liberal internationalism. However, since September 11, 2001, the counter-hegemonic potential associated with genuinely free elections has reappeared, with particularly destabilizing implications for some of the new emerging democracies in the Middle East. The third deals with the narrower issue of whether democratization alters a state's foreign policy and if so, in what way.

Philippe Schmitter then turns to the evaluation of the impact of democracy promotion and protection, as autocratic regimes in the Middle East and North Africa liberalize, and as the democratic regimes in Central and Eastern Europe become consolidated. He suggests that there has been a constant rhetoric of democracy promotion but, until recently, little was done to consolidate such developments. One reason for this, he suggests, is that there was a general presumption that external actors could not and should not interfere. It was the comparative tranquillity of the democratic transition in Portugal that began to change this perception, together with the surprising way in which the Cold War and the authoritarian regimes in Eastern and Central Europe came to an end. He then goes on to outline what he describes as "thirteen sceptical propositions" on democracy promotion and protection, and discusses ways in which they might be tested. His chapter concludes with a quantitative evaluation of democratization models for the Middle East and North Africa.

Geoffrey Pridham considers the role of international factors in Eastern and Central Europe in the post-Cold War world. Regime change in former Communist countries has been accompanied by far-reaching international change in which each has influenced the other, suggesting an overall dynamic of external–domestic interaction. Most importantly, this led to the reconfiguration of the international system with the disappearance of global confrontation and the structures that had marked the Cold War period from the late 1940s onwards. However, this, in turn, led to the emergence of new, more regionally focused, forms of international conflict, some of which – notably the wars in the former Yugoslavia between 1991 and 1995 – influenced the nature of regime change, delaying transitions to democracy in the countries affected, and helping to buttress quasi-authoritarian regimes in Croatia and Serbia.

Geoffrey Pridham goes on to argue that, in the post-Cold War period, certain developments increased opportunities for democratization and highlighted the importance of international factors. These included the use of political, economic or financial conditionality by international organizations, democracy promotion as an aspect of national interest and security for regional actors, international human rights discourse; and, more recently, doctrines of intervention based on international ethics. At the same time, new information and communications technologies and their influence on socio-economic and political attitudes, given their potential for transnational networking, has increased the scope for a more immediate and widespread transmission of international influences than ever before, a development that has been facilitated by globalization. It is therefore no coincidence that the role of international factors in democratization since 1989 is now more clearly recognized. Indeed, democratization is itself an international phenomenon whose potential limits are still unknown.

Nuno Severiano Teixeira, the editor of the book and the convenor of the original conference, considers Portugal's process of democratization and its foreign policy, re-examining this and other early transitions in light of new theoretical models and thereby highlighting the hitherto undervalued (and even ignored) role of the international dimension in Southern European democratization processes, namely the foreplanned transition in Spain and the transition through political rupture of the established order in Portugal. The goal is not to outline a model of the impact of the international context on the transition and on the process of democratic consolidation in Portugal or on the impact of democratization on the system of international relations; rather, it is to analyse the relationship between democratization and foreign policy in order to show how the former influenced the latter. The focus is on outcomes, rather than process – on foreign policy writ large rather than any specific aspects of what is a multidimensional affair.

Juan Carlos Pereira focuses on the international factors involved in the Spanish transition to democracy, particularly on internal political change and the consequences it had for Spanish foreign policy. International factors in this context are seen from two perspectives: in terms of the impact of the international context on domestic actors and in terms of consequent changes in foreign policy which mirrored domestic political change, producing a democratic foreign policy. This approach involved a revision of the political science and international relations literature in Spain and abroad. Six main hypotheses that arise from the literature are considered: first, that international factors play a role in the origins, development and outcomes of transition processes; second, that such processes vary according to the "geo-historical" area under consideration – European transition processes are broadly similar, for example; third, that a transition from authoritarianism to a democratic state entails a transition in foreign policy; fourth, that such a transition in foreign policy occurs in the same way; fifth, that in the Spanish transition the international context was extremely important; and sixth, that there was also a transition in foreign policy in Spain, from Francoist authoritarianism to a democratic foreign policy.

Andrés Malamud, who examines the case of Argentina, argues that both the frequent democratic breakdowns and processes of re-democratization that followed in Latin America were linked to international factors. He describes the cycles of political instability in Argentina from 1930 to the present day, tracing their link to the international context. He then analyses the democratization process that took place during the 1980s in order to single out the international factors that influenced it. He concludes by examining the ways in which Argentina's renewed democracy has affected its international environment, especially in the region in which it is embedded – the Southern Cone of South America.

Alexandra Barahona de Brito considers the role of the international environment on the democratization of Brazil. She points out that the international dimension was not very relevant in the early years of the transition to democracy in Brazil, but it did acquire some prominence after 1989. This was due to both the work of transnational networks of activists shaping key issue areas in order to affect the process of deepening democracy, and because the values permeating the international order of the post-Cold War period became internalized and part of the new Brazilian political scenario.

Lawrence Graham considers the situation in Central and South-Eastern Europe, arguing that two dates stand out in the reconfiguration of a region which for forty-five years was defined as Eastern Europe. They are 1989 and 2004, the former marking the ending of Soviet domination, itself a consequence of the outcome of the Second World War; and the latter best capturing the reconfiguration of Europe over the last decade with the expansion of the European Union from fifteen to twenty-five member states. Today, the old political landscape is gone and in its place are three distinct groups of states: the Baltic states in the North, the Visegrad group in Central Europe and then South-Eastern Europe as a separate unit. Graham argues that the way in which these countries were incorporated into the Soviet sphere of influence or the way in which they secured their autonomy from direct Soviet control after 1948, as much as their prior historical experiences before the Second World War, is reflected in their realignment during 1989 and 1990 and how they have handled their external relations since.

Richard Youngs deals with the Middle East from a unique point of view by considering the relevance of international factors in democratic transitions in a context, such as that of the Middle East, where democratization has not yet occurred. He assesses the role played in the Middle East by a number of international factors, such as Western relations with authoritarian regimes across the region; the role of transnational networks; and the relationship between the global economy and the prevalence of rentier economic structures across the Middle East. He argues that, in each of these situations there are factors that have been influential in rendering democratization more difficult in the Middle East. Some of the standard categories of positive, pro-democracy international influences posited in the academic literature have either been weak or had the reverse effect in the Middle East. At the same time, he suggests that these international factors contain the potential for a more positive impact. Increasing variety and diversity within the Middle East, along with apparent changes in outside perspectives of the region, demand a more balanced assessment of the impact of international factors on the prospects for political change.

George Joffé suggests that there is an increasingly widespread view that the root causes of social and political tensions in the Muslim world, alongside economic failure, arise from poor governance. In the Middle East and North Africa in particular, the persistence of despotic regimes is adduced as the source of regional failure, quite apart from the specific political issues in the region or the economic problems associated with the rentier states resulting from dependence on hydrocarbon production as the source of economic wealth. There is thus growing pressure on Arab states to engage in the process of democratization, in the belief that this will, alone, provide the basis for a resolution of the region's problems. This, certainly, is the view of the neo-conservatives who currently dominate the foreign policy and intellectual establishment in Washington. As a result, it has also become the normative theme in much international relations discourse throughout the West and in the Middle Eastern and North African region itself. However, the real bar to democracy lies in its mode of legitimization which in the Western model requires populist support, but in the Islamic model refers to the divinity. Nonetheless, the classical Islamic model shares very similar values to those connected with democracy so there is no a priori reason why democratic pluralism cannot be established there. Indeed, contemporary thinkers in the Islamic world are anxious to develop indigenous political models which will be consonant with their Western counterparts. Success, however, will require a sensitivity on the part of international actors that is all too often missing.

In his concluding chapter to the volume, Laurence Whitehead argues that there are two ways to address the problems of the role for the international arena in democratization, one temporal and the other geopolitical. In terms of periodization, it would be instructive to contrast the first half of the 1990s – the highpoint of international consensus and optimism concerning the pace and coverage of democratization around the world – with the first half of the following decade – a much changed international context, full of security fears and characterized by an "overstretch" of the rhetoric of democratization. In terms of geopolitical coverage, he contrasts the western hemisphere, strongly under the influence of the United States and its closest allies, with Europe – also influenced by developments in Washington and the expansion of the North Atlantic Treaty Organization but, above all, structured by the enlargement of the European Union itself. It is an argument that highlights the potential conflict between America and Europe over democracy promotion and its many related issues. The author argues that if the American paradigm is the key to spreading democratization, then Europe may have to learn to accept American power-projection as part of an imperfect bargain for the future.

It is a sobering point upon which to conclude, but it highlights the loss of optimism that has been generated by the past decade. There is now a debate about the way in which international actors can best influence the democratization process, in view of the unhappy experience of Iraq and the implications of the neo-conservative cast of American foreign policy. It could be argued that the role of external influence, in certain parts of the world, has been discredited by the policy of pre-emptive intervention. But Europe cannot ignore the implications for its own security of the growth of democratic governance along its periphery. It is condemned to encourage such developments and thus to engage in democratic transition. Its only problem remains how this might best be done – the question that this book addresses.

1 The international politics of democratization from Portugal (1974) to Iraq (2003)

Laurence Whitehead

Introduction

From the "revolution" in Portugal (April 1974) to the "liberation" of Iraq (April 2003), the so-called "third wave" of democratizations has triggered various types of "transition" from authoritarian (or even totalitarian) rule. Over the past thirty years this has affected almost half of the sovereign states recognized by the United Nations (UN). In some countries, a clear-cut episode of regime change separates an old (undemocratic) order from a new (more or less "consolidated") electoral democracy. In many other cases, the political trajectory has been more erratic and the outcome more ambiguous, but even so what has come to the fore has been the norms and structures of competitive politics within a relatively neutral institutional framework. There remain large regions that have proved resistant to this global tendency (most notably in the Arab world), and there have been a small number of significant reversals (as in Pakistan). In some cases democratization has come about through delicate negotiations between rival domestic political elites, but there are also numerous examples of regime change through rupture, perhaps precipitated by external crises, or even (as in Iraq) imposed through military conquest. The old established democracies remain securely in place but there is quite widespread evidence of growing disenchantment with the way that "really existing" democratic politics works, and in some important countries there have been significant signs of "decay" in the observance of basic democratic norms. Quite a few of the new democracies display substantial levels of citizen disenchantment, and in some cases even institutional dysfunctionality. Whereas the early democratizations of the 1970s all took place in long-established and securely implanted nation states, those of the 1990s were more likely to occur in institutionally fragile nations (perhaps newly created), where basic elements of the underlying political order remained subject to contestation. Overall, then, the record of the past thirty years presents a mixed picture. Democratization has advanced, but initial theories and models of democratic transition have been stretched (and even undermined) by the resulting diversity of paths and outcomes.[1]

Surveying this thirty-year period, it is evident that individual instances or even regional clusters of democratization cannot be fully understood if studied in isolation from the broader international context and intellectual climate. For example, the tentative nature and uncertain prospects of the early democratizations of the 1970s partly reflected an anxious and indeed somewhat pessimistic outlook for the Western democracies. This was a time of bipolar tension, or international economic difficulties, and of radicalized youth movements. By contrast, the later 1980s were characterized by growing optimism about the prospects of Western victory in the Cold War, together with a more positive economic climate for the corporate sector, and the decline or even eclipse of many radical movements. Whereas democratization was viewed with anxiety in the 1970s (given the fear that it might lurch out of control, or could unleash counter-hegemonic instability, as in Portugal), by the late 1980s the re-democratization of, say, Chile was viewed as a safe way to lock in "pro-market" reformism and to bury disagreeable memories of ideological polarization. Then, during the 1990s, the international climate was one of still further optimism about the prospects for the old Western democracies. There was no longer any Soviet alternative, either military or ideological. Market liberalization could be extended, linked to the promotion of democracy, and lubricated by the "peace dividend" arising from the resolution of world conflicts. In this climate it became possible to regard the extension and indeed universalization of liberal democracy as an almost "natural" state of affairs. Diverse individual processes of transition were all too easily treated as further confirmations of a single ineluctable logic. This led to progressively more ambitious interpretations, as everywhere from Albania to Zimbabwe was assigned a position on a presumably unilinear continuum destined to converge on a pre-determined "end of history." The implausibility and over-reach of this *zeitgeist* had become apparent to many well before the end of the 1990s, but in any case the reversal following September 11, 2001 was brutal and has been extended. Over a cycle of two political generations the international context for individual national experiments with democratization has clearly undergone huge swings, and these background conditions have powerfully affected the course of development of different processes of democratization.

The early regime changes (such as the Greek and Portuguese) were rare, and seen as precarious. But as the "third wave" gathered momentum in the 1980s, the perception grew that democratization had become easy and perhaps even unstoppable. This optimism crested with the dissolution of the Soviet bloc after 1989. During the 1990s impediments and uncertainties become more evident, as the most recent claimants for inclusion in the list of new democracies tended to lack many of what earlier theorists had regarded as the basic "prerequisites" for democratic stability (a minimum level of per capita income, literacy, urbanization, and a middle class, among others). From Albania to Zambia, the later "democratizers" presented a range of adverse characteristics that may help to explain why, as the "wave" has spread, the spectrum of processes has broadened and outcomes diverged. What initially appeared as a relatively small and coherent cluster of cases suitable for tight comparative analysis (Portugal, Spain, the Dominican Republic, Uruguay and others) has become a sprawling, and perhaps unmanageable, crowd. Certainly the attempt to apply established categories and models to such recent instances of "regime change" as Afghanistan and Iraq involves extrapolation on a heroic scale.

Nevertheless, the comparative study of democratization processes has developed into one of the most flourishing growth industries in comparative politics, and on some important topics this has generated substantial advances in methods and understanding. One area of methodological advance is of particular interest and relevance to the theme of this chapter – comparative historical analysis.[2] This macro, and potentially holistic, perspective helps us to view each democratization process as a long-term, multidimensional, and partially open-ended and perhaps even potentially reversible historical reality. It also facilitates theoretically informed comparison of analogous processes, undertaken with the principal aim of enhancing the understanding of each specific instance. From this perspective, the test of a good comparison might not be whether it uncovered a "law-like" regularity applying to a multitude of cases, still less to "predict" outcomes, or to prescribe "best practices." Rather, it would be to identify themes and hypotheses that merit further inspection when "telling the story" of each particular democratization. Ideally, in addition, these themes might (if supported by detailed historical corroboration) generate tentative "middle range" generalizations applicable to suitably defined clusters of cases.

This is the approach guiding the rest of this chapter. The universe of democratizations subject to reassessment in what follows is all the attempted or achieved regime changes that began after April 1974 and before April 2003. Out of this large universe, the focus will be on a limited number of "telling" examples, cases where a historically grounded reconsideration uncovers hitherto underestimated indications of the importance of international variables and dimensions. This volume contains several such studies. In particular, the Portuguese regime change was reinterpreted as an episode of European decolonization, and the reorientation of mainland Portugal away from its maritime empire (seen as a counterweight to Spain's dominance of the Iberian hinterland) and towards full integration in a democratic European Union (EU). Likewise, the democratization of Spain following the death of Franco was also reinterpreted, uncovering historical evidence to demonstrate that this supposedly archetypal instance of a domestically driven "pacted" transition was also strongly conditioned by hitherto neglected international components. Thus, subsequent democratizations in, say, Argentina, Poland, Taiwan or East Timor can no longer be classified as mere "exceptions" to the general rule that international dimensions of regime change are typically of no more than secondary significance, since this new research demonstrates their centrality in even the classic initial cases. Moreover, Washington's recent ambition to bring democracy to the large world region it has recently constructed (the "Greater Middle East," which extends from Pakistan to Morocco) underscores the continuing policy significance of comparative work on the international politics of democratization.

This overview chapter highlights three comparative and theoretical issues that have, in my opinion, so far received inadequate attention from the democratization studies community. With the benefit of thirty years of hindsight, it would be illuminating to reassess prevailing interpretations of many key democratic transitions from an international politics perspective. More specifically, the chapter suggests the following three axes of comparative historical analysis: first, the increasing emphasis on the links between democracy and security, in contrast to an earlier perception of democratization as liberation; second, the associated possibility of a declining "counter-hegemonic potential" of democratization during the 1990s period of unipolarity and ascendant liberal internationalism although since September 11, 2001, the counter-hegemonic potential of free elections has reappeared with particularly destabilizing implications for some new democracies in the Middle East; third, the narrower issue of whether democratization alters a state's foreign policy (and, if so, what parts of it, and how). The following three sections of this chapter outline an exploratory research agenda on these inter-related topics. It does not aspire to resolve the questions it raises (that requires more detailed historical analysis of key cases, as exemplified in other chapters of this volume), but only to stimulate further work. The final section of the chapter sketches some provisional suggestions and conclusions.

Democracy as security, or as liberation

Every democratization process involves a change of political regime. Every regime change presupposes the demise of a prior regime. But, of course, an undemocratic regime can come to an end without being replaced by any equally coherent successor regime; and a change from an authoritarian regime may not result in democracy. Therefore every transition generates uncertainty, and raises the spectre of potential insecurity (both domestic and in relation to neighbours and allies of authoritarian incumbents). Every regime change also raises fears of betrayal, reversal or collapse. So those who struggle for democratic regime change are aiming to introduce a new political order in which old authoritarian practices are permanently ended, not just temporarily interrupted. In this sense they aim for "liberation" of their society from its repressive traditions and heritage. This dialogue between hope and fear, between liberation and security, is inherent in all democratizations.

Even when a regime change does culminate in the establishment of a durable democracy, it must nevertheless obey the logic of order that applies to the implantation of every effective political regime. Even democracy is a form of "domination," in the sense that only certain patterns of political conduct can be tolerated. Others lie outside the range of what can be permitted by even the most liberal of constitutional orders. All beliefs and forms of peaceful expression may be allowed, but even then some more aggressive forms of behaviour will have to be prescribed, and even in the last analysis repressed. Those political actors who remain wedded to the promotion of outlawed behaviour will ultimately have to be sanctioned (always within the law, and subject to constitutional guarantees and due process, if the new regime is indeed to qualify as a fully fledged constitutional democracy). For example, those engaged in attempts to restore the previous authoritarian system in violation of the new rules will have to be restrained or ultimately punished. Similarly, those who welcome the breakdown of the old regime but refuse to accept constraints legitimately put in place to defend the new order will also have to be disciplined.[3]

So the dialogue between freedom and security in democracy always requires the striking of a balance. Within a democratic framework, liberation cannot be confused with anarchy. But at the same time any incoming democratic regime will want to offer its newly enfranchised *demos* a menu of political and civic freedoms that were not previously available. This is the inherent "liberation" component of a democratic transition. Admittedly this terminology carries a baggage unacceptable to many contemporary liberals, who prefer to speak in terms of "building the rule of law" or "promoting the rights of citizenship." But there is a cost to this substitute terminology. Correctly understood, "liberation" is an objective that people struggle for, rather than a target that is merely set for them from above.

Now let us put these theoretical reflections into some comparative historical perspective. Twenty years ago democratic transitions were infrequent, and their outcomes were uncertain. In a bipolar world the two dominant blocs generally promoted loyal protégés, and discouraged the security risks associated with democratic experimentation. Political democratization also raised anxieties about the stability of economic arrangements – as voters oscillated between left and right parties this might produce shifts between socialist and capitalist economic orientations. So democratization was plausibly viewed as an uncertain undertaking, one that would have to be internally driven, one that was potentially counter-hegemonic, and therefore a project most likely to succeed when domestic strategic interactions favoured agreement, and when external destabilizing pressures could be minimized. The relevant unit of analysis was therefore the individual state (or national political regime), and attention was focused on those states that possessed sufficient internal autonomy to screen out international intrusions.

This panorama has now been transformed. Whereas in Cold War conditions the struggle for democracy often prioritized national liberation and downplayed the issue of security, in the post-Cold War world the balance of emphasis has swung in the other direction. There is currently one main source of political orientation (Washington) instead of two rival centres. During the 1990s, under Washington's influence, democratization was more commonly viewed as the norm, rather than the exception (outside the Islamic world). Unsatisfactory outcomes are most often presented as temporary setbacks to a predetermined course. There has been an explosion of international political and economic incentives for states to qualify as "democracies," and these external reinforcements are widely expected to "lock in" democratization processes in most or all properly administered states. Where such expectations are clearly being frustrated, the leaders of international opinion reach for such labels as "rogue states," or "collapsed" or "failed" states, thereby paving the way for encroachments on state sovereignty. There has been a proliferation of so-called "humanitarian interventions" that are supposed to end when transitional administrations construct new democratic regimes. This radical shift in the outlook of international actors reflects the end of the bipolar conflict and the discredit of socialist economic models. More recently, it has been reinforced by a perception that Western-led security interests are best served by managing the risks of controlled democratization.

In the 1990s an academic consensus argued that democracies do not go to war with one another, and therefore that democratization is a means to abolish war. This justified democracy promotion as a policy that was both virtuous and cost-effective (on the "all good things go together" principle). But with the passage of time this automatic linking of democracy with security has been seen to be simple-minded. The emphasis has therefore shifted to more intrusive forms of Western intervention that may promote security in troubled regions without necessarily cherishing democratic values, although official discourse still assumes the promotion of pro-Western security through controlled withdrawal, supposedly leaving new democratic regimes in place after the intervention ends. Although this is mainly a Western (above all US-led) approach to democratization it has been taken up by the United Nations, and so has acquired the status of a new international orthodoxy.

This was not the way democratization was viewed in the early, Cold War, stage of the "third wave." At that time, given its confrontation with the Soviet Union, the West embraced quite a few clearly undemocratic regimes, and disavowed many of their typically democratic opponents as either willing or naive agents of Soviet imperialism. In response, emerging democratic coalitions in Southern Europe and Latin America tended to view authoritarian rule and the violation of human rights as a tolerated expression of Western security interests. In consequence, when opposition forces argued for democratization and the return of the military to barracks, they tended to associate regime change with a certain degree of "liberation" from the straitjacket of repressive anti-communism. More concretely, democracy might require the legalization of an outlawed Communist Party, and a return of exiles, and even a reassessment of the role of military bases and external security alliances (which could only be renewed subject to popular democratic endorsement). In the Soviet-controlled countries of Eastern Europe, the association of democratization with "liberation" was even more direct and indeed stark. Since a transition from communist rule would mean escaping Soviet control, it almost inherently involved "national liberation."

Since the end of the Cold War this logic has faded. Now that the richest, most powerful and most secure nations of the world are so predominantly rated as democracies, it has become possible to forge agreements between leading states in the international system, extending "democratic conditionality" to a widening range of regional and functional arenas. The intention was to press the remaining (mostly poor, weak, and insecure) nations to conform to standards set by these leading nations (not themselves necessarily subject to much external scrutiny). So during the 1990s, the idea that international organizations should attach a higher priority to democracy promotion than in the past became increasingly fashionable, at least in the West. This probably also reflected the increased proportion of member states in most such organizations that are now, at least formally, classified as "democracies," and that gain international prestige and even benefits from such a status. It also reflects the fact that some international organizations include commitments to democracy (or, failing that, at least to some basic universal values concerning human rights and respect for international law) among their goals. Increasingly, they even make democracy a requirement for membership. In addition, since the end of the Cold War, if not before, Western liberal thinkers have tended to downgrade the claims of "national sovereignty" and "non-intervention," and to extend the scope attributed to shared international norms as arbitrators of the conduct of nations.

For a mixture of these reasons the international community has over the past decade or so become increasingly committed to democracy promotion, and these practices are becoming more institutionalized and perhaps more effective. Even before the end of the Cold War, the five permanent members of the UN Security Council (UNSC) had begun coming round to a more positive view of the possibilities for promoting both political reform and regional conflict resolution through the UN system (the 1988 Namibia Agreement provided an early indication of this new trend).

Since the end of the Cold War the UNSC has been much freer to authorize "humanitarian interventions," which start with the determination (under Chapter VII of the UN Charter) that there is a threat to international security justifying the temporary suspension of state sovereignty until the fault has been corrected. International interventionism is therefore conceived as no more than an interlude to be accompanied by a variety of measures, including the convocation of a competitive election, prior to the withdrawal of UN or other internationally mandated forces. The key point to note here is that democracy promotion is typically embedded in a broader set of conflict-resolution objectives, rather than pursued in isolation. There may well be a tension between the UN desire to terminate its peace-making activities and withdraw its forces (which implies the early convening of an election, even though conditions for a durable democratization may not be present) and the goal of democracy-building. It is also important to note that the typical arenas of such UN operations are centres of international turbulence which may well consist of very weak, or even "failed" states. This is neither the most representative nor the most propitious setting for democratization. At times, the UN has also found itself drawn into democracy-promoting activities in states where the UNSC has not determined that there was any threat under Chapter VII (Kosovo, for example). And occasionally the UN has felt obliged to terminate a democracy-promoting mission on the grounds that the local situation had become too unstable (as in Angola in 1999 and Haiti in 2000, for example – although it returned to the latter country after the ousting of President Aristide in 2002).

Another area of anxiety concerns the dynamics of a UN transitional administration, once an international intervention has been sanctioned and carried out.

Cambodia, Namibia and East Timor all offer relative reassurance that – at least in the limited number of suitable cases – the process can be kept on track, and the outcome can be achieved with reasonable punctiliousness at a bearable cost, and without adversely affecting the basic security of neighbouring states. But these were all "post-Cold War" episodes, and even that category contains some less reassuring experiences – Angola, for example, or, arguably, Kosovo.

In this new context, the notion of the UN taking responsibility for the administration of "failed states" that can only be restored to independence once they have been "democratized" has attracted new sources of support. It has also stirred up new sources of anxiety. First in the Balkans, then in Afghanistan and then, briefly, even in Iraq, the UN was called upon to legitimize the installation of new and purportedly "democratizing" governments in the wake of external invasions and "liberations." But the basic tests of procedural democracy (a level playing field, and a fair count, for instance) are subordinated to the security interests of the occupation forces.

The terrorist atrocity of September 11, 2001 precipitated a dramatic reorientation of Western geopolitical and security objectives, and resulted in a severe downgrading of the role Washington and London were willing to assign to the United Nations. NATO was brought to the fore as a more easily controlled and security-focused instrument for stabilizing the allegedly "democratic" regimes under construction in the wake of invasions and coercive regime change. In Afghanistan this formula is currently being tested, with deeply discouraging results (at least so far).[4] In Iraq, the US-led "coalition of the willing" was much more ad hoc and short-lived. In both cases it has proved easier for Western security forces to precipitate civil war than to engage in effective democratic reconstruction. The West's highly charged post-9/11 rhetoric of "democratization throughout the Middle East" has appropriated concepts and techniques that previously enjoyed substantial support and approval, and has applied them in a manner likely to produce lasting resistance and indeed discredit. When democratic elections were held (partly in response to international urgings) in the Lebanon and Palestine, they produced results that were deemed threatening to Israel and therefore Western security interests. As a result, the fruits of competitive elections in the few Middle Eastern countries that have experimented with them have proved extremely bitter, both for the voters involved and for international sponsors of such experiments.

Although the assault of September 11, 2001 has elicited a new enthusiasm in Washington for more "transformational" policies aimed at forceful regime change and democratizations of whole large regions, this security-driven logic has also elicited new sources of resistance in other parts of the international community. None of the permanent members of the UN Security Council need envisage a diminution of their sovereignty as a result of the new logic, since they all enjoy the right of veto over initiatives that might otherwise adversely affect them (for example, in Chechnya, Tibet, Corsica, Guantánamo, or indeed Gibraltar). But of course all those UN members that are listed as "rogue" or "failed" states" are bound to take a much more critical view. In addition, many ordinary members of the General Assembly have learnt a cautionary lesson though observing the selective application of the Bush doctrine. It has been particularly instructive to discover how quickly individual regimes are first taken up and then discarded (the "Orange Revolution" in the Ukraine, the "Cedar Revolution" in Lebanon, Georgia, and Kyrgyzstan, to cite just some examples).

To conclude this section, we can now revert to the more theoretical considerations introduced at the outset. Authoritarian regimes typically promise to strengthen security, and ask in exchange for heightened discipline and the reduction of personal freedoms. In reaction against such regimes, democratic transitions are typically associated with increased uncertainty, and perhaps even insecurity, compensated by a restoration of lost liberties. This exchange was a familiar feature of past democratizations, and it still has some currency even today. But durable and legitimate democracies require a firm basis of public security; where it is not present it must be created, and where present it must be preserved. However, since September 11 in particular, the liberating dimension of regime change has been downgraded, replaced by a new emphasis on security. Security concerns have the potential to crowd out procedural democracy altogether, but in current conditions the greater danger could be that they merely drain it of deliberative content. Electoral processes may still allow some limited freedom of choice, access to information, and the right to organize and petition, all freedoms lacking under authoritarian rule. But the freedom to choose may be limited to a narrow range of safe alternatives; the information available may well be manipulated to serve the requirements of order and stability; and the right to organize and petition may be kept selective and incomplete. Only those portions of the national territory most "securely" under the control of the central authorities may be allowed to vote, thus unbalancing the outcome to the advantage of foreign-backed incumbents.

This confirms the broader point that debates about democratization are also invariably about *what kind* of democracy is desired, or considered feasible. The early "transitions" literature, with its focus on strategic interactions between opposing currents of domestic opinion, privileged a version of democracy structured around the building of consent, and the establishment of local credentials of political authenticity. This was a "dialogical" as well as a domestically oriented conception of democracy. But other conceptions of democracy are also possible. Democracy can be conceived as the expression of a majority will to affirm collective values, and to silence discordant challengers. In that case, those who control the state apparatus and define the official discourse can use the argument of security to exclude opponents as troublemakers. Democracy can be characterized as at the opposite pole from "liberation." This shift from an emphasis on building consent to one of exerting control seems to be occurring not only within some new democracies, but within some old ones as well. And it occurs not only within individual countries, but also at the international level.

Variable "counter-hegemonic" potential

As the focus of attention shifts from well-established nations to weak or even "failed" states, and as Western and UN-led suspensions of sovereignty come to precede democratization, the international security imperative tends to over-ride the domestic drive for liberation from authoritarian constraints. In this context, it would not be surprising if the resulting "democratic" regimes were to prove compliant or indeed subordinate to their external mentors. If so, the post-Cold War democratizations would tend to display less counter-hegemonic potential than their pre-1989 precursors.

Certainly, since the early 1990s the structure of the international order has shifted. Many campaigners for democracy in Southern Europe and elsewhere in the 1970s and early 1980s thought that they might also renegotiate their country's place in the international alliance system, and even that a democratic electorate might also exercise the option to practice re-distributive economic policies, both internally and internationally. But since the mid-1980s inter-national economic arrangements have become more universal, rule-bound and – at least for most new democracies – constraining than the ad hoc arrangements that used to precede "globalization." The scope for domestically driven policy experimentation has accordingly been reduced. Where sovereign democratic rights are respected, they are accompanied by powerful associated obligations and responsibilities. This applies to political alliances and military security arrangements as much as to economic commitments.

In this way, for example, the voters of, say, newly democratic Mexico or Turkey find their international options to be substantially limited (by the North American Free Trade Agreement (NAFTA) and the EU respectively), and even their internal socio-economic choices are hedged in by manifold external restrictions. Perhaps some such constraints were always present, but under the preceding authoritarian regime it was possible to hope that with the removal of artificial internal restraints on citizen pressures and demands there would be some increased scope for choice at the international level. Typically, illusions of this kind have been dashed by recent experiences of democratization. If this is true even for such major and weighty players as Mexico and Turkey, it is all the more evident in lesser and more fragile democracies (think of Benin, or East Timor, or Nicaragua). Some observers may consider such constraints to be reas-suring, or even aids to the stabilization of democracy. For others they may be less welcome, since they undermine the authority and perhaps even the legiti-macy of locally elected governments. Whichever view one takes, this shift over the past thirty years would seem to constitute a major and durable change in the international politics of democratization as the "third wave" has progressed.

Afghanistan and Iraq are so recent, and so controversial, that it may seem polemical to cite them in evidence here. But their significance should not be overlooked. As mentioned in the previous section, the claim that the military interventions there are paving the way for "transitions to democracy" is heavily contested, and lacks empirical support, at least for the time being. At the time of writing, neither the Karzai nor the Allawi administrations can claim electoral legitimization. They were both ratified in office by handpicked assemblies that were convoked during continuing civil conflict under the supervision of foreign occupying armies. From these externally created positions controlling state patronage they plan to convene elections, which seem designed to confer a mantle of electoral legitimacy on those most loyal to the occupiers. If these processes succeed, the international community will be invited to classify them as further examples of "democratization." But this either involves stretching the term to cover outcomes far different from an earlier period, or it is a straight-forward misnomer.[5] Only time and future scholarly analysis will reveal which. In either instance, these are telling cases for analysts interested in the declining counter-hegemonic potential of contemporary democratizations. If the term can be stretched to embrace the election of Karzai and Allawi, these will be limit cases of democratizations tailored to reinforce a prevailing international hege-mony (military supremacy at that, rather than a broader-based political hege-mony). If not, then the counter-hegemonic potential of regime change in Afghanistan and Iraq will involve the expulsion of the occupation forces. It is questionable whether such a regime change could now take a democratic form.

Afghanistan and Iraq inevitably colour contemporary debate on the broader issue. They could be aberrations, but they could also foreshadow further regime changes along the same lines. That, at least, is what the Bush administration's GME initiative seemed to promise (its subsequent discredit is another matter). For the purposes of this chapter, a thirty-year time horizon introduces some necessary perspective. But how much counter-hegemonic potential did the earlier democratizations really contain? If that potential declined after 1990, how, and why, and with what implications for our general models of democrat-ization?

These latest examples are not historically unique. The 1966 elections in the Dominican Republic (following the US-led invasion of 1965) provided a clear precursor. In that case, it is arguable that democratization came to the country not in 1966 but in 1978, when the party representing the losers from the US intervention won a majority and (narrowly) secured the right to take office. Here, the Cold War shaped the security agenda, just as the so-called "war on terror" is doing in Afghanistan and Iraq. The Dominican Republic was close to communist Cuba, and the US intervention was motivated by a determination to block any possibility of a second Castro-type takeover in the Caribbean. For that reason only, protégés of the invading force could be allowed to win the 1966 election. In 1978, it was (narrowly) decided that an electoral victory by the opposition party of the democratic revolution would not constitute an unaccept-able rebuff to Washington. Thereafter, the US came to view competitive elect-oral politics in the Dominican Republic as the best way to insulate that nation from the temptations of Castroism.

As the "third wave" gathered momentum in the late 1970s and early 1980s, an increasing number of democratizations began to generate demands for the renegotiation of Cold War security commitments. Greece and Portugal always remained formally within the North Atlantic Treaty Organization (NATO), but commitment to the alliance was questionable during the early years of these new democracies. Newly legalized left-wing parties drew attention to the complicity linking NATO authorities to previous anti-communist military authoritarianism. Similarly in Spain (which had a military alliance with the US, outside the frame-work of NATO), the incoming Socialist party was initially opposed to member-ship of NATO – a policy that the party subsequently reversed through a democratic referendum. In the Philippines, the fall of the dictator Marcos led to an upsurge of opposition to US military bases. Similar security doubts arose concerning Argentina after the Falklands War, or in South Africa after apartheid, for instance. It is true that, over time, nearly all these new democratic regimes became reconciled to the Western security system, but this was brought about through processes of democratic deliberation, and was justified in terms of the modifications that could be secured, to adjust Western defence priorities in accordance with pluralist politics. The counter-hegemonic potential of the democratizations may thus have helped to reform and liberalize the Western alliance system at a time when the Cold War was in any case winding down.

In East-Central Europe, no such negotiated repositioning was on the agenda. For understandable reasons (including the use of Soviet tanks in Budapest in 1956 and in Prague in 1968), democratization included freeing these countries from the military, political and economic domination of Moscow. Here (and in the Baltic states), the counter-hegemonic content of democratization was not just potential but integral. Throughout the successor states to the former Union of Soviet Socialist Republics (USSR), democratization was similarly identified with escaping control from Moscow.

However, after 1990, subsequent democratizations took place not in a bipolar but within a basically unipolar international security framework. In this changed setting, counter-hegemonic potential would involve democratizing regimes against the wishes and interests of the US. Although Washington took care to minimize the scope for such possibilities, this was not a purely hypothetical con-tingency. In Mexico, for example, to have accepted the outcome of the 1988 presidential election might have complicated the Reagan administration's regional security agenda, most notably in Central America. By contrast, in 2000, when an opposition victory in a Mexican presidential election was finally recog-nized as legitimate, the democratization of Mexico was no longer a security problem for the US. Similar points could be made concerning the democrat-ization of El Salvador in the early 1990s. More generally, by the end of the Cold War new democratic regimes (whether post-communist or post-authoritarian rightist) were increasingly enmeshed in networks of economic and political obligations to their neighbours, and to the international community, that limited their room for destabilizing policy discretionality, and that therefore diminished their counter-hegemonic potential.

An important test case for this general thesis would be the democratization of Turkey. Here, the victory of a moderate Islamic party could (on some interpreta-tions) be seen as an affirmation of national aspirations in the face of Western disapproval. After all, the Turkish parliament voted down a proposal to send troops to Iraq, and Washington accepted this decision as the free choice of a democratic parliament. So some leeway is still possible, although Turkey's wish to join the EU exerts a powerful constraint on its policy discretionality in most arenas (even on such improbable topics as the outlawing of adultery).

Democratization and foreign policy

This section tackles the question of how democratization may affect a country's foreign policy. Note that the enquiry concerns a relatively uncertain "may," and not a tightly causal "does." In principle, foreign policy could be reshaped as a consequence of regime change. However, much depends on the international context. Some states have low-profile foreign policies, and some enjoy a considerable degree of foreign policy discretion. If democratization occurs in this kind of setting, there may be significant scope for foreign policy variation in response to a shift in the internal political balance. But high-profile foreign policy commitments may be less optional. The international balance of forces may leave little scope for innovation. Alternatively, democratization may be driven more by external than by internal dynamics (the lifting of an external veto, or even democratization as a result of invasion). In these cases, the same forces that produce the democratization may determine the re-orientation of foreign policy, and we would be mistaken to refer to the former as causing the latter. For all these reasons, a comparative historical analysis should explore possible linkages, rather than causal necessities.

When addressing this broad question, it might be helpful to distinguish between negotiated democratizations and regime changes brought about through "rupture." April 1974 in Portugal, the defeat of the Greek colonels later that year, and that of the Argentine Generals in 1982 all led to major domestic turbulence ("regime change" in the strong sense), and foreign policy was transformed as an almost inevitable counterpart. The same was true of the "triple transitions" in post-communist Eastern Europe in 1989. But negotiated (or "pacted") democratizations may be much more carefully controlled, with foreign policy disruptions thereby excluded from the agenda for change. Thus, for example, in the 1980s and 1990s South Korea achieved a negotiated transition to democracy without in any way altering its security alliance with the US (necessitated by its still unresolved state of belligerence with North Korea). Over a similar period, Chile and Mexico both democratized gradually and without disturbing basic foreign policy alignments.

The example of South Korea highlights the fact that foreign policy may sometimes be so heavily intertwined with external necessity that domestic regime change can have little impact. This leads to a third area of clarification. There are many dimensions to a country's foreign policy, and we need to be clear which aspects are to be included in our "dependent variable." This section focuses on "general foreign policy orientations," and not on key detailed or specialized sub-fields (voting patterns at the UN Commission on Human Rights, for instance) unless these acquire a broader significance. In addition, foreign policy can be roughly divided into "process" and "outcome," both of which could be affected by democratization. The questions of most interest here normally involve elements of both, and that is how the issue is addressed here.

In synthesis, then, the impact of democratization on foreign policy may be examined under four sub-headings, and in what follows the opening question is disaggregated into five sub-sections: types of democratization; components of democratization; foreign policy instruments; foreign policy areas; and discretionary outcomes.

Components of democratization

Thus far, "democratization" has been treated as a holistic process. However, from the foreign policy standpoint it may be equally important to consider its distinct institutional components, and their respective international consequences. For example, under democratization it is normal for the executive to lose its hitherto exclusive control over foreign policy, and to be required to share responsibility for key operations (the ratification of treaties, the appointment of ambassadors, the casting of votes in international organizations) with the Congress. Where bicameralism prevails, it is typically the Senate or the Upper House that is assigned the major formal foreign policy prerogatives. But the lower house may control the power of the purse, and also take an active interest in the more controversial issues of international and diplomatic action. Another significant component of democratization may be the communications media. Under authoritarian rule their coverage of international politics and foreign policy is typically constrained by the need to endorse official government stances, whereas in a more pluralist and competitive political environment the incentives may shift towards a much more critical treatment of the official line, and much more independent coverage of alternative perspectives. Reports concerning human rights, humanitarian interventions, and electoral observation overseas may be particularly affected. Authoritarian regimes are usually defensive about such forms of international monitoring, but official attitudes can change drastically following a transition. By taking a "forward line" on such issues, both domestically and internationally, a new democratic government may hope to capitalize on its new legitimacy and to underscore its moral superiority compared to its predecessors. If so, this is likely to be expressed through other components of democratization, such as the incoming government's relations with both domestic and international NGOs. There may also be significant legal repercussions (such as the ratification of international legal instruments protecting human rights of domestic citizens, and changed expectations of the domestic courts concerning immunity for past violations). Under democratization the security forces are also likely to lose some autonomy, with consequences for that dimension of foreign policy as well.

It should not be imagined, however, that all democratizations produce equally strong effects across all these various components of regime change. Indeed, the courts and the military may both be much slower to adopt than the Congress and the media, if only because whereas the latter see new opportunities for themselves in the course of democratization, the former may fear institutional damage.

Foreign policy instruments

Under authoritarian rule, foreign policy is usually controlled by a small, closed elite which aims to monopolize information about the issues at stake, and which may be under very little constraint to explain or justify its decisions to the wider society. Democratization tends to broaden the range of foreign policy decision-makers, and to open up the relevant sources of information to wider scrutiny. It may also require much more negotiation, persuasion and formal justification. International commitments that were previously opaque and potentially unlimited may have to be reformulated in more precise language and with clearly specified time limits and procedures for review. As individual foreign ministers (or trade ministers, or ambassadors, or economic negotiators) rotate in office, the commitments they enter into have to be made more impersonally binding on their successors (who may come from different party political backgrounds). State governors and opposition candidates for national office may acquire their own foreign policy voices, and may need to be included in the machinery of decision-making (at least in a subordinate role). The differences between competing agencies and bureaucracies working on the same international agenda may have to be more formally aired and arbitrated. The whole ethos of foreign-policy making may therefore become more complex and more impersonal. However, democracies may also engage in personalist diplomacy, at least on those fronts where electoral competition can be affected by a candidate's image or international stature. This is especially true of presidentialist democracies.

Foreign policy arenas

Under conditions of electoral competition, what count as the most salient issues in foreign policy may shift in accordance with voter preferences. In Hungary, for example, the shift to democracy uncovered a strong sentiment of solidarity with "ethnic Hungarian" minorities in neighbouring countries, whose misfortunes became a domestic political issue (as they had not been, at least not to the same extent, under communist one-party rule). Similarly, in democratic South Africa international criticism of Mugabe's Zimbabwe is an issue of substantial internal political significance, and has to be treated accordingly. Thus, the change to a democratic regime may enhance the salience of some foreign policy arenas and downgrade others. Where the dominant party or the outgoing military conducted its own foreign policy outside formal channels, these sources of expertise and orientation may be disbanded or at the very least demoted. Where opposition constituencies such as the Church, labour unions or academics had previously been excluded from foreign-policy making, under democratization they can no longer be silenced, and may promote influential new arenas of action, with alternative sources of information and hitherto unconsidered proposals for foreign policy innovation. Again, these potential shifts in emphasis are not automatic or uniform. Old agencies may find ways to reposition themselves to avoid demotion. Not all new voices will succeed in creating effective arenas for action to change foreign policy priorities. These processes may be contested and delayed. But democratization can certainly produce foreign policy effects through this medium.

Discretionary outcomes

As already noted, in some countries there may be very little scope for policy discretion on issues of external relations. Thus, when we consider the impact of democratization on foreign policy processes and outcomes we need to focus on the limited areas where some discretion is available. One outcome of particular interest would be the decision to work more closely with an international community of democratic states, and to make the support of democracy elsewhere one of the new objectives of foreign policy action. A related outcome could be to stress the value of international law and of international organizations as sources of orientation in world affairs. Linked to these two could be an enhanced emphasis on voluntary multilateralism as opposed to the unilateral pursuit of national objectives in the external arena. There could also be outcomes related to redefinitions of the conditions under which force would be used to pursue foreign policy objectives, and also the renegotiation of security arrangements (bases, alliance links, membership of denuclearized zones, for example) insofar as these can be varied by domestic choice. As noted in previous sections of this chapter, it should not be assumed that the installation of a democratic regime necessarily or immediately generates large effects in these areas of discretionary choice. Nor should it be assumed that eventual changes are necessarily unidirectional. A democratic regime might be more reckless than before in its military deployments (like the Poles in Iraq), and the electorate of a new democracy may favour more intense security commitments (the Baltic States in NATO) rather than neutrality. The mantra that "democracies do not go to war with each other" was always vulnerable to the charge of circularity (if it went to war, it couldn't "really" be a democracy). But Western analysts have never wavered in their conviction that Israel is a democracy, and until it launched military operations against Gaza and southern Lebanon these were said to have held democratic elections – albeit ones in which "terrorists" performed well.

Reassessing democratizations from an international politics perspective

This chapter has revisited the international political dimensions of the "third wave" of democratizations that took place between 1974 and 2003, highlighting three relatively neglected issues – the shift from a conception of democracy as liberation towards one stressing security; the associated declining counter-hegemonic potential of recent "democratizations" (especially those induced by military intervention since 2001); and the foreign policy changes associated with democratization. It has sought to illustrate the range and importance of these neglected issues, but has painted with a broad brush. More conclusive reassessments would require detailed re-evaluation of critical cases, some of which can be found elsewhere in this volume.

In conclusion, as new experiences destabilize initial theories and interpretations, and as older episodes of democratization are re-interrogated in the light of current concerns, the international politics of this type of regime change is acquiring heightened prominence. This shift in perspective is important for scholarship, and it is also of considerable policy significance. What can we expect of regime changes when these are justified in the language of democracy, but are imposed by coercive means that generate anxieties about their security implications? What is the value of democratization that leads to a policy strait-jacket, in which newly enfranchised electorates may conclude that their margins of choice have been constrained to vanishing point by internationally imposed limitations? Do such democracies develop foreign policies that are in any way different from (better than) what would otherwise have been adopted? Such questions touch on quite profound theoretical problems. The sovereignty and discretionality of "really existing" democracies affects the moral basis of their claims to legitimacy. The idea that international politics can improve with the dissemination of such regimes, and the displacement of authoritarian alternatives, rests on certain assumptions about what democratic regimes are like and how they behave – assumptions that seem to require critical re-examination in the light of recent developments.

These international political dimensions of democratization require extended re-evaluation, of the type initiated in this volume. However, this is not the only area of comparative democratization studies requiring further consideration. Elsewhere, I have identified two other relatively neglected fields of enquiry that could change our analysis and prescriptions.[6] These are "lustration" (the degree to which democratic state institutions are "purged" of individuals and groups associated with the previous undemocratic order), and "epistemic communities" (the extent to which under democratic conditions key areas of policy-making are guided and filtered by open and pluralist communities composed of "experts," namely those with the requisite minimum levels of technical understanding required for effective modern government in each area).

This is not the place for further elaboration of these topics, except insofar as they bear on the international political dimensions treated in this chapter. But it is worth noting certain interconnections. Thus, key arenas for lustration would include the intelligence apparatus, the security forces, the apparatchiks of the ruling party, and foreign service personnel. The extent to which these are replaced, retrained or allowed to continue with their previous practices will have a profound effect on the balance between "liberation" and "security" in a new democracy, and may well bear on its counter-hegemonic potential. Similarly, the capacity of a new democratic regime to undertake effective foreign policy innovations (supervised by congress, monitored by an independent press and accountable to an informed electorate) may be strongly affected by the presence (or absence) of an appropriate "epistemic community" in this field. "Expertise" in foreign affairs is a scarce resource, and not all democracies can count on a ready public understanding of the issues involved. Thus, the comparative study of democratizations can be reinvigorated by fresh thinking and new research in three separate fields – international dimensions, lustration, and epistemic community building – with the contributions from each of these reassessments feeding into parallel work in the other two areas.

Notes

1 This theme is more fully elaborated in the final chapter of my *Democratization: Theory and Experience*. Oxford: Oxford University Press, 2002.
2 For a good recent survey, see James Mahoney and Dietrich Rueschemeyer (eds), *Comparative Historical Analysis*. Cambridge: Cambridge University Press, 2002.
3 At first there may be negotiation over just how much leeway to allow those who contributed to the downfall of the old regime. New rules may be leniently applied until the transition to democracy is complete. However, eventually even the most generous of democratic regimes has to take a stand if some of its initial backers press an incompatible project too far.
4 Afghanistan is the first of the new "war on terror" international interventions, and the implications of generalizing this type of operation are seen by the sceptics as considerably more troubling. If the result had been to bring peaceful and legitimate authority to post-intervention Afghanistan, and to remove the country as a source of instability and security threat to its neighbours and the world, the UN and NATO would both be entitled to receive some of the credit. But equally, if warlordism and narco-criminality prevail, if Afghanistan remains a "failed state" and if its neighbours continue to experience spill-over disturbance from its unresolved internal tensions, the consequences for these international institutions will be long-lasting and severe.
5 Iraq's interim Prime Minister Allawi, for example, was reported as stating on 11 September that the elections planned for January 2005 would go ahead whatever the security situation: "If, for any reason, 300,000 people cannot have an election, if – a very big 'if' – then frankly 300,000 is not going to alter 25 million voting." *Financial Times*, 13 September 2004.
6 My keynote address to the Brazilian Association of Political Science (*Associação Brasiliera de Ciência Política*, ABCP), Rio de Janeiro, 22 July 2004.

2 International democracy promotion and protection

Theory and impact

Philippe C. Schmitter

Introduction

A novel "international policy industry" was born in the early 1980s: Democracy Promotion and Protection (DPP). It has expanded rapidly, almost monotonically, and still shows no signs of abating. The aim of this chapter is to evaluate the impact of DPP on the liberalization of autocratic regimes in the Middle East and North Africa (MENA), and on the consolidation of democratic regimes in Central and Eastern Europe (CEE).

An unprecedented effort has been made for DPP in terms of the financial *magnitude* of resources expended and in the geo-cultural *spread* of countries involved. Although it represents only a relatively small proportion of the total of public and private transfers from donor to recipient countries (roughly 10 per cent), this is still a great deal more than was spent in the past. And at the public discursive level, DPP has become a very prominent theme, at times eclipsing the previous emphasis on economic development, social equity or political stability. Transfers from the established to the deserving in the name of democracy are justified in terms of their contribution to domestic growth and international peace, rather than vice versa.

Even more surprising than the donors' enthusiastic embrace of these object-ives has been the way in which they have been received. Whereas such manifest intrusion by outsiders would have been rejected in the past on the grounds of unwarranted "interference in the domestic affairs of a sovereign state," DPP has not only been accepted (often willingly, sometimes grudgingly) in contexts of regime liberalization but also actively encouraged by elites seeking to consoli-date democracy. This is especially puzzling since the assumption had always been that attempts to consolidate regimes, and democratic regime consolidation in particular, were uniquely autochthonous affairs, heavily overlaid with national symbols and domestic calculations, such that manifest intrusions of this kind by outsiders could only diminish chances of success.

The principles and practices of political democracy have long been an object of international diffusion. All regimes that claim to be democratic have pro-claimed a permanent national interest in having other regimes adopt similar rules and ideals – even if they have done little to promote or protect such an outcome explicitly, and have, not infrequently, supported autocratic regimes when it suited their other national interests. Particular events, such as revolutions conducted in the name of democracy, and choices of rules established to implement it in a particular country, have spread from one place to another, although again this was only rarely the subject of deliberate effort. One might invoke the images of Thomas Jefferson, Benjamin Franklin and Thomas Paine in the salons of eighteenth century Europe, but this hardly constituted a concerted policy initiative of the new American Republic.

Diffusion was, moreover, strictly limited by spatial and cultural boundaries. For example, the first real "wave of democratization" – the so-called Springtime of Freedom (1848–52) – began in Naples and was quickly diffused to neighbouring countries on the continent, but it had little effect across the Atlantic or even across the Channel (although it did get as far north as Denmark). Subsequent waves associated with the First and the Second World Wars widened the circle of affected countries and involved a more explicit recourse to policies of DPP. The former involved attempts to democratize the newly independent units of the former Austro-Hungarian and Ottoman Empires, and the international supervision of plebiscites, as well as approval of constitutional guarantees of minority rights by the League of Nations, were part of that effort. The latter wave leapt across several oceans to produce regime change within units of European empires in Asia, Africa, the Caribbean and the Pacific. In virtually every case, the former imperial power was itself a (more or less) successfully established democracy and sought to transfer its institutions to newly independent ex-colonies. The role of the newly created United Nations (UN) was limited to supervising the transfer of authority in protectorates under its mandate. With a few notable exceptions (such as India, Botswana, Jamaica and some other Caribbean island republics, as well as a few Pacific micro-states), this most recent precursor of DPP was not a success. Most of the transplanted institutions failed to take root, and many were rejected on the grounds that they were antithetic to cultural norms and popular aspirations.

This brief historical *excursus* serves to show that while democracy has always been an international subject of discourse and object of policy, until recently relatively little was done *deliberately* and *specifically* to promote or protect democracy across national borders. And the evolutionary trends were hardly favourable for DPP: as the practice of citizenship expanded to include forms of equality beyond the strictly legal and political, democracy itself become inevitably more "national" and discriminatory against "non-nationals." Disparities emerged between the rights and entitlements of persons in particular countries, which inhibited exchanges of international pressure and solidarity from below; while a tightening system of inter-state alliances (and national neutralities) made cooperative action at the top more difficult. It may be the case, as the well-worn saying goes, that "democracies have not gone to war with each other," but it is also true that they did relatively little to help each other become or remain democratic – unless it was clearly in their national security interests to do so. Even then, intervention ostensibly to make a particular country "safe for democracy" did not always turn out very well, as the cases of Central America, Haiti, the Dominican Republic, the Philippines, South Korea and South Vietnam show (not to mention innumerable cases in sub-Saharan Africa).

A theory vacuum

This dismal historical record may help to explain why the practice of DPP was so devoid of any theoretical backing when it began in earnest in the early 1980s. In striking contrast to the initiation of foreign economic aid to Third World countries in the 1960s and 1970s, which came fully equipped with a widely respected (at the time) set of justifying concepts (remember the idea of "take-off to self-sustained growth"?) and an expanding professional cadre of "development economists," one looks in vain for any serious attempt to ground DDP in existing theories of democracy or democratization. The obvious reason for this was not that there were no such theories available or in the making. If practitioners had dared to take seriously what scholars had written on the subject (and managed to sift through their inevitable *querelles de famille*), they could only have drawn a negative lesson: that they should not intervene directly in the internal affairs of a fledgling democracy, since they would have either little or no impact because virtually all the relevant countries lacked the elementary "prerequisites" that were deemed necessary in the past, or they would not know what to do because such a highly uncertain enterprise depends on contingent power relations within a relatively small sub-set of actors inside the country.

Had they listened to the prevailing orthodoxy in academe at the time, DPP practitioners would have been encouraged strongly to act indirectly (if they had to do so at all) by promoting the allegedly indispensable economic or cultural conditions that make stable liberal democracy possible. In other words, they would have been told to go back to what they had been doing before, if only in a more focused and selective fashion by rewarding the countries that were at least trying to move from autocracy to democracy, but to have no illusions. The message would have been that democracy-building is a very lengthy and largely autochthonous process, and that all that established democracies could do directly was to cultivate their image of material and ethical superiority and hope that those who were less economically and culturally fortunate would eventually get the message and revolt against their authoritarian or totalitarian rulers. All this, unless, thanks to highly unusual conditions of international insecurity, these democracies were willing to go to war, were capable of defeating their autocratic opponents and then motivated enough to occupy them for a protracted period of time. Post-war Germany, Austria and Japan demonstrated that this could be done successfully, but then these countries already had many of the allegedly indispensable economic, if not cultural, requisites before they underwent externally induced and protractedly applied regime change.

Had the practitioners eager to engage in DPP bothered to read the emerging literature on democratization that was subsequently labelled "transitology," they may have felt slightly more encouraged. Here, the emphasis shifted from probabilistic analyses of what had been associated with the advent of liberal political democracy in the past, to "possibilistic speculations" about what actors might do in the present to come up with ("craft") mutually acceptable rules for channelling political conflict into competition between parties, associations and movements. This strategic rather than structural conception of the process of regime change quite explicitly failed to mention the importance of material or cultural requisites, and thus implied that efforts to democratize in "unfavourable" settings were not a priori doomed to failure. Had such advocates of DPP read a little further, however, they would have learned that this "possibilism" placed great emphasis on *domestic* elites, be they incumbent authoritarians or challenging democrats. In the context of the exaggerated uncertainty of transition, only those with "local knowledge" of rapidly changing interests and with "credible capacity" to deliver the compliance of key groups stood any chance of making a positive contribution (precisely the qualities that foreign DPP experts are least likely to have). It was only once the transition was over and reversion to autocracy more or less excluded that politics would begin to settle into more predictable behaviours reflecting (and reproducing) pre-existing patterns of socio-economic inequality and cultural differentiation. During this subsequent process of "consolidation" or "institutionalization," programmes of foreign democracy assistance might have a more important role to play, but by then the range of probable outcomes would have narrowed considerably. Many, if not most, of the crucial decisions would have already been made. The most that DPP could reasonably expect would be to make a marginal contribution, more to the type and quality of democracy than to its emergence or persistence.

The DPP industry seems to have been blissfully unaware of either of these "schools," and to have gone ahead on a more practical and immediate basis. The logic it followed seems to have been that if people were (or should have been) trying to democratize their respective national regimes, then well-established democrats should help them – although there may have lurked behind these public proclamations some less other-regarding motives. The fact that such a policy tended to funnel additional resources into donor agencies that already existed to promote economic and (sometimes) military aid certainly made the choice to intervene initially more palatable. Subsequently, it galvanized into action a wide range of non-governmental organizations, many of which took advantage of the "sub-contracting" opportunities offered by national and, in the case of Europe, supra-national authorities.

Timing seems also to have played an important role. It is very important to observe that DPP began in earnest in the early 1980s – *before*, not after, the fall of the Wall and the end of the Cold War. Doubtless, these events at the very end of the 1980s gave an additional impetus to the policy, but they cannot be assigned initial responsibility for it. One should not forget that the very first case of democratization in the most recent wave occurred under very special circumstances: the Portuguese *Revolução dos Cravos* in 1974 sent the (in retrospect, erroneous) message that regime change from protracted authoritarian rule was going to be a tumultuous process. Not only might it lead to aspirations for radical forms of "popular power" and the expansion of the role of the state, but it might also call into question well-established international alliances and thus endanger the external security of existing liberal democracies. Events in Portugal were not only unexpected, but also caught these powers unprepared with any *instrumentarium* to deal with such a threat (with the notable exception of the German party foundations and the usual deployment of national intelligence services) by surprise.

Ronald Reagan's famous speech before the British House of Commons in 1982 has been widely and rightly regarded as the "kick-off" event for DPP. The Council of Europe had a long-standing commitment to democratization that it implemented through its own membership requirements and a growing network of treaties. The German party foundations (Friedrich Ebert, Konrad Adenauer and Friedrich Naumann, at the time) were also active, giving aid to "sister parties" and sponsoring academic encounters in countries with authoritarian or totalitarian regimes. But it was not until the Americans entered the arena aggressively in the early 1980s that DPP can be said to have begun *in serio*. And when they did so, they were unequivocally motivated by the desire to prevent experiences such as the Portuguese and those just beginning to emerge in Latin America from upsetting the international balance of power and/or producing types of democracy that would be much less compatible with American economic interests. It is not too much of an exaggeration to claim that their interest in democracy was secondary to their concern with containing the spread of the "evil empire" and, not coincidentally, with insuring the health and welfare of capitalism. Had it not been for two quite unexpected developments and one lucky guess, I suspect that DPP would never have attained its subsequent prominence. It would have been (accurately) perceived as just another weapon in the US anti-communist arsenal (and a relatively minor one at that). Europeans at that time were experimenting with various forms of *Ostpolitik*, and would certainly have distanced themselves from the endemic excesses that have plagued such policies in the past: the Manichean vision of politics divided into "good guys" and "bad guys;" the tendency to support right-wing and sometimes even reactionary political groups; the propensity to confuse "free politics" with "free markets;" and, of course, the unwillingness to admit that the enemy itself might be changing.

The first development was the discovery that democratization might not be such a tumultuous process of change as was implied by the Portuguese Revolution, and subsequently reinforced by the Philippine experiment with "people power." The spectre of radical popular democracy proved to be a mirage. In case after case, domestic groups struggling against autocracy rather quickly came to realize that, whatever eventual changes might be forthcoming in property relations, income inequality or social justice, the route to attaining them passed through – rather than around or on top of – the limited and prosaic procedures of institutionalizing "liberal political democracy." The lessons of Cuba, Nicaragua and other abortive revolutionary or populist breakthroughs had been learned, and were not going to be repeated in the post-1974 wave of democratization that began in Southern Europe and then moved on to South America and Asia.

The second development was the *divine surprise* of 1989 in Eastern Europe and the subsequent collapse of the Soviet Union. Not only did this manifestly knock the props out from under the whole edifice of anti-communism, but it also vindicated the European strategy of "constructive engagement." Moreover, it virtually doubled the number of potential recipients of DPP overnight. Deprived of their enemy and overwhelmed by the demands of their new friends, the US architects of DPP seized the opportunity to intervene, although, interestingly, they emphasized the absolute priority of economic over political reform. Presumably this reflected their primary underlying goal, since it was by dismantling the structure of economic management and state ownership that the communist system would be most irrevocably destroyed, not just by decreeing the end of single-party rule and introducing competitive political institutions. They also prudently "off-loaded" the operational responsibility for many specific DPP programmes in Eastern Europe to a "consortium" run predominantly by Europeans and channelled through the European Community (later the European Union).

The "lucky guess" was that the more optimistic "strategic" theories of democratization turned out to be better descriptors and predictors of the process of regime change and its outcome than were the more pessimistic "structural" ones. Country after country that should have been condemned to immediate failure and regression to autocracy somehow managed to craft its way through the transition, and many have already made substantial progress towards consolidating a mutually acceptable set of rules for competition between political groups, rotation in power and some degree of accountability of rulers. DPP promoters were probably ignorant of this underlying academic controversy, but they could not help but notice that even some countries as initially unpromising as Bolivia, Mongolia, Nepal and Romania did not succumb to the temptations of "heroic leadership" or "populist power." Whatever the actual impact of their various programmes for the organization and observation of elections, the promotion of civil society, the enhancement of the independence of the judiciary or the rule of law, these efforts were only rarely associated with manifest regime collapse. Even with the (by now habitual) references to the low quality of the democracies that are being crafted under these conditions, there can be no denying that the strategic choices of actors have been making a difference – and this leaves open the possibility (but does not prove) that external democracy promoters and protectors have contributed positively to that unprecedented successful outcome.

Fourteen sceptical propositions about DPP

For the reasons mentioned above, DPP seems to be one of those topics in which theory and practice are unusually difficult to combine successfully. With very few exceptions, those who reflect in a generalizing and comparative way about attempts by outsiders to guide and improve the process of democratization are destined to be sceptical about the effort. With few exceptions, the "foreign agents" involved in designing and implementing policies of DPP are very likely to complain that "abstract theoreticians" are insensitive to their practical problems and, hence, that their efforts are not properly appreciated. Most of the time, however, the former do not waste much serious research time and effort on what they see as naive and misguided policies; the latter do not even bother to read attentively such irrelevant "scribblings," and when they do, they complain that the theoreticians adopt contrary perspectives and do not provide clear and compelling guidelines for action.

As card-carrying members of the "theory party," we cannot pretend to resolve this intrinsic clash of perspectives – not even to present a balanced view on the issue. The best we can offer is a set of sceptical propositions suggested by the literature on democratization that focuses on why DPP is such a difficult and paradoxical activity, with an impact that may only rarely correspond to the "good intentions" of its practitioners. What follows are fourteen sceptical propositions about DPP.

1   The net contribution of DPP can be potentially significant (and positive), but it is rarely more than marginal in determining the outcome of democratization.

2   The very existence of DPP is normally voluntary and reciprocal in principle, but is almost always semi- to in-voluntary and asymmetric in practice.

3   The presence of DPP in a given country usually involves a formal contractual arrangement between public authorities, but its performance is largely contingent upon informal relations between non-governmental organizations and private persons.

4   The epistemological basis of DPP is the presumed superiority of well-established liberal democracies, and yet democracy in these donor countries is often in serious crisis – and precisely in the areas they are most insistent on transferring to recipients (electoral politics and competitive party systems).

5   The success of DPP is intrinsically problematic and long term (not to mention, marginal in impact), and yet donors require repeated evidence of immediate, visible and significant accomplishments in order to ensure continuous support from their citizens or taxpayers.

6   The success of DPP is likely to be greater where it is least needed; hence the tendency for donors to "cherry-pick" by concentrating their effort on those countries where liberalization or democratization would have occurred anyway.

7   Inversely, the success of DPP is likely to be greater when the desire of donors to provide it is weakest (namely, when it is not used as a "cover" for the pursuit of other donor objectives such as national security or commercial advantage).

8   The institutional transfer inherent in DPP is often the greatest where it leaves the least perceptible traces (namely, where the practices and rules that it encourages look the most remote from those of the foreign donor and the closest to the native or national traditions of the recipient countries).

9 The net contribution of DPP is most positive when it is "self-cancelling" (namely, when the practices and rules of its specific programmes are most quickly taken over by national authorities and politicians and require no further foreign input).

10 The long-term probability of a successful transfer of institutions from donor to recipient is greatest when grounded in a generic understanding of what democracy is, and yet the short-term chance that a given programme will work well depends on specific knowledge of conditions in an individual country.

11 DPP works best from the point of view of recipients when there is a multiplicity of competing donors such that they are capable of picking and choosing the programmes or projects that they prefer.

12 DPP works best for donors when they can collude or divide up the market in a way that enables them to compel recipients to accept the programmes or projects they think are most effective.

13 Since success in democratization involves "hitting a moving target" of actors and objectives, DPP must change its programmes or projects correspondingly, and this is likely to mean disrupting and even abandoning previous exchange relations between donors and recipients.

14 The more that DPP becomes a salient and well-funded component of donor foreign policy, the greater will be its appeal for ambitious organizations and individuals in these countries, and the more they will seek to professionalize and control access to its provision. A similar process of closure is likely to emerge on the recipient side, particularly in those countries with the least "domestic capacity" to absorb DPP and, hence, the greatest potential need for it. Professionalization becomes a mutually reinforcing process and, accordingly, programmes and projects tend to become less and less responsive to the county's needs and more and more to the aspirations of providers on both sides.

It will not be easy to convert all of these fourteen sceptical propositions into discrete and testable hypotheses, although all of them are, at least in principle, falsifiable. Some are obviously worded in too abstract a manner; others contain "essentially contested" concepts that it would be difficult to measure in an objective manner. Not a few refer to trends whose effects it may be too soon to evaluate. Hopefully, however, in the project dealing with the macro-measurement of DPP on which this chapter is based, and the macro-assessment of its impact, we will be able to test several of them. The rest will have to await the next stage of our research, when we shift to meso- and micro-analyses of specific programmes and projects in particular countries. The best we can expect to extract from this preliminary (but nonetheless essential) analysis is to describe the total magnitude of the DPP effort and its distribution across CEE and the MENA, as well as its distribution according to generic types of programmes. Then, we can attempt through statistical estimation procedures to assess the probability that DPP has made a significant difference in either promoting the liberalization of autocracies or the consolidation of democracies – not on particular institutions or practices, but upon the polity as a whole.

Assessing the macro-impact of the DPP effort

At this point, we seem to have all the necessary empirical material for assessing the aggregate impact of DPP upon democratization during the period from 1980 to 1999: multiple indicators of DPP Effort (DPPE) and separate scales for liberalization (LoA), transition (MoT) and consolidation (CoD) for the eleven countries in CEE and the MENA. What we now need is an apposite strategy for analysing this material comparatively and a plausible basis for inferring causality from whatever patterns of association we find. However, as discussed at the outset, my expectation has always been paradoxical. I do *not* expect to find a positive and significant direct correlation between the DPP effort and progress toward LoA and CoD, and if I were to find such a correlation, my inference would be that it is spurious.[1] In other words, I would interpret this to mean that donors had deliberately "cherry-picked" (chosen to give democracy assistance to countries that they knew, or suspected, would have in any case been successful in liberalizing their autocracies and/or consolidating their neo-democracies).

My working hypothesis has been that the impact of DPP will only be marginal (but potentially significant) and positive: the aggregate effort (DPPE) – measured in monetary terms – by all DPP donors and DPP programmes in a given country is likely to have a net effect on the success of democratization, but only once other, more significant, domestic factors have been taken into account. In other words, if I simply add all the DPP contributions together (with and without controlling for variation in the size of recipient countries), ignore the identity and mix of donors, set aside the content of the programmes and projects involved, pay no attention to the timing and sequence with which they were disbursed, and presume that there are no differences in overhead costs and the efficiency of actual disbursements – I should still be able to discern a *positive net effect* upon both the extent to which recipients' liberalize their previously autocratic regimes (in the MENA) or consolidate their newly founded democratic regimes (for the CEEC), but only *after* taking into account a number of structural and situational factors.

To a limited extent,[2] this strategy of inference implies that my data-gathering so far has been insufficient. I need to introduce, in some systematic fashion, a set of control variables. These will measure conditions that might have contributed independently to the success of liberalization, transition and/or consolidation, and it is only after assessing their impact on outcomes that I will be able to test for the marginal contribution of the DPPE.[3] Fortunately, however, there exists an abundant literature on the so-called "prerequisites" or "facilitating conditions" for democracy, and it should be possible to manipulate data on them in such a way as to predict how easy or difficult it is likely to have been to be to produce a successful outcome.[4] Once I can introduce variables to control for those characteristics that allegedly favour such successes, my estimate of the contribution of DPP to the outcome should diminish – although I do anticipate some enduring (and positive) effect.

Of course, we might even discover the inverse. The independent contribution of DPP could be significant, but negative. In this case, my initial suspicion of spuriousness would be inverted. Instead of "cherry-picking" the easy cases, donors may have been "basket-casing" – concentrating their efforts on cases where impediments to liberalization and/or democratization are most likely to emerge. Needless to say, if these economic, social and cultural variables cannot be combined into a statistically significant model that predicts the subsequent course of regime change in CEEC and the MENA, the potential for a positive contribution by DPP would be considerably enhanced, but not proven. It is still possible that other variables, especially ones intrinsic to the process of democratization itself, determined the outcome – whether or not the actors involved in making these "transitional" choices received any support from foreign donors.

Tracking the direct impact of DPP effort

Table 2.1 displays the Pearson Product Moment Correlations and two-tailed significance tests between three indicators of DPPE and three indicators of the cumulative progress that ten of the eleven CEE and MENA countries made toward the consolidation of a liberal democratic regime from 1980 to 1999.[5] It will be immediately noticed that all of the coefficients are positive. In other words, *the more in absolute, logged or per capita terms a country was given in democracy assistance, the further that country tended to advance on all three Scales of Democratization.*[6] *This relation was less significant for the absolute and the logged amounts than when the DPP effort was controlled for the size of country's population.* The unweighted cumulative scores of all three processes (TDS) hardly differed from the sum of just the liberalization and the consolidation scales (LoA and CoD), and hence the correlations were virtually identical. Interestingly, the two scores weighted by their relative difficulty of acquisition – TDS (W) – proved to be predicted to about the same extent as the simple cumulative scores, except for per capita DPP where the weighted one was predicted significantly better.[7] Using the sum total of DPP from 1980 to 1999 in US dollars, all the relationships were statistically insignificant. Controlling for the

Table 2.1 Correlation matrix of DPP measures and scales of democratization

Measures of DPP	TDS	LoA + CoD	TDS (W)
Total DPP in US$ million (1980–99)	+0.421 (0.225)	+0.431 (0.214)	+0.419 (0.228)
Total DPP in US$ per capita (1980–99)	+0.604 (0.064)	+0.572 (0.084)	+0.642 (0.046)
Total DPP logged in US$, (1980–99)	+0.619 (0.056)	+0.579 (0.080)	+0.612 (0.060)

Note
N = 10.

size of each country's population, the coefficient became considerably more significant, even reaching the magic >0.05 level in the case of TDS (W). Logging the total DPPE produces a positive but less statistically significant result.

This is *not* what I expected. Not even the most enthusiastic proponent of DPP has argued that it alone is capable of ensuring either liberalization or a successful consolidation. The financial sums have been manifestly too modest, and the expert advice, however good, still had to compete with "domestic priorities and values" in the receiving countries. My first suspicion, therefore, is that DPP promoters could be accused of "cherry-picking." The results are consistent with a strategy of giving a priority to those recipients that were likely to do well anyway, so that the donors would look good to their funding sources "back home." Inversely, at this aggregate level (including both the CEEC and the MENA countries but excluding Palestine), there is no evidence that they preferred the countries that one might have expected (and subsequently had) the greatest difficulty in democratizing themselves.

However, when I split the data into two samples – one with six CEE countries and the other with four MENA countries – the accusation of "cherry-picking" becomes radically less compelling. What I have captured initially is simply the two core differences between CEE and the MENA: namely, first that the countries in the former region have received more DPP per capita over the period (from US$8.23 in Poland to US$28.2 in Bulgaria) than the latter (from US$0.15 in Algeria to US$2.84 in Egypt); and second, the former have progressed through the transition well into consolidation, whereas the latter are still mired in hesitant processes of liberalization. As can be seen from Tables 2.2 and 2.3, when examining the distribution of DPP within the two regions, there is no longer any evidence at all that more was given to successful countries.

Table 2.2 The macro-impact of DPPE: CEE scales of democratization

Measures of DPPE	TDS	LoA + CoD	TDS (W)
Total DPP in US$ (1980–99)	–0.225 (0.668)	+0.052 (0.922)	–0.306 (0.555)
Per capita DPP (1980–99)	–0.029 (0.956)	–0.305 (0.555)	+0.096 (0.856)
DPP logged (1980–99)	–0.327 (0.526)	–0.064 (0.904)	–0.401 (0.430)

Note
N = 6.

Table 2.3 The macro-impact of DPPE: MENA scales of democratization

Measures of DPPE	TDS	LoA + CoD	TDS (W)
Total DPP in US$ (1980–99)	–0.266 (0.734)	–0.480 (0.531)	+0.328 (0.672)
Per Capita DPP in US$ (1980–99)	+0.217 (0.783)	–0.469 (0.520)	–0.321 (0.679)
Total DPP in US$ logged (1980–99)	+0.132 (0.869)	–0.101 (0.899)	+0.062 (0.938)

Note
N = 4.

In CEE, the direction of many of the correlations has even changed from positive to negative, but the major finding is that none of them is remotely close to significant. Based on the simple bivariate relation between DDPE and the scales of regime change, there is no evidence either that it contributed directly to regime change, or that donors systematically picked winners or losers. The impression for CEE is simply that of randomness.

In Table 2.3, we find a quite similar picture for the smaller MENA sub-set. The coefficients are positive, but utterly insignificant. DPP (in much smaller amounts except for Palestine, which has not been included) went neither to those recipients who liberalized more nor those who liberalized less. For example, Turkey was the only country in the region that made any progress towards consolidating democracy, and it received much less DPP than Egypt (US$23.77 million compared to US$189.13 million), although both have about the same population (65.7 million inhabitants compared to 66.7). What makes this finding especially compelling is that, unlike a random division of variance for which the two sets should have approximately the same means, these two sets almost do not overlap with each other, with the exception of Turkey. Finding the same (non-)significance implies that the relation of DPP to the process of regime change holds constant for both its liberalization and its democratization "phases," and holds across units at very different levels of development. Moreover, it holds for two sub-sets of countries with quite different political histories and cultural heritages.

I can also partition the data to address another controversial issue in the democracy assistance literature; namely that of whether DPP given by the EU and European countries is more or less effective than that given by the United States, at least at the macro-level. Several articles have suggested that their greater "local knowledge" (and secrecy in the case of the German party foundations) makes the former perform more effectively.[8] One might also add that, given the fact that all of the CEE countries in our sample were on the list of front-runners for membership of the EU, Western Europeans have a potentiality for exercising political conditionality that the Americans do not. Regardless of the sums that they spend, the mere threat that failure to produce a liberal democratic outcome will exclude the recipients from entry into the EU club provides a powerful incentive to conform.

Juxtaposing Tables 2.4 and 2.5 and including both CEE and the MENA, there

Table 2.4 The macro-impact of European DPPE on democratization (scales of democratization, CEE and MENA)

Measures of DPPE by Europe	TDS	LoA + CoD	TDS (W)
Total DPP in US$ (1980–99)	+0.674 (0.032)	+0.719 (0.019)	+0.672 (0.033)
Total DPP in US$ per capita (1980–99)	+0.773 (0.009)	+0.739 (0.015)	+0.804 (0.005)
Total DPP in US$ logged (1980–99)	+0.809 (0.005)	+0.792 (0.006)	+0.802 (0.005)

Note
N = 10.

Table 2.5 The macro-impact of US DPP upon democratization (scales of democratization, CEE and MENA)

Measures of DPPE by USA	TDS	LoA + CoD	TDS (W)
Total DPP in US$ million (1980–99)	+0.193 (0.593)	+0.179 (0.621)	+0.191 (0.597)
Total DPP in US$ per capita (1980–99)	+0.458 (0.183)	+0.430 (0.215)	+0.496 (0.145)
Total DPP in US$ logged (1980–99)	+0.510 (0.132)	+0.467 (0.174)	+0.504 (0.138)

Note
N = 10.

is some evidence that "Europeans do it better," but it will only be discernable later, whether this is because they have been better at assessing who would have done well anyway or because their DPP really has been better placed or more efficiently administered. As was the case with Table 2.1, the correlations are positive for both "camps of donors," although they are higher and more significant for the Europeans in every category. As before, the weighted cumulative scale is best predicted by the DPP indicators, with an astonishingly high correlation of 0.804 (0.005) between European per capita aid and TDS (W). We may, of course, subsequently discover that this is spurious when we control for the other factors that predict success in regime change. It is important, however, to note that the putative superiority of European DPP is not due to its concentration on CEE. In fact, the US was a larger contributor to four of these six recipients (Poland and the Czech Republic were the exceptions). The Europeans gave more DPP money to Morocco, Algeria and Palestine than did the United States.[9] However, whether they should be castigated for picking the cherries that are easier to reach or congratulated for helping to produce a better *tarte aux cerises* remains to be seen.

Creating a model of democratization without DPPE

Having examined the direct relation between DPP and LoA and CoD, we can now get down to the more serious and challenging business of trying to build a model that predicts the likelihood of successful liberalization–transition–democratization, and then discovering whether the absolute, per capita or logged amounts of DPP differs (positively or negatively) from the expectations established by this model. Specifying such a model with so few and such diverse countries is not going to be an easy task. As mentioned previously, the political science literature has produced long lists of alleged prerequisites for democracy, far too many to be tested simultaneously with the ten cases available. Upon closer inspection, these variables can be separated into no less than five theoretical clusters: "structural;" "cultural;" "realist or geo-strategic," "state-ness," and "transitological." Each has a mutually exclusive set of causal or enabling conditions and is capable of generating its own distinctive predictions concerning the probable outcome.[10]

Structural variables

Let us begin with a standard list of allegedly favourable structural conditions obtaining at the moment of departure, and see how well indicators of them predict the subsequent course of LoA and CoD. These are: first, estimated gross domestic product (GDP) per capita (the higher the average income, the greater the probability of successful liberalization/consolidation); second, the United Nations Development Programme (UNDP) Human Development Index (HDI) (the higher the quality of life prior to regime change, the greater the probability of successful LoA and CoD); third, income distribution (the more egalitarian the distribution, the greater the probability of successful LoA and CoD); and fourth, the rate of economic growth (REG) (the higher the growth rate before and/or after the initiation of regime change, the greater the probability of successful LoA and CoD).

Even a cursory glance at Table 2.6 demonstrates that some of the structural variables that are suspected to "cause" or "facilitate" democratization are indeed significantly correlated with this outcome, and their signs run in the anticipated direction. For example, GDP per capita at the beginning of the period (1990) is positively correlated with the total democratization scale at a quite significant level: +0.709 (0.022) and even more closely correlated with the weighted scale: +0.771 (009). The correlations are virtually identical at the end of the period (1999). The HDI does better than both in 1990: +0.837 (0.003) and only slightly less well in 1999: +0.750 (0.012). And, again, the correlation with TDS (W) is higher. Surprisingly, from a strictly "liberal" point of view, the share of government revenues in GDP (1990) is also a good predictor of later success – +0.736 (0.015) with TDS and +0.765 (0.010) with TDS (W) – but this may be due to a "regional specificity" (the much higher value for this variable in CEEC at point of departure). In any case, it had declined in magnitude and significance ten years later: +0.517 (0.126) and +0.556 (0.095). The other two structural conditions – income distribution and REG – were insignificant, although their signs were in the anticipated direction.[11] Once I partition the variance into our two regions (Tables 2.7 and 2.8), the correlations persist in terms of their signs (with

Table 2.6 Correlation matrix of structural variables and democratization scales

Structural variables	TDS	TDS (W)
GDP per capita (1990)	+0.709 (0.022)	+0.771 (0.009)
HDI (1990)	+0.837 (0.003)	+0.913 (0.000)
GINI index of income distribution	−0.372 (0.289)	−0.399 (0.253)
REG (1990–9)	+0.165 (0.649)	+0.140 (0.699)
GDP per capita (1999)	+0.712 (0.021)	+0.753 (0.012)
HDI (1999)	+0.750 (0.012)	+0.833 (0.003)
Gov. revenue as % GDP (1990)	+0.736 (0.015)	+0.765 (0.010)
Gov. revenue as % GDP (1999)	+0.517 (0.131)	+0.556 (0.095)

Note
N = 10.

Table 2.7 Correlation matrix of structural variables and democratization scales in CEE

Structural variables	TDS	TDS (W)
GDP per capita (1990)	0.661 (0.153)	0.745 (0.089)
HDI (1990)	0.830 (0.041)	0.904 (0.013)
GINI index of income distribution	0.137 (0.795)	0.032 (0.952)
REG (1990–9)	0.532 (0.277)	0.420 (0.407)
GDP per capita (1999)	0.712 (0.113)	0.718 (0.108)
HDI (1999)	0.786 (0.064)	0.767 (0.075)
Gov. revenue as % GDP (1990)	0.399 (0.433)	0.484 (0.330)
Gov. revenue as % GDP (1999)	0.176 (0.739)	0.305 (0.557)

Note
N = 6.

Table 2.8 Correlation matrix of structural variables and democratization scales in MENA

Structural variables	TDS	TDS (W)
GDP per capita (1990)	+0.345 (0.655)	+0.638 (0.362)
HDI (1990)	+0.309 (0.691)	0.607 (0.393)
GINI index of income distribution	+0.716 (0.284)	+0.790 (0.210)
REG (1990–9)	+0.325 (0.675)	+0.421 (0.579)
GDP per capita (1999)	+0.097 (0.903)	+0.422 (0.578)
HDI (1999)	0.129 (0.871)	+0.222 (0.778)
Gov. revenue as % GDP (1990)	−0.309 (0.691)	−0.300 (0.700)
Gov. revenue as % GDP (1999)	−0.225 (0.775)	−0.215 (0.785)

Note
N = 4.

one exception), but not their significance. Everything is less tightly related in the MENA: GDP per capita, the HDI and the REG. Interestingly, the GINI Index of income inequality across deciles of the population is *positively* correlated with democratization in both CEEC and the MENA countries, rather than negatively when the entire sample is considered. In other words, the more unequal the initial distribution of income is *within* both regions, the greater is the likelihood of democracy at the end of the period (although the correlation is not highly significant for either sub-set).

When I take the variables from Table 2.6, place them in an OLS multiple regression and eliminate those that contribute nothing to our ability to predict the outcome in terms of the simple or weighted total democratization score, I obtain the best fit by using HDI (1990) and REG (1990–9), with the former contributing a lot and the latter very little. All of the other structural variables are eliminated. The problem in Table 2.9 is that HDI does too good a job – and that can safely be attributed to the fact that the communist regimes in CEE with their superior education and health systems did much better on this index than the

Table 2.9 Multiple regression TDS and TDS (W) estimate with the best combination of structural variables

Equations	TDS	TDS (W)
HDI + GDP growth	R = 0.847	R = 0.919
ANOVA		
GDP growth		
Standardized beta	0.132	0.105
T	0.657	0.702
Sig.	0.532	0.505
HDI		
Standardized beta	0.831	0.909
T	4.135	6.104
Sig.	0.004	0.000

Note
N = 10.

capitalist (or, better, state-nationalist) regimes in the MENA at comparable levels of economic development. Once capitalism had arrived "in such a shocking manner" in the former, so did their relative performance on the HDI decline and, hence, its correlation with TDS and TDS (W).

This has led me to prefer a "second-best" strategy on the grounds that a less impressive, but nonetheless highly significant, indicator (GDP per capita) should be preferred on the grounds that the results obtained by using it are more likely to be universally valid, especially when entered into comparisons with fewer post-communist cases (Table 2.10). Therefore, as I move towards a "consolidated" model, I will use it along with whatever is discovered from the cultural, strategic and other variables.

It should be noted that, as has usually been the case, the weighted indicator of democratization is better predicted than the simple cumulative one. Also, the

Table 2.10 Second-best combination of structural variables

Equations	TDS	TDS (W)
GDP per capita + GDP growth	R = 0.715	R = 0.774
ANOVA		
GDP growth		
Standardized beta	0.093	0.062
T	0.351	0.257
Sig.	0.736	0.804
GDP per capita		
Standardized beta	0.700	0.765
T	2.637	3.177
Sig.	0.026	0.016

Note
N = 10.

level of GDP is a much more significant predictor of TDS and TDS (W) than the rate of its growth. The two countries whose accomplishments are least well predicted are Romania which did better than expected, and Algeria which did worse.

Cultural variables

"Culturalist" explanations for the success of democratization abound, but are characteristically difficult to specify or to operationalize. Many authors have stressed the imperative of having a "civic culture," and even measured this in one well-known study, which applied survey research in several settings in order to discover whether mass attitudes resembled those found in the two allegedly most successful cases, namely, the United Kingdom and the US.[12] Needless to say, countries such as Italy and Germany failed to replicate this standard. Even so, their respective democracies persisted, and, indeed, today there are no grounds for judging them markedly inferior to the UK or the US. In any case, we do not have any such carefully crafted research that covers the cases that interest us here with attitudinal surveys, so I had to improvise. Below, I specify three historical and relatively enduring conditions that might be expected to make it culturally easier or harder to consolidate a democratic regime (Table 2.11):[13]

1   *years of previous democracy* (the longer the prior experience with some form of democracy, the greater the probability of successful TDS and TDS (W));

2   *religious homogeneity* (the more that the society has a single dominant religion, the greater the probability of success in the same categories); and

3   *ethno-linguistic homogeneity* (the more the society is dominated by a single ethno-linguistic group, the greater the probability of a higher TDS & TDS (W) score).

Only one of these variables is correlated to a statistically significant degree within our eleven-country sample, and its sign is *contrary to theoretical expectation*. The more the society is dominated by a single religion, the less likely it is that its polity will make progress towards democracy! Needless to say, it might have been more interesting to test for the identity of that dominant religion, but

Table 2.11 Correlation matrix of cultural variables and democratization scales

	TDS	*TDS (W)*
Years of previous democracy	−0.052 (0.886)	+0.025 (0.945)
Religious homogeneity	−0.605 (0.064)	−0.631 (0.050)
Ethno-linguistic homogeneity	+0.098 (0.788)	−0.045 (0.901)

Note
N = 10.

that would simply split the sample into a (mostly) Catholic CEE and a (thoroughly) Muslim MENA. With a larger number of societies and a greater range of religious affiliations, we might eventually be able to test for the alleged propensity for the more "Westernized" and secularized Christian societies to be more democratic than "Easternized" Christianity, Islam, Buddhism or Confucianism. Those with a longer previous history of democracy and greater ethnolinguistic homogeneity did do better, but only very marginally so among our ten cases. Whether this "non-finding" – which goes very much against the literature – holds up in a larger sample of neo-democracies is, of course, another matter.

Realistic or geo-strategic variables

The next set of theorists who have had something to say about democratization come from the so-called "realist" school of international relations. All of the following are alleged to be associated with a more prominent location on the security agenda of donor countries, and hence likely to attract higher relative DPP and greater concern with the resulting democratic outcome. The underlying assumption, repeatedly stressed by former US President Bill Clinton, is that "democracies do not go to war with each other." This desirable end from the perspective of well-established democracies should vary with:

1   *proximity to Europe* (measured by the distance from the national capital to Brussels);
2   *proximity to the US* (measured by the distance from the national capital to Washington, DC);
3   *special security situation* (as measured by the country's importance as a raw material supplier, particularly petroleum;
4   the presence or absence of *civil conflict or internal war* (particularly one that involves neighbouring states);
5   *geo-strategic location* (especially the presence of a foreign military base or prospect for refugees);
6   the level of previous *Western fixed foreign investment*; and finally
7   the proportion of *imports from and exports to Western countries*.

It should be noted that several of these variables would require some "artful" transformations since, in some situations, the "realist" assessment places much higher priority on political stability of any kind, and hence may lead to no DPP at all if that would endanger the perpetuation of compliant autocracies (as in Saudi Arabia or Algeria). Moreover, it is precisely because potential donors may not agree on the nature of the threat or opportunity posed by the international system that they may disagree in their willingness to engage in a DPP effort, or may decide to compete with each other in doing so.

Thus far, I have only been able to operationalize three of these variables, and only one of them looks highly promising from the results in Table 2.12 – namely, *distance from Brussels*. The closer the national capital of a neo-

Table 2.12 Correlation matrix of strategic variables and scales of democratization

Strategic variables	TDS	TDS (W)
Distance from Brussels	−0.652 (0.041)	−0.667 (0.035)
Distance from Washington	−0.265 (0.459)	−0.183 (0.612)
Exports and imports as % GDP (1990)	+0.374 (0.287)	+0.406 (0.244)

Note
N = 10.

democracy is to the EU, the more likely is it to have made progress towards con-solidating its regime. Distance from Washington DC is much less significant, and the extent of integration into the world economy (as measured by exports and imports as a percentage of GDP) is only slightly less insignificant.

"State-ness" variables

There has been a renewed concern with the impact of "state-ness" upon processes of regime change.[14] The underlying theme dates back to a (belatedly) influential article by Dankwart Rustow, who argued that there was only one prerequisite for democracy: "the vast majority of citizens in a democracy-to-be must have no doubt or mental reservations as to which political community they belong to" and this, in the contemporary age, means that they must be organized into a economic-ally viable and territorially unique state.[15] Needless to say, there are no ready-made operational indicators of "state-ness," and we have already seen that ethnic-national homogeneity alone is no guarantor or even correlate of successful democratization. I have not yet been able to assemble the necessary data, but the following indicators might be capable of capturing variation in the context of "state-ness" once the previous autocracy has fallen or transformed itself:

1   change in central government revenue as a percentage of GDP once liberal-ization or democratization has begun;
2   years during which the unit has continuously enjoyed external recognition (has been a member of the UN).

The code for state-ness in the context of regime change is as follows: 1=no change in either external or internal borders; 2=no external, some internal border changes; 3=contestation about external borders, but no change in them; 4 =peaceful change in external borders; 5=violent conflict over appropriateness of borders leads to change in them.

"Transitological" variables

Finally, the recent and burgeoning literature sometimes referred to as "transitol-ogy" has tended to focus on the peculiar conditions and choices made during the highly uncertain period between one regime and another, with the assumption that these momentary balances of power and improvised solutions to immediate problems can have long-lasting effects on both the likelihood that some form of democracy will be consolidated and the quality of that democracy. The following conditions might be expected to affect these outcomes:

1 *the mode of transition*, in order of promoting a favourable outcome: 1= "pacted" between the *ancien régime* and its opponents; 2=imposed by the *ancien régime*; 3=reformist, generated by peaceful mass mobilization from below; 4=revolutionary, brought about by violent insurrection from below; 5= "black hole," an indeterminate and confused mix of the above);

2 the *timing of transition* (years since this "wave of democratization" began in 1974);

3 the *regional context* (1=all neighbouring regimes are established democracies; 2=some neighbours are established, some neo-democracies; 3=all neighbouring regimes are neo-democracies; 4=some neighbours are neo-democracies, some liberalized autocracies; 5=all neighbouring regimes are autocracies of some type or another);

4 *regional organization* (1=the country is an early candidate for EU membership; 2=the country is a candidate for later EU membership; 3=the country is already a candidate or is a candidate for associate status with EU; 4=the country has no foreseeable link to the EU but is involved in some regional international governmental organization (IGO) with a proclaimed commitment to democracy, such as the Organization of American States (OAS) or the Organization of African Unity (OAU); 5=the country has no significant political links to a regional IGO with democratic objectives, such as the Association of Southeast Asian Nations (ASEAN) or the League of Arab States; and finally,

5 the *type of previous autocracy* (1=bureaucratic authoritarian; 2=traditional monarchy; 3=populist authoritarian; 4= "partialitarian" or degenerate communist/totalitarian; 5=totalitarian/communist).

Again, I have not had the time or resources to gather or code these data, but intend to do so in the future.

Since it is by no means clear which of these models (if any) DPP donors might have had in mind to guide their "cherry-picking" (or what signals they may have used to trigger their "basket-casing"), all that I can do is to try to construct the best possible predictive model from the indicators so far assembled. Now that we have explored each of them separately, it is time to combine them in multiple regression equations and eliminate those variables that make no contribution to our ability to predict the subsequent course of liberalization/democratization. It is only after having examined the predictive validity of these differing sets of assumptions that we can turn to the task of estimating the direction and significance of the independent contribution of DPP.

Estimating a multi-variate equation for democratization (with and without DPP)

We now have a rich list of "suspects." The following have all been found to have been conducting significantly intimate bivariate relations with TDS and TDS (W):

1   HDI
2   GDP per capita
3   religious homogeneity (negative)
4   distance from Brussels.

Doubtless, some of the "state-ness" and "transitological" variables might eventually contribute something once I have measured them adequately. Once I had opted for the "second-best" option (preferring economic to human development for the reasons advocated above), I came up with the equations in Table 2.13:

A glance at the statistics reveals that none of these "finalists" made equally significant contributions to either TDS or TDS (W). GDP per capita alone is by far the most reliable "competitor." The total estimate jumps only from 0.709 to 0.733 in the case of TDS, and from 0.771 to 0.783 in the case of TDS (W) when the strategic variable is added, and makes virtually no improvement with the religious variable. The proportion of variance predicted is quite high, but not so high as to preclude any effect for DPP. In terms of specific cases, the ones with the highest residuals (the least well predicted) were Poland and Romania, which did better

Table 2.13 Multiple regression model predicting TDS and TDS (W) using the (second) best combination of structural, cultural and strategic variables

Equations	TDS	TDS (W)
GDP per capita/religious Homogeneity/Distance from Brussels	R = 0.736 R square = 0.541	R = 0.784 R square = 0.615
ANOVA	0.171	0.105
GDP per capita		
Standardized beta	0.446	0.580
T	0.920	1.307
Sig.	0.393	0.239
Religious homogeneity		
Standardized beta	−0.098	−0.066
T	−0.226	−0.165
Sig.	0.829	0.875
Distance from Brussels		
Standardized beta	−0.253	−0.190
T	−0.591	−0.483
Sig.	0.576	0.646

Note
N = 10.

than might have been expected, and Algeria, which did worse. Morocco also did better than it was "supposed to," but still within the standard deviation.

Finally, we have arrived at "the moment of truth," at which I can apply the most strenuous possible test for the (positive or negative) impact of DPPE on the macro-process of regime change from autocracy to democracy in CEE and the MENA. In Tables 2.14 to 2.16, we find the results of inserting the three DPPE variables into the previous "second-best" equation.

Table 2.14 Multiple regression model predicting TDS and TDS (W) using the (second) best combination and total DPP

Equations	TDS	TDS (W)
GDP per capita/Distance from	R = 0.821	R = 0.867
Brussels/Total DPP	R square = 0.674	R square = 0.752
ANOVA	0.066	0.016
GDP per capita		
Standardized beta	0.557	0.672
T	1.582	2.193
Sig.	0.165	0.071
Distance from Brussels		
Standardized beta	−0.185	−0.113
T	−0.522	−0.365
Sig.	0.620	0.728
Total DPP		
Standardized beta	0.375	0.378
T	1.583	1.832
Sig.	0.164	0.117

Table 2.15 Multiple regression model predicting TDS and TDS (W) using the (second) best combination and logged DPP

Equations	TDS	TDS (W)
GDP per capita/Distance from	R = 0.866	R = 0.895
Brussels/Total DPP	R Square = 0.750	R Square = 0.801
(constant)		
GDP per capita		
Standardized beta	0.340	0.465
T	1.078	1.654
Sig.	0.323	0.149
Distance from Brussels		
Standardized beta	−0.326	−0.251
T	−1.059	−0.916
Sig.	0.330	0.395
Logged DPP		
Standardized beta	0.479	0.450
T	2.257	2.380
Sig.	0.065	0.055

Note
N = 10.

Table 2.16 Multiple regression model predicting TDS and TDS (W) using the (second) best combination and DPP per capita

Equations	TDS	TDS (W)
GDP per capita/Distance from	R = 0.763	R = 0.813
Brussels/DPP per capita	R square = 0.583	R square = 0.660
(constant)		
GDP per capita		
Standardized beta	0.360	0.473
T	0.831	1.209
Sig.	0.438	0.272
Distance from Brussels		
Standardized beta	–0.255	–0.183
T	–0.642	–0.511
Sig.	0.544	0.628
DPP per capita		
Standardized beta	0.266	0.271
T	0.806	0.910
Sig.	0.451	0.398

Note
N = 10.

The findings are surprising and convincing. *On all three measures, DPP contributes positively to both the simple and weighted scales of democratization.* Despite the fact that in Table 2.1 the per capita measure was most significant in predicting the extent of regime change, once the controls have been added, it is the absolute and, especially, the logged measures of DPP that win hands down. The larger total sum of DPP a country received, the greater its progress towards liberalization or consolidation was likely to have been – not more significant than having a higher GDP per capita, but definitely more than just being nearer to Brussels. But the most astonishing finding is in Table 2.15, in which the log of total DPP has become *the most significant* predictor of such progress, at the 0.065 level for TDS and the 0.055 level for TDS (W). It even displaces GDP per capita in relative importance, and the distance from Brussels literally evaporates as a contributor. So, for the moment I can affirm that *DPP when distributed in a certain fashion does seem to produce a positive effect – and this is so regardless of the stage of regime change or differences in cultural or historical context.* Given the "most different systems" nature of the comparative design – one in which CEE and the MENA are clustered at the opposite ends of a continuum, with only Turkey in between – this makes the finding especially compelling from a theoretical perspective, even if its statistical basis is not very "robust."

Moreover, this finding – that it is the total and logged amounts of DPP that are particularly significant, not the per capita amounts – has potentially important policy implications. It does not seem to make sense to divide DPP funds evenly, or calibrate them according to the size of a country's population. What apparently counts is the ability to assemble a critical mass of financial support. Only then can it have a discernable and positive impact, regardless of the absolute number of beneficiaries or magnitude of the problem. The fact that it is the logged rather than the total amount that is even more significantly associated with both TDS and TDS (W) suggests (but does not prove) that there are diminishing marginal returns to DPP, and that it is not necessarily the "big ticket items" that have the greatest impact.[16]

Since the sample is too small to estimate the slope (the beta coefficient) separately and reliably for CEE and the MENA, we can only speculate about the discrete impact of DPP upon liberalization among the former countries and consolidation among the latter. The fact that the MENA four received significantly less support (except for Palestine, the outlier) and made less progress leads us to add probability to the earlier hypothesis that *DPP is better at protecting democracy than at promoting it in the first place.* This is not to say that that its contribution has been irrelevant in the former instance, since both sub-sets seem to have received a significant positive boost from DPP funding.

Striking as they are, these findings are tentative, and may well "evaporate" when similar tests are performed on larger samples. CEE and the MENA do make an odd "pair," in that they have been engaged in different aspects of the complex process of regime change – very rapid transition and consolidation in the case of the former, and hesitant liberalization and very little evidence of transition among the latter. Turkey does provide the "missing link" between the two samples, and, interestingly enough, its score on TDS and TDS (W) is well predicted by the final multiple regression equations. It is not an outlier, and this is encouraging in terms of future research, which will almost certainly "discover" many other polities crowded into that difficult "transitional" space between liberalization and democratization. The real test will come not just when I insert other contextual and situational variables into the existing sample, but when its number and range of variation is enlarged to include such challenging cases as the republics of the former Soviet Union and the former Yugoslavia – not to mention Albania and Mongolia.

Concluding with some doubts

Ultimately, what counts for the future regimes in these neo-democracies is their *legitimacy.* This may well be where the contribution of DPP is most problematic, since virtually none of its programmes and projects can be demonstrably shown to contribute positively to such an outcome, and there is even the suspicion that the intervention of foreign agents may undermine long-term regime legitimacy in the eyes of national citizens. Moreover, legitimacy has proven notoriously difficult to measure empirically. It can be presumed that a fully consolidated democracy is more likely to persist over time, but this could be the product of habit, inertia or the lack of an alternative.

It is the *quality of democracy* – not its consolidation as a set of rules – that is likely to have the determining influence on legitimacy, and hence on the regime's presumptive capacity to persist when faced by serious exogenous challenges or dramatic endogenous declines in performance. The presence of legitimacy, however, is usually inferred from what does *not* occur, rather than what can be directly observed or who has directly benefited. Whenever and wherever certain forms of collective violence, resistance or struggle do *not* manifest themselves (whenever or wherever resourceful and conflictful protagonists agree to play by established rules rather than try to eliminate each other from contention, or whenever and wherever subordinates defer without a fight to the commands of "superior" rulers), one tends to assume that the democratic regime must be legitimate, and hence that its quality must be satisfactory according to the prevailing standards of that citizenry.

Admittedly, this is not a very satisfactory state of affairs from the point of view of normative democratic theory. It can mask the hegemony of "prepolitical" forces of social and economic oppression. It can fail to disclose the manipulative effects of mass media. It may be more a product of resignation and apathy than of respect for the decisions of authorities or the political rights of fellow citizens. However, it is still a safer base for inference than relying on the opinions of those theorists and intellectuals who are inevitably disappointed that the advent of neo-democracy has not brought along with it all the qualities that they had hoped for.

Notes

1 This may be a "first" in empirical social science. One is always testing for the "null hypothesis" that operative variables are not related to each other, but it is very rare that an analyst is predisposed to reject a significant correlation if and when it emerges from the data-set.

2 This "macro" approach differs substantially from the myriad of efforts to evaluate the impact of specific DPP programmes and projects. The indicators and estimators are quantitative, but they are based on theories of democratization, not numerical measures related to the activities or (allegedly) discrete effects of such programmes or projects. Moreover, thanks to its theoretical grounding, it is possible to stipulate plausible counter-factuals (how a given country might have performed without DPP, for instance) and thus estimate its marginal contribution. Of course, any findings at this level tell us nothing about which specific programmes or projects worked well, but only that a certain "package" of spending by different donors over a lengthy period of time seems to have produced a positive or negative effect across a sub-set of countries. In fact, it is logically possible that none of the programmes or projects worked as intended and that it was only the overall volume of resources injected into the regime change process that produced the observed effect.

3 The issue is actually rather more complicated. I was not just interested in the extent to which national and international variables "retrodict" the course of the democratization process – independently of DPP – but also the extent to which donors might have "predicted" eventual success and adjusted their strategies to conform to it. Since I had no way of knowing which (if any) of these factors were present in the minds of donors, the best I could do is presume that they were consciously or unconsciously influenced by the "prevailing wisdom" in the social sciences.

4 There is a serious statistical problem, however. The number of potentially relevant variables greatly exceeds the number of cases – even more so if we divide our vari-

ation in outcome into distinctive CEE and MENA sub-sets. All I could do is use multiple regressions as a device to eliminate variables that are insignificant, although this is bound to produce a less than "robust" solution.

5 Palestine is not included in the calculations, in part because data on it are especially deficient since it is a "non-state," and in part because it is such an "outlier." Palestinians received more than ten times the average DPP per capita expenditures (US $63.95), and they had the poorest record of performance on regime change for the period! Its inclusion (where possible) has a significant (if unique) effect on correlations between per capita and logged measures of DPPE and of both TDS and TDS (W). In effect, this exclusion amounts to a recognition that European and American DPP (and economic aid in general) to Palestine obeys a different logic.

6 The log of the total amount of DPP was used on the grounds of diminishing marginal utility or costs (in other words, a certain initial amount of support was necessary for virtually any DPP programme regardless of the size of the country, but beyond that "seed money," its impact might be expected to decline either because it became less expensive to extend it to larger numbers, or because it was less likely to have an impact upon those receiving it).

7 In the subsequent analysis I have eliminated LoA+CoD since it performs no differently from the TDS scale. The correlation between the two is a very high at 0.987 (0.000).

8 See: Ann Phillips, "Exporting Democracy: German Political Foundations in Central Eastern Europe," *Democratization*, 6 (2), 1999: 70–98; Stefan Mair, "Germany's Stiftungen and Democracy Assistance: Comparative Advantages, New Challenges", in Peter Burnell (ed.), *Democracy Assistance: International Co-operation for Democratization*. London: Frank Cass, 2000, pp. 128–149.

9 It should be noted that, had Palestine not been removed from the calculations, the relative prowess of the Europeans would have suffered a considerable blow. They gave US$106.70 million to Palestinians (compared to US$78.11 million from the US), and very little progress was made even towards liberalization, not to mention democratization, during this period.

10 For each model, the number of operative variables is reduced to a maximum of four, given the restricted number of cases.

11 There is another "structural-cum-strategic" variable that might have contributed to predicting TDS or TDS (W): Overseas Development Aid (ODA). According to this argument, democracy is best promoted not directly but indirectly, by raising the level of economic development, and foreign aid is the instrument to accomplish this. Leaving aside the fact that almost no one seems to be able to find any correlation between ODA and growth rates, the data show a negative (but not significant) correlation between this indicator and the democratization scales: ‡.498 (0.143) with TDS and ‡.389 (0.267) with TDS (W).

12 See: Gabriel Almond and Sidney Verba, *The Civic Culture: Political Attitudes and Democracy in Five Nations*. Princeton, NJ: Princeton University Press, 1963; Ronald Inglehart, *Modernization and Post-Modernization: Cultural, Economic and Cultural Change in 43 Societies*. Princeton, NJ: Princeton University Press, 1997.

13 I have chosen not to include a fourth "cultural" variable in the analysis, on the grounds that it clusters too much within our two regional sub-samples. The "better" the colonial heritage (the more democratic and/or benevolent the previous colonial power, roughly in the following order: American, British, French, Dutch, Belgian, Austro-Hungarian, Ottoman, and none at all), the greater the probability of successful democratization. Needless to say, in subsequent analyses with larger samples, this variable should be taken into account.

14 As expressed most forcefully and recently in Juan Linz and Alfred Stepan, *Problems of Democratic Transition and Consolidation: Southern Europe, South America, and Post-Communist Europe*. Baltimore, MD: Johns Hopkins University Press, 1996,

pp. 16–19. Along with "state-ness," these authors attach considerable importance to "nationhood." To the extent that being a nation is defined in terms of either ethnic and/or religious homogeneity, we have just learned that the former has no significant correlation with democratization, and that the latter is significantly correlated with it – but in the direction opposite to the hypothesis. Again, these are the findings for a small number of cases from two quite distinct regions and they may not hold up in larger, more comprehensive samples.

15 See: Dankwart Rustow, "Transitions to Democracy," in: Lisa Anderson (ed.), *Transition to Democracy*. New York: Columbia University Press, 1999, p. 26 (first published in *Comparative Politics* 2 (3), 1970: 337–365).

16 These findings do not allow us to infer anything about the impact that DPP has had at the *meso* (programme) level or at the *micro* (project) level. The macro is never a simple aggregation of individual cases in the world of politics – that is the main insight embedded in the notion of "the ecological fallacy." There is every reason to believe that, hiding behind the complexity of total, logged and relative effect, there exist specific DPP programmes and projects that do make a quite significant contribution to either liberalization or democratization and do so without a predictable relation to their financial cost. There may even be instances of this that work successfully in otherwise quite different national and regional contexts.

3 International factors in democratization, their scope and limitations

European comparative perspectives on the post-Cold War world

Geoffrey Pridham

Introduction

Regime change in former Communist countries has been accompanied by far-reaching international change. Indeed, this regime change provided the opening and stimulus for that transformation, and, in turn, the latter had a significant impact on continuing regime change, suggesting an overall dynamic of external–domestic interactions. Most importantly, there was the reconfiguration of the international system with the disappearance of the global confrontation and the structures that marked the Cold War period from the late 1940s onwards. Soon there emerged new, more regionally focused forms of international conflict, some of which – notably the wars in the former Yugoslavia between 1991 and 1995 – influenced the nature of regime change, in particular delaying transitions to democracy in the countries affected, and helping to buttress quasi-authoritarian regimes in Croatia and Serbia.

During this new period in international relations, from the start of the 1990s onwards, democratic regimes spread across different areas of the world (leaving aside for the moment the question of the nature of the new democracies constructed and, indeed, whether some of them were really democracies or only nominally so). This reinforced the view that there was a true wave of democratization in process, controversially written up as a "triumph of democracy;" however, the term "wave" as used in the literature[1] has more descriptive than analytical value, particularly when applied as it is to broad historical periods – in this instance, to patterns of pro-democratic regime change since the Portuguese revolution of April 1974. It is of little merit when assessing the actual dynamics that drive democratic transitions in terms of international impacts. The term is only seriously relevant when looking at much shorter periods of time when there are transnational effects between contemporaneous transitions, especially in the same region: the regime changes in the Central and Eastern European countries (CEEC) in the autumn of 1989 provide a classic example of this.

In this post-Cold War period, a variety of developments especially increased the chances of a push towards democratization, and also underlined the growing importance of international factors – including a distinct increase in the use of political or democratic conditionality on the part of a variety of international organizations (both economic and financial); the upgrading of democracy promotion as a factor of national interest alongside (and often intermixed with) other motives, most notably security ones in the case of some specific external actors in the same region; greater attention paid to international human rights discourse; and, more recently, the emergence of a doctrine of intervention in the cause of international ethics. At the same time, the new technology and its varied influence on socio-economic and political attitudes – not to mention its potential in terms of transnational networking – has increased the scope for a more immediate and widespread transmission of international effects than ever before. And then there are wider globalization patterns. It is therefore no coincidence that international factors in democratization are now more clearly recognized – a recognition initially prompted by the historical events of 1989.

Indeed, it can be claimed that democratization is itself an international phenomenon. Thus, the issue at stake here is not *whether* but rather how far and in what ways international factors influence and drive democratization. This question is analysed by considering the role of four operative tasks: hypothesizing, identifying, analysing and demonstrating.

Hypothesizing: lessons from history

The purpose of hypothesizing about international factors is to contextualize and orient the discussion of regime change. Two questions arise from that exercise: first, if the international dimension of democratization has been so important since the end of the Cold War, is this a cyclical development that may conceivably end, or are we witnessing the incremental long-term growth of international influences?

The evidence points both ways: on the one hand, it is possible to identify historical periods in which the international context is especially important (this conventional chronological structure is preferred to the vague concept of "waves"). The inter-war period in Europe saw the rise of Fascist or right-wing authoritarian regimes, which encouraged one another through their transnational influence, representing a mounting threat to democratic systems that was only resolved by world war. The post-1945 period in Europe saw, with the defeat of the Axis powers, the restoration or reconstitution of parliamentary democracies. Given that direct support for these democracies came from the victorious countries, notably in the case of occupied West Germany, one may speak of international factors also being important in this later period, albeit in a very different setting (one given added urgency by the coming of the Cold War). This was a period that saw the securing of parliamentary democracy in the Western part of Europe and, simultaneously, the construction of Soviet-supported "people's democracies" in the Eastern half. Three decades later, Southern Europe experienced three parallel transitions to democracy, in Spain, Greece and Portugal.

International events played a part in instigating these transitions as well, but international factors were generally not so pervasive there, having less of an influence over the subsequent course of events than was the case in the previous historical period. Clearly, however, international factors in the post-1989 period were very much at the forefront of developments in the post-communist countries. In short, looking back over the history of this region of the world, it is apparent that the importance or otherwise of international factors in regime change may vary between different periods in time.

On the other hand, some of the above-mentioned developments – notably the emergence of new technologies, but also the wider effects of globalization – appear to be progressive and to have longer-term consequences. At least at some levels, the world has become more interdependent than ever before and, as the effects of this are probably irreversible, it is unlikely that we will witness any return to the kind of international state of relations of confrontation between hostile political systems that characterized the Cold War years. This does not mean that there will be no serious dangers. The current "war on terrorism" suggests otherwise: while this newly devised conflict seeks actively to promote if not provoke transitions to democracy in countries under despotic rule, it also poses challenges to civil liberties in established democracies, particularly those most threatened by Al-Qaeda activity.

The second question regards the relative importance of international factors compared with domestic ones. In the past, the debate among "transitologists" about the one (usually the international) being subordinate to the other missed the crucial question: it is the *balance* between them, and how they interact in particular, that really matters. The dynamics of regime change may well be domestic – after all, the key actors are to be found in that domain – but domestic dynamics are not exclusive, and are becoming less so in what is an increasingly interdependent world. What matters, then, is how and why international factors feed into processes of regime change. It is very unlikely that international factors will in any way exclusively determine what happens in processes of regime change, short of extraordinary occurrences such as invasion from abroad (which put an end to the Czechoslovak First Republic in 1939 and the French Third Republic in 1940, for instance) or defeat in war (which led to the occupation of Germany and provided the frameworks for two very different new political regimes in a country divided into two halves). So the question that should guide us is not whether international factors are important – they are indisputably so – but rather under what conditions and in what ways they have an effect on democratization. When speaking of the "international dimension of democratization," one needs to differentiate rather than make bland references to a presumably unified force acting beyond the borders of countries undergoing regime change. With the above in mind, this chapter focuses on conditionality as the most prominent post-Cold War transnational concept, and the most suggestive of deliberate external efforts to influence the course of democratization, as it applies to CEE countries (referred to as CEEC) and to the enlargement of the European Union (EU).

Identifying: patterns and problems

There are numerous historical and contemporary examples of the role of international factors in regime change. Historical events provide the benefit of hindsight. Subsequently released information provides detailed insights and inside knowledge about what actually happened, and can reveal how different and sometimes inconsistent witnesses interpreted the impact of international factors. The picture is invariably one of greater subtlety than that conveyed in early theoretical work on external and domestic interactions in democratization processes. Most importantly, the historical evidence challenges the view, in traditional comparative studies on regime change, that international factors are at best of second-order importance and essentially subordinate to, if not dependent on, domestic factors of change.[2]

It is obviously more difficult to assess contemporary events because of the absence of comparable inside information, but this can be partially remedied by well-chosen elite interviews with key actors and by consulting the best informed sections of the quality press, in which relevant "indiscretions" sometimes surface. Further, Internet material now provides access to a greater amount of official documentation than ever before, and this makes it possible to ascertain modes of policy-thinking to some degree. And there is, of course, the opening of archival sources as a result of regime change, which sometimes bring about a flood of revelations, although these are usually about the past regime rather than transition-related events. Thus, more often than not, close observation makes it possible to substantiate the international impact on domestic developments and to test working hypotheses. For instance, is it not possibly the case that international factors, far from depending on domestic openings, now actually impose confining conditions[3] which either constrain or stimulate change?

The focus here is on the most recent period of regime change in CEE countries, since 1989, in an attempt to make sense of patterns and problems that have arisen concerning the role of international factors in democratization. One basic precondition for this kind of assessment is to recognize the variety of such factors and to unscramble the "international dimension." Failing to do so makes it impossible to undertake a meaningful analysis. Five patterns and problems are discussed below: types of external actors, the priority accorded to democratization, the nature of the democracy being promoted, cross-national variations, and levels of interaction.

Types of external actors

External actors may be categorized as national governments, international organizations (IOs) and international non-governmental organizations (NGOs). In the period under consideration there was a marked expansion of democratic conditionality (DC) by IOs, and considerable growth of relevant activity by NGOs, including new ones such as the influential Soros Foundation, particularly in the area of human rights. NGOs may also include politically aligned foundations, notably those attached to the main party forces in Western Europe, as these have contributed to political education in new democracies whether in a partisan way or more broadly (as in the case of the important German foundations). Transnational political parties also play a part in professionalizing their fraternal partners in emerging democracies. Some, like the party internationals, operate worldwide, but it is the EU party federations that are now most influential as a result of the institutional development of the European Parliament (EP). The latter provide various forms of training and political socialization for aspiring member parties, but also apply fairly strict procedures of democratic conditionality that parallel official European Commission conditionality. EU parties were all the more influential in CEE because of EU leverage over accession countries, since the accession dynamic drove forward compliance with their conditionality demands on parties from candidate countries. At least in the case of the main political parties in CEE, the EU party federations have strengthened their own democratic practices, defined more clearly their left-right identities, and confirmed or strengthened their commitment to European integration (with the exception of a few prominent Euro-sceptical parties).[4]

Some international NGOs have focused particularly on democratization tasks, and have sometimes proved to be quite powerful, as when they gave significant support to the disorganized opposition to the Milosevic regime in Yugoslavia in 1999–2000, allowing it to play a decisive role in his fall from power in the autumn of 2000. Other kinds of external actors cannot concentrate on furthering democratization and on checking authoritarian legacies or tendencies in the same way. Naturally, national governments have different – and often competing – priorities, and national interests invariably play a predominant role, although not necessarily to the exclusion of democracy promotion. Apart from the German state-funded political foundations, some EU countries have their own programmes for democracy promotion, including support for NGOs. For the most part, national governments have tended to make a link between strengthening or stabilizing new democracies and international security. Germany's eastern border – which shifted eastwards with unification – is no longer an "Iron Curtain" but contiguous with new democracies (the Czech Republic and Poland most importantly), while beyond Poland there are the new democracies of the Baltic states and, further eastward, the Ukraine – a still uncertain democracy with aspirations to join both the EU and the North Atlantic Treaty Organization (NATO).

The role of IOs in democracy promotion or conditionality is different again. The most influential and ambitious is the EU, of course, which applies a tight and detailed form of DC to countries wishing to become official candidate states. Conditionality is crucial to opening membership talks, and continues in the form of annual monitoring by the Commission throughout accession talks until accession itself. The EU has promoted democracy through the PHARE Democracy Programme. Other IOs, be they global (the International Monetary Fund (IMF) and the World Bank (WB)), transatlantic (NATO) or regional (in the case of Europe, the Council of Europe (CoE) and the Organization for

Security and Cooperation in Europe (OSCE)), developed more assiduous conditionality policies in the 1990s, but they have varied in the specificity of conditions and the rigour with which they have been applied. The CoE, for instance, has been just as insistent as the EU on human rights conditions, but its menu of conditions is much narrower and its attitude much more lenient (conditions are usually met after rather than prior to membership). By contrast, NATO supports broad conditions (including the establishment of a constitutional state and civilian control over armed forces), while international financial institutions (IFIs) have subsumed the conditions under the "governance" heading. In short, it may be said that DC is strict in the case of the EU, loose in the case of the CoE, bland in the case of NATO, and vague in the case of the IFIs. These IOs also vary in the extent to which they prioritize democracy promotion, and the EU is well ahead of the others in this respect.

The priority accorded to democratization

National governments rarely make DC or democracy promotion the priority in the way some IOs or NGOs may do. However, states' degree of commitment varies, as indeed does that of the other two actors, as illustrated by the above comparison between IOs. Even international NGOs tend to focus on a particular area, such as civil society, without embracing the whole gamut of democratic conditions demanded by the EU. These may be divided into institutional (executive accountability and the stable functioning of democratic institutions, as well as free and fair elections and an independent judicial system) and behavioural (fighting corruption, promoting gender equality, and protecting human and minority rights) requirements. Democracy concerns have not always been uppermost even for the EU, which has the most developed of DC policies. These are particularly visible immediately before decisions on possible candidate countries, and especially when conditions become controversial, as in the case of Slovakia (when Meciar was in power 1994–1998), Turkey at different times and, intermittently, Romania (in recent years over the issue of institutionalized children). During membership negotiations, which last several years, there is a less intense focus on EU political conditions, which are subject to an elaborate bureaucratic procedure and the regular reports of the European Commission on each candidate country. These reports cover economic conditions as well as the third condition, the "ability to assume the obligations of membership," namely state capacity. During the negotiation process, prospective member countries are tested more thoroughly for "Europeanization" of institutional procedures and policies than for their democratic standards. In the two years leading up to the Copenhagen Summit of December 2002, at which the final decision on enlargement in 2004 was taken, the regular Commission reports paid increasingly more detailed attention to progress in the adoption of European legislation under the thirty negotiation chapters.

Two issues qualify the priority accorded to democratization: inter-linkage with other priorities and conditions, and diachronic variation. It is possible to argue that, as with the EU, political conditions may benefit from other ones. Strengthening state capacity, for instance, is likely to influence governmental performance in a positive way and thereby possibly contribute to the credibility of new democratic institutions (in fact, a major problem in CEE). At the same time, the way Brussels approached DC in candidate countries suggests that efficiency was of greater immediate concern than democratic requirements.[5] At times, the EU focus on political conditions has been subordinate to other issues: in the early 1990s, for example, Brussels (along with other IOs and Western governments with their assistance programmes) was more interested in the business of economic transformation in the new post-Communist countries; but the idea behind this policy was that the shift to a market economy would promote economic and thereby political pluralism. Now that eight of these countries have recently joined the EU, political conditions are no longer monitored, although there are treaty provisions to deal with violations of democratic standards.

Generally speaking, the end of the Cold War significantly boosted democracy promotion, as the balance between international security dictates and democracy promotion favoured the latter more. US governments are no longer prepared to buttress gruesome dictatorships abroad in the name of fighting Communism. However, even now, when US presidents refer to "democratic transition" (as Clinton did about the Balkans) or "regime change" (as Bush has done quite frequently in the context of the war on terror), these aims are still linked to strong security concerns. For the US, democracy appears to be a means to an end. EU governments have tended to adopt a rather more committed attitude to the cause of democratization and international law issues. This difference is highlighted by the blunt pressure Washington has put on the EU to grant accession to a strategically important Turkey, with the EU resisting pressure to abandon strict DC in this case. At the same time, some EU states appear to want to use DC as an "excuse" or "screen" to obscure the fact that they do not want Turkey to enter the EU for reasons that have nothing to do with human rights or democracy.

The nature of the democracy promoted

One noteworthy contrast with the 1990s is that greater attention is now paid to qualitative and not just formal democratic standards. In other words, DC now embraces substantive democracy, whereas the concern was formerly with formal democracy (having the requisite institutions and an appropriate constitutional order) or even – more narrowly – electoral democracy (a term which unfortunately may apply to some hybrid regimes, such as that of Tudjman and, formerly, Milosevic). The increasing power of international discourse on human rights has played a major role in this shift. As noted above, the EU has moved furthest in this direction, as some of the conditions it imposes concern human and minority rights and the development of aspects of civil society, notably NGO promotion. The Council of Europe is also involved because of its special interest in human rights. Nevertheless, there remain differences among external actors: IFIs continue to concentrate on governance (institutional) issues, although they now insist more on democratic conditions broadly speaking; and, more often than not, US governments have tended to be content with formal democratic conditions, although important American NGOs have been promoting substantive democracy, notably with NGO development work in the CEE countries.

Whatever the extent of the change, there has been little alteration in the methodology of DC. Even the EU has retained the "checklist approach," as is evident in the regular Commission reports on candidate countries. This is understandable, as it facilitates what is essentially a bureaucratic procedure, but it also means that DC is not driven by an overarching sense of the desired democratic outcome. The regular reports have used the term "democratic consolidation" quite liberally, but it lacks a clear conceptual basis. As one high-ranking Commission official remarked, any conceptual debates would cause disagreements among EU member states, so democratic consolidation is conveniently taken as read when a country joins the EU. For similar reasons, the EU does not engage in discussions about the structure of new democracies, primarily because they have usually progressed beyond constitution-making by the time its DC starts to apply, but also because EU member states themselves have different democratic models and would be likely to disagree over structural prescriptions. In effect, most countries have adopted various kinds of parliamentary systems (although Poland toyed with a form of French semi-presidentialism in the 1990s). Interestingly, the successor regimes to the Soviet Union are, with the exception of the Baltic states, presidential, but, given their weak democratic standards, they are unlikely to develop serious EU membership prospects for some time.

Cross-national variations

When speaking about cross-national variations, the focus shifts to the recipients rather than the providers of democracy assistance. What factors favour a response to outside support for democratization and thus account for cross-national variations in terms of success? There are five such factors: structural factors; foreign policy orientation; bilateral links with established democracies; the commitment of ruling elites; and the balance of domestic pressures.

For the most part, structural factors relate to the geopolitical situation (like the historically vulnerable position of the Baltic States, for instance). Understandably, for some years the focus was on Euro-Atlantic integration and security arrangements, although this also translated into meeting conditionality requirements, which is significant because of the difficulties of overcoming Soviet legacies. A fairly clear link has been evident between external policy orientation and the readiness to meet EU demands. While most CEE countries have re-oriented their policies since 1989 towards a "return to Europe," a few have occasionally hesitated. One example is Meciar's sympathy for links with the East, while formally claiming EU membership for Slovakia, which gave added meaning to his flouting of democratic standards. The proclaimed wish of Belarus for a union with Russia is an extreme example, given Lukashenka's persistent suppression of political opposition. This is less because Russia is a political model and more a result of a failure to follow a path to "return to Europe."

One less remarked-on aspect of the "return to Europe" has been the fostering of close bilateral links with specific EU countries for geographical or historical reasons, but also in an attempt to find patrons inside the EU. Such links, like that between Poland and Germany, Estonia and Finland, and Latvia and Sweden and Denmark, have encouraged transnational elite socialization with some beneficial transmission of democratic experience. This pattern has furthermore been evident at the level of party organizations, as when local and regional branches from two often neighbouring countries cooperate based on the model of European town twinning. It is difficult to measure the actual influence of such regular contacts; but it may be supposed it has added some depth to the democratization process at the micro-level. Sub-national activity is barely taken into account when looking at international factors, but this is an example of why it should be.

Most important, too, is the elite commitment to Euro-Atlantic integration, for this drives compliance with DC criteria as a strategic necessity. There may be problems with the implementation of the political conditions, however, depending on the level of public support for integration, the alignment of political forces (or the strength of consensus), and the influence of the media and socioeconomic actors. It is worth noting one area of cross-national differentiation at this point: some problems with conditionality are greater in some countries than others because of the varied incidence of particular problems (the Roma question is especially difficult in Slovakia because of the large Roma population there, while minority problems have loomed large in Latvia and Estonia because of the high proportion of Russians in those two countries). In most CEE countries achieving judicial independence has been problematic not least because of the persistence of Communist legacies. The institutionalization of children is peculiar to Romania, however, being a consequence of a particular legacy of the Ceausescu regime. Romania has also had a special problem with state capacity, which has inhibited the implementation of DC, notwithstanding the commitment of the country's ruling elites to Euro-Atlantic integration; this problem has also been present in other post-communist countries.

Levels of interaction

Research on international factors in democratization should differentiate between different levels of government when considering compliance with DC and the actual impact of international factors. There are three broad levels: governance (the institutional dimension), the intermediary level (particularly parties, the media and their relations with the public), and the socio-economic arena (different economic interests and active elements of civil society like NGOs). Governments seeking to meet conditionality requirements may be assisted, constrained or even obstructed by domestic factors. It may be necessary to use pressure or persuasion when addressing these other domestic actors, although problems may well vary depending on differing conditions. Making the necessary institutional changes for the sake of executive accountability is rather easier and is speedier to implement than rooting out corruption or banishing social prejudice against minority groups or the Roma. Making personnel changes in and instilling a sense of democratic values among the judiciary involves much more effort than introducing legal provisions for an independent judiciary. This illustrates how, as transnational relations theory posits, internal structures mediate or filter transnational organizations' policy impacts, among other things, by changing attitudes (new perceptions of reality) and increasing dependence of domestic actors on such organizations for networking and information.[6] Some domestic factors may resist transnational influences, however, and thus complicate the implementation of DC. This reflects the view that external actors are most effective when they have domestic partners. In the case of the EU, an entity with a sustained leverage over accession countries (provided their ruling elites are strongly committed to Euro-Atlantic integration), outside pressure and a growing prospect of membership provides the crucial incentive for meeting DC requirements.

Analysing: scope and limitations

To summarize, the scope of international impact has increased greatly in the decade and a half since the end of the Cold War. The changed structure of international relations and strategic priorities, and the increase in external actors with a democratization programme – or, in some cases, an enhanced programme – has widened that scope. At the same time, there is greater variability in terms of policy objectives and impacts. It is therefore appropriate to assess the scope for and the limitations on international factors and DC in this new period, in terms of timing, tipping and dynamic functions, incentive structures and regional environments.

Timing

It is safe to assume that international impacts may vary significantly at different stages of the democratization process. The kinds of problems that force domestic actors to seek outside assistance differ in the turbulent moments of democratic transition from those in the subsequent, more settled, period of democratic consolidation, when assistance may still be welcome but to develop established democratic structures or, more commonly, empower civil society after institutions are in place. One further variation on this theme relates to democratic institutionalization. Here, it is useful to distinguish between three stages that overlap to some extent: the primary stage (basic choice of regime type, whether liberal democratic or other); the secondary stage (usually consisting of a constitutional process, or a structural version of this, which is a choice between parliamentary or (semi-)presidential, centralized or federal government); and the tertiary or stabilizing stage (when new institutions or agencies are set up but the democratic settlement has been more thoroughly institutionalized or articulated, with obvious implications for democratic consolidation).

In this respect, the scope and limitations for the EU become clearer. The EU's DC has benefited both from the general international trend to use conditionality (as evident in the greater attention to human rights), and from the enhanced international weight of the EU itself and expansion of its policy concerns in the past two decades. Nonetheless, its more ambitious DC regime (as compared to that applied to new Southern European democracies from the late 1970s onwards) only really works during the tertiary stage of democratic institutionalization. This is also largely true for other external actors, although those that emphasize formal democracy (and the "triumph of democracy" rhetoric) are really referring to the first stage. In the decisive first year after the 1974 revolution in Portugal, when antagonistic regime models competed with one another, external actors at times played an important role in determining the liberal democratic outcome that was formalized with the 1976 constitution.[7] External concern with the secondary stage is rare, although there are some historical examples – such as the role of the occupying powers in choosing a federal system for post-War West Germany. The EU, however, is rather limited by timing and choice. The Copenhagen conditions for the CEEC were not drawn up until 1993, nearly four years after the transitions began, and monitoring only began four years after that with the Commission *avis*. The conditions established in 1993 ("stability of institutions guaranteeing democracy, the rule of law, human rights and respect for and protection of minorities") were brief and rather vague. However, with the advent of the annual regular reports in 1998, the EU conditions were monitored in some detail. It can be said, then, that while their scope was indeed limited by the timing factor (in effect, therefore, concentrating on the third stage), within that stage their scope for action was enhanced by general conditionality trends and by the expanding role of the EU itself, including its shift to substantive democracy concerns.

Tipping and dynamic functions

International impacts may be divided into two groups according to the function they have in democratization processes. A *tipping function* occurs when an outside event determines or provides an opening for democratic transition when an authoritarian regime has the potential to collapse. This happened with the Turkish invasion of Cyprus in 1974, which finally brought about an end to the already much discredited Colonels' regime in Greece. In CEE countries, the obvious tipping function during the historic autumn of 1989 was the dismantling of the Berlin Wall, which thereby acquired enormous symbolic importance. Its effect was to demonstrate the failure of Communist systems; but it also decidedly pushed forward the transition in other countries, particularly Czechoslovakia. The events in Prague that led to the democratic revolution in that country happened just ten days after the dramatic events in Berlin. Thus, tipping events may play a first-order role in some transitions, although they may have no or little carry-through effects. In this, they differ from *dynamic functions*, which occur when external pressures interact continuously with regime change and may have a longer-lasting and perhaps deeper effect. The EU is very obviously in the second group. Rather differently, during the events of late 1989 the EU was a potentially important but rather nervous bystander. In other words, in given circumstances these two functions may both influence regime change, but in the first instance (the tipping function) that influence is very time restricted. With dynamic functions, there is clearly more scope time-wise, but limitations may arise as a result of the above-mentioned lack of responsiveness of domestic actors.

Incentive structures

Incentive structures may be conceptualized broadly as push and pull effects. External actors push specific countries or actors in a certain direction (over conditionality demands, for instance), but not all exert a strong pull effect. This consists of incentives such as urgently needed financial aid and training programmes, policy advice and, above all, the prospect of membership. Training was a compelling incentive in the early 1990s, when CEE countries found they needed speedy assistance to manage their first free elections and set up democratic procedures. It has remained an incentive ever since, but in a less urgent way, and the EU has pushed this strongly as part of the accession process. At times there may be a direct trade-off between push and pull. Following Milosevic's fall in 2000, Belgrade was put under pressure to hand over war criminals to The Hague, and financial aid was made conditional by the USA. Pull effects are also present in the case of reliance on policy advice from IFIs in the process of economic transformation, with the imposition of policy prescriptions in return for assistance. More difficult to assess in terms of push and pull effects is the promotion of particular causes. Humanitarian issues like minority rights and the situation of the Roma evince undoubted push effects from some international NGOs and IOs, such as the EU and the Council of Europe, but influences vary, and pull effects are sometimes weak in the face of domestic prejudice or lack of consensus. It is a combination of new legal instruments and a commitment of some domestic actors (such as domestic NGO leaders) that helps slowly to drive forward change in this area.

In the final analysis, motivation is a determining factor in international impacts on democratization, and one that merits much more attention than that so far received in the literature on regime change and international actors. Obviously, the motivation has to come from external actors in the form of policy strategies and choices, and from domestic actors in the form of positive responses. But incentive structures must be taken into account when assessing the motivation of the latter. Membership of international organizations has the greatest pull effect, offering new democracies various advantages such as international recognition and status (with possible gains in terms of democratic credibility at home), the chance to play a sometimes leading policy-making role at the international level, access to greater resources, and openings for careers in international organizations. The pull effect of European IOs varies considerably, with EU membership clearly being superior to all others. One can thus hypothesize that the scope of and the limitations on external actors depends on the extent and consistency of their pull effects.

Regional environments

Regional environments can enhance international impacts on new democracies in many ways. Geographical proximity, for instance, means that official external pressures can be supplemented by close transnational or cross-border contacts; a systemic environment marked by the prevalence of a certain kind of political regime such as liberal democracy; and, very importantly, the existence of regional IOs that may have in this respect greater powers than would ever be possible for IOs with a global or international membership. Europe, more so than Latin America or Asia and its sub-regions, provides the best enabling regional environment because its IOs are stronger than those elsewhere. International NGOs are active in other areas of the world, but in Europe they are more powerful because of the prevalence of established or consolidated democracies (with many new democracies in CEE well on the way to consolidation, Europe has become the heartland of democratic rule). Client relations with a superpower usually have a mixed impact on democratization because, for such powers, democracy promotion is often an ambiguous motive and usually subordinated to strategic objectives. By contrast, multilateral allegiances tend to be more benign, as they are not dominated by a particular set of national interests. In this respect as well, Europe provides a stronger regional environment because it has the most integrative IOs in the world. Indeed, the EU appears to be moving towards becoming a political system in its own right. In sum, this kind of regional environment offers considerably more scope for a thorough and even deep effect on democratization than does a more "diffuse" international environment. Its limitation, of course, is that it is territorially confined.

Demonstrating: lessons from research

This section presents some empirical observations to elaborate on the above points, focusing on EU democratic conditionality over the last decade vis-à-vis CEE candidate countries. Not only has the EU expanded its policy in recent times, making it a decidedly more politicized organization; it has also adopted a much more ambitious conditionality approach compared with that used in Southern Europe. Moreover, DC is now largely in the hands of the European Commission, so pressure is more consistent compared with the conditionality of two decades ago, which was in the hands of member states that usually differed over the issue.[8]

The crucial role of national governments

As noted above, elite commitment to Euro-Atlantic integration is vital for accession and a positive responsive to conditionality. This applies especially to governments in candidate countries, although a broader elite consensus is important, particularly in the event of a change of government. Governments are the central actors in accession, by leading negotiations and by acting as intermediaries between Brussels and domestic politics, and because of their leverage over other domestic actors. It follows that any serious lapse in their commitment to join the EU can easily weaken the overall accession effort. In a context where integration is the strategic objective, implementation of DC is driven by accession dynamics. DC usually follows a bureaucratic path – albeit not always a smooth one – parallel to negotiations, and failure to advance with political conditions has sometimes been noted as an accession problem, as with judicial reform in the Czech Republic in 1999 and 2001, and the absence of decisive action to improve the lot of institutionalized children in Romania. Scarcely veiled threats that negotiations would be halted in the latter case led the Nastase government to pass legislation and spend public money to address the problem. It is therefore not very surprising that DC has been sometimes treated instrumentally by CEE elites as a means to attain the much desired goal of EU membership. This is another aspect of how DC can benefit from accession dynamics, which in turn raises the question of how far political conditions have been internalized in these countries. This question can only really be answered in the course of time, after accession has taken place.

Meanwhile, it is worth noting that political elites in post-communist countries have been driven by different motivations, which can be referred to as four imperatives: the *historical*, reinforcing the policy reorientation to "return to Europe" and break with the Communist past, complicated in some countries by concern with losing recently gained national independence; the *security*, as in the desire to avoid international isolation and to benefit from the support mechanisms of Euro-Atlantic integration; the *modernizing*, involving socio-economic change, which is best accomplished within the European framework; and the *democratic*, with integration regarded as a guarantee that new democracies will be sustained and consolidated.[9] Thus, democratization is far from being an exclusive, and neither is it necessarily a superior imperative. However, as things turned out in CEE, these four imperatives tended to reinforce one another so that the democratic imperative gained in strength.

An elitist process?

During the accession negotiations, it was commonly stated that negotiations were asymmetrical, and DC imposed. This is literally true, since the terms of accession and its pre-conditions are set by Brussels, and while there is room for manoeuvre over transition periods, this cannot be said about all policy chapters. This does not officially apply to DC, although the Commission came to understand that it would take time to satisfy fully some difficult conditions that might only be definitively solved after accession. However, where this was the case, as with fighting corruption and ameliorating the situation of the Roma, Brussels made it clear that significant movement in the right direction was expected. DC is essentially a top-down process. Nevertheless, implementation and compliance required cooperation from other domestic actors, such as NGOs in the field of human and minority rights. NGOs could play an important complementary role, especially when working at the local level. The media could sometimes create additional pressure over DC as well, although not always in a way convenient for government circles. This was especially noticeable immediately after the publication of the annual regular reports, as these provided an opportunity to criticize any lack of government action with all the backing of EU authority. Opposition parties also used such occasions for similar reasons. Contrary to the view that accession could have a de-politicizing effect, especially with the broad cross-party backing it enjoyed in most CEE countries, in fact negotiations gave an immense stimulus to elites and opinion-makers in political learning concerning integration affairs, and provided an occasion for debate between governments and oppositions over the terms of membership. At the same time, governments benefited from the usually high levels of public support for EU membership in CEE countries.

Direct effects

What are the direct effects of the EU implementation of DC? Because of the relative brevity of time since the beginning of regular monitoring of the political conditions by the Commission (little over half a decade), one cannot expect deeper problems like corruption, anti-Roma prejudice, and relations with large Russian minorities and ethnic Latvians and Estonians in the Baltic states to be resolved before EU entry, although the situation differs depending on the actual depth of the problem. The situation of the fairly large Hungarian minority in Slovakia has improved, but then the problem was largely caused by nationalist attitudes within the Meciar government and among the power elites. Once these were replaced and a more democratically minded government came to power, and when, with discreet EU pressure, the Party of the Hungarian Coalition (*Slovakia Strana Maïarskej Koalície*, SMK) was included, the path was cleared for improvement. The role of the SMK in government was important in symbolic terms (highlighting Hungarians' political integration) and in legislative terms (with laws favouring that minority). EU influence was important in many ways, and on one or two occasions it was used to sustain government unity and preserve its relations with the SMK, assisted by the momentum of accession.[10] This, then, is an instance in which the EU went out of its way to promote a particular minority diplomatically (although it should be added that Slovakia was always the CEE country that was politically controversial in Brussels). The Hungarian minority situation was not as deeply rooted as that of the Russian minorities in the Baltic States. Historical memory plays a role in this, as Russian hegemony under the Union of Soviet Socialist Republics (USSR) remains a recent and very painful memory for Latvians and Estonians, while Hungarian rule over the Slovaks is a more distant memory. Generally, EU DC has been rather more successful in bringing about formal change than in changing reality on the ground.

Anti-corruption laws and mechanisms have been introduced with prodding from Brussels, although corrupt practices continue to be a major problem in most of the accession/new member states. This reflects time limits and the rooted nature of some political problems, but it is also a consequence of the limited abilities of the EU to promote socio-economic behavioural change. By the time of enlargement in 2004, the DC record was mixed. Time will tell whether it has deeper effects than are evident at present.

Indirect effects

Indirect political effects are those that are not the deliberate result of DC policy but derive from the accession process in general. These may be somewhat less positive, although they tend to be short term rather than long term in their impact on democratic consolidation. The burdens of accession have undoubtedly magnified government overload in these new democracies, although they have accumulated much democratic experience through the hard grind of transformation. Political elites have evidenced fatigue and frustration with the pace of change, the relentlessness of negotiations, and persistent monitoring by the EU and other IOs, which may have had some negative impact on government performance. There has also been concern over the bureaucratization of relations between CEE and EU institutions, with possibly distorting institutional or procedural effects on these still unconsolidated democracies. The business of accession usually favoured national executive over parliamentary institutions (these were often scarcely consulted during negotiations and had practically no scope to alter the terms of membership when under domestic pressure), and administrative superseded democratic values at times. What is more, elite-mass relations have been a problem since the fall of Communism – partly as a legacy of former regimes when political institutions were not trusted, and partly because of public awareness of elite corruption. It was feared that elite credibility might deteriorate with accession due to the over-concentration on executive power, but this has not happened. The problem remains, and there is hope that the greater credibility and prestige of the EU vis-à-vis national institutions may alleviate it. Further, there is much public ignorance about integration and its realities, and such ill-informed views are likely to have a gradual effect after accession, and even generate disillusionment once the realities of integration set in. In sum, different indirect political effects have diffuse implications for democratic consolidation, but it is as yet unclear what their deeper impact might be.

The differential pull of the EU

It has been suggested that EU leverage varies according to perceived prospects of accession,[11] and indeed, the dynamics of accession have done much to push forward DC. Countries are on major alert with political conditions in the phase leading up to a decision to negotiate accession. Once negotiations begin, countries are locked in procedurally, bureaucratically and politically, which places the onus on success – not least because of the rivalry between countries negotiating simultaneously. This explains the desire to fulfil DC at almost any cost, and the reluctance of CEE elites to risk derailing the accession process by openly contesting conditionality (the cause of intense behind-the-scenes annoyance). This suggests that the invitation to negotiate is the vital turning-point. By contrast, this drive is absent for countries out of the accession loop (such as Belarus), and those struggling to please Brussels politically but without real or immediate prospects (such as the Ukraine). At the time of writing, Turkey is clearly in limbo, having recently made heroic efforts to break with past reluctance to accept conditionality and yet lacking a clear positive response from the EU, notwithstanding the start of negotiations. Croatia, however, is moving forward with accession, and progressing slowly with DC. By contrast, Serbia has not shown much flexibility regarding the war criminals issue. Its obduracy owes more to the deteriorating situation and nationalist feeling in Serbia than it does to poor EU prospects, however. In short, there are limits to the argument about integration dynamics that are rooted in national politics. As shown above, this may also affect candidate countries with reasonable prospects of joining the EU.

Conclusion

What can one conclude about the impact of international factors on democratization? Some general conclusions may be drawn from this overview of European experiences with democratic conditionality. First, and most obviously, it is fallacious to see international factors separately from "domestic factors" in democratization processes; and, this is now basically understood in the regime change literature. But the point needs to be taken further. Given the ever increasing impact of interdependence, the key issue is the interaction between different external factors and different levels of domestic systems. In other words, both the international environment and the domestic arenas need to be unscrambled, not descriptively but dynamically. It is obviously important to differentiate between different actors on both external and internal fronts, and it is also necessary to accommodate diversity, especially between regional environments.

Secondly, work on international factors in democratization needs to move beyond hypothesizing – hence the attempt to outline various approaches to studying actual effects in this chapter. Interactions between democratization and parallel processes of change are important, as indeed are the indirect and direct effects of outside pressures. Clearly, with the wide variety of possible international impacts it is analytically most feasible to concentrate on conceptual themes such as conditionality and study their effect in particular cases. All this suggests that research should focus on individual regional environments, while taking note of essential differences in other environments.

Third, and last, more attention needs to be paid to what generates compliance with outside pressures. Motivation is crucial here. However, whatever the central role of national governments with their executive powers, it must be remembered that domestic pressures or counter influences may complicate the effects of outside pressure in favour of democratization. More effort needs to be made to balance different sets of international and domestic factors and their diversity in empirical research. The scope for and limitations on these interactive dynamics provide the key to understanding how and why one impacts on the other.

Notes

1 Samuel P. Huntington, *The Third Wave: Democratization in the Late Twentieth Century*. Norman, OH: University of Oklahoma Press, 1991.
2 See: Geoffrey Pridham, *Designing Democracy: EU Enlargement and Regime Change in Post-Communist Europe*. London: Palgrave/Macmillan, 2005, Chapter 1.2.
3 The term "confining conditions" was first used in regime change studies by Otto Kirchheimer in his article "Confining Conditions and Revolutionary Breakthroughs," *American Political Science Review* 59, 1965: 964–74. He was referring essentially to socio-economic conditioning on regime change; but of course such a thesis may be applied to an international environment where the structures are rather institutionalized. Most of all, this applies to European politics and the EU, especially in recent times.
4 Geoffrey Pridham, *Designing Democracy*, op. cit., Chapter 5.3.
5 Ibid., Chapter 4.4.
6 See the introduction in Robert Keohane and Joseph S. Nye (eds), *Transnational Relations and World Politics*. Cambridge, MA: Harvard University Press, 1973, pp. xvi–xxii.
7 See my chapter on the European Community and transnational networks in: Geoffrey Pridham (ed.), *Encouraging Democracy: The International Context of Regime Transition in Southern Europe*. Leicester: Leicester University Press, 1991, pp. 236–238.
8 Geoffrey Pridham, *Designing Democracy*, op. cit., Chapter 2.
9 Ibid., Chapter 3.4.
10 Geoffrey Pridham, "EU Enlargement and Consolidating Democracy in Post-Communist States: Formality and Reality," *Journal of Common Market Studies* 40, 2002: 964–65.
11 See, for instance: Alex Pravda, "Introduction," in: Jan Zielonka and Alex Pravda (eds), *Democratic Consolidation in Eastern Europe: International and Transnational Factors*. Oxford: Oxford University Press, 2001, pp. 23–4.

4 Portugal

Democratization and foreign policy

Nuno Severiano Teixeira

Introduction

The Portuguese Revolution of 25 April 1974 and the process of democratization that followed it affected not only domestic politics but also foreign policy. Newly democratic Portugal set up a new social model and new political institutions, and adopted a new model of insertion into the international system as the process of democratization evolved. Indeed, the more than three decades of democratic governance have left a clear mark on both domestic structures and Portugal's international position. In short, Portuguese democratization had an unequivocal international dimension and an impact on the country's foreign policy.

In the early literature, transition theories and models initially focused on domestic politics. The view was that endogenous factors were the fundamental drivers of political change. The international dimension and the play of exogenous factors were considered secondary or marginal.[1] Such early theories were partially a reflection of the democratizations of the first "wave" in Southern Europe and Latin America. Still in the thick of the Cold War, and thus dominated by the rigid logic imposed by two competing blocs, experiences with democratization were highly risky in terms of security because they had the power to generate international instability. For that reason, such experiences were rare and their fate uncertain. Success depended more on domestic political capabilities than on international factors. It is hardly surprising, then, that the focus of analysis was initially on national states, and that theoretical explanations centred on domestic forces and its political and institutional autonomy from international factors.[2]

All this changed dramatically with the 1989 revolution and the post-communist transitions of Eastern and Central Europe, as these called attention to the impact of international factors on processes of democratization. To this shift in reality, there corresponded a theoretical shift: traditional transition theories were broadened and reconfigured. In the more recent literature on democratization, the international dimension has become a central focus, and explanatory models are built around the central role of exogenous factors.[3] With the end of the Cold War and the triumph of the "Western model," democracy became a universal norm. An exception thirty years ago, democratization is now the apparent rule.[4] Indeed, the failure of democracy is regarded as a precarious and transient state of affairs, so it is seen as a threat to international security and stability. Policies to "promote democracy" have become common international practice. In short, the "international dimension" has become decisive. It is hardly surprising, then, that analytical models changed so radically, focusing now on the international components of democratization. The contributions of Philippe Schmitter and Geoffrey Pridham are essential, but the most central reference is the work by Laurence Whitehead. From his pioneering study to the present, he has not just developed a general model but also followed the historical evolution and taken on board the multidimensional nature of this phenomenon in a global and systematic fashion.[5]

If one re-examines the first transitions in light of new theoretical models, it becomes clear that the international dimension of the Southern European democratizations was significant. This was the case of the pacted transition in Spain,[6] and of the transition through "rupture" in Portugal. The goal of this chapter is to examine the Portuguese case. The aim is not to assess that case using an "outside-in/inside-out" all-purpose model (or, put differently, to examine the impact of the international context on the transition and the process of democratic consolidation,[7] or of the impact of democratization on the system of international relations), but rather to undertake an analysis of the relationship between democratization and foreign policy. Thus, the aim is to know how democratization affects foreign policy. The focus is on foreign policy writ large, rather than any specific aspects of what is a multidimensional affair; equally, the focus is less on process than on outcomes.

Two questions are addressed in the domain of foreign policy analysis and have dominated the theoretical debate about democratization: first, whether there is a chronological "fit" between transition to and consolidation of democracy at the domestic level and foreign policy shifts; and second, the extent to which there is continuity or a rupture with past foreign policy options with the advent of democracy. The analysis is divided into three parts: the first examines historical foreign policy models and the way in which Portugal inserted itself into the international system; the second examines the international dimensions of the process of transition to and consolidation of democracy; and the third reflects on the relationship between democratization and foreign policy.

Historical models of international integration

Portugal is simultaneously a European and an Atlantic country. It is a small peripheral power with a geopolitical feature which weighs decisively on the formulation of its foreign policy: the possession of only one terrestrial frontier. For this reason, it has always experienced an unstable geopolitical balance between land and sea. These geopolitical realities and Portugal's attempt to ensure a balance between them are what established the historically dominant features of Portugal's foreign policy options and its place in the international system. Portugal has adopted three models of insertion into the international system, each corresponding to a different historical period. Under the first, from the medieval period until the fifteenth century, Portuguese foreign relations operated within an Iberian peninsular framework, between five political units, all of them more of less similar in size and power: the peninsular kingdoms of Castile, Leon, Navarre, Aragon and Portugal. Because of the battle against Islam in the interior of the Peninsula, as well as resource and scientific-technological limitations, it was not possible to sustain extra-Peninsular relations. Thus, during the Middle Ages, Portuguese foreign relations were essentially intra-Peninsular relations in an international context of near "natural" equilibrium.

This dispensation changed dramatically from the fifteenth century onward, with the emergence of the geopolitical conditions and *longue durée* trends that reshaped the historical mode of Portuguese integration into the international system. The new model lasted for five centuries and ended, precisely, with the process of democratization. With the victory over Islam and the unification of Spain by the Catholic kings, the Iberian Peninsula was divided into two units of unequal size and power. At the same time, scientific and technological evolution permitted the sustained development of extra-Peninsular relations. Thus, a new peninsular imbalance replaced the medieval peninsular balance, and Portugal tried to compensate it by looking towards the Atlantic. Portugal engaged in an ongoing attempt to compensate for the continental pressure exerted by Spain with a maritime outlook.[8]

This dual reality is the pillar of the historically constant features of Portugal's strategic options and foreign policy. The latter are characterized, first, by an antinomic attitude, one that tilts sometimes towards the Continent and sometimes towards the sea, one caught between Europe and the Atlantic. Second, as a result of the former, it is characterized by distance from Europe and the continent (perceived as "the Spanish threat") and the predominance of a maritime orientation in external relations (the so called "Atlantic option"). Third, as a result of the above, Portuguese foreign policy and its international position are characterized by two long term trends: the search for special alliances with a maritime power (historically, the Anglo-Portuguese alliance, the US after the Second World War, and the North Atlantic Treaty Organization (NATO) at the multilateral level); and the colonial project (with the various cycles of Empire, ranging from India to Brazil and Africa). Fourth, as a result of all three of the above, it is characterized by the adoption of different extra-Peninsular alliances from those adopted by Spain, and a bilateral diplomacy based on the Lisbon–Madrid–London triangle (or the Lisbon–Madrid–Washington triangle after 1945).

These are the strategic options that shaped the foreign policy of the so-called authoritarian "New State" (*Estado Novo*) regime, and dominated Portuguese diplomatic culture from the Ambassadorship of Teixeira de Sampayo to that of Franco Nogueira, guiding Salazar's foreign policy from 1935 to the end of his regime.[9]

The contours of Portugal's foreign policy were already apparent in 1935. The regime was critical of the "international parliamentarism" of the League of

Nations, which was regarded as the political centre of the Continent and "opposed" to Portugal's Atlantic vocation and the its distance from central-European issues; it revaluated the traditional axes of Portuguese foreign policy, reaffirming the Anglo-Portuguese alliance and the Peninsular Friendship; and, last but not least, it adopted an intransigent defence of its status as a colonial empire.

These same principles – distance from European affairs, the affirmation of a Portugal attuned to the Atlantic and its colonies, and a balance based on the Lisbon–Madrid–London triangle – constituted the strategic pillars of Portuguese foreign policy in the 1930s and 1940s, particularly during the Spanish Civil War[10] and the Second World War.[11] In this, the Anglo-Portuguese Alliance and the Iberian Pact were central features. This dispensation remained in place after the Second World War, and shaped the international positions adopted by Salazar. The dictator did not seem to understand – or accept – that a new world order was emerging. First, there was the decline of Great Britain and the emergence of the United States as a new maritime power, which was only recognized with accession to NATO. Second, there was the suspicious attitude towards the new international organization with a global reach, the United Nations – a dislike previously focused on the parliamentarism of the League of Nations. Third, Salazar did not see that the reconstruction of Europe called for international cooperation and could not be undertaken within a national framework only. Finally, he also failed to understand and accept the principle of self-determination (which carried the General Assembly of the United Nations), and he rejected decolonization out of hand.

These positions shaped the evolution of Portuguese foreign policy towards Atlantic security, European integration and the colonies up until the demise of the authoritarian regime.

Salazar was suspicious of the US and reluctant to recognize the decline of British power and the rise of the United States as the new hegemonic maritime Atlantic power, but he was forced to acknowledge this changing reality. A first sign of the shift was the signature of the Lajes Agreement, a bilateral defence cooperation agreement between Portugal and the US dating from February 1948. At the multilateral level, the shift was signalled with the accession of Portugal to the Atlantic Pact in April 1949 despite all the reservations and resistance of Salazar. The Lajes Agreement and accession to NATO marked the integration of Portugal into the Atlantic security system, Portuguese recognition of the new maritime power, and emergence of a new alliance. They constituted Portugal's foreign policy response to the new post-war international context and a return to its Atlantic traditions.[12]

The position of Portugal regarding Europe and European integration was very different, as indicated by the reservations about the Marshall Plan, which led Salazar to refuse to participate in the first phase of the Plan in 1947–1948. The dictator agreed to participate in the second phase, but the evolution of Portuguese foreign policy towards European integration was nonetheless marked by aloofness and ambivalence: Portugal participated in the economic cooperation organizations, but remained hostile to integration or supranational projects. It participated in "economic Europe" for pragmatic reasons, but refused to have anything to do with "political Europe" for strategic ones.[13] Further, the great novelty in Portuguese foreign policy was the "European option," which was conditioned by a prior commitment to democratic governance.

This strategy – participation in the Atlantic security system, aloofness from European integration, the obstinate refusal to accept decolonization, and an intransigent defence of the colonies until the onset of the thirteen-year-long colonial wars fought on three simultaneous fronts – dominated foreign policy until the demise of authoritarianism.[14] They are the central elements of the second historical model of insertion into the international system adopted by Portugal. First, there was the antinomic perception of Europe and the Atlantic, which culminated in a "paroxysm" with the end of the New State regime, as exemplified in the political debate between those advocating an African strategy and those favouring a European one. Second, there was aloofness from Europe and the predominance of the Atlantic and colonial policy option. This predominance was both political and economic. In the former sphere, the focus was on NATO and a special alliance or relationship with Washington and London, a policy implemented by a strategic-diplomatic apparatus entirely dedicated to the Atlantic sphere. In the latter, the apparatus was geo-economic and essentially focused on the overseas and colonial arenas. Even when Portugal was forced to work more closely with European economic institutions for pragmatic reasons, that rapprochement only occurred within the Atlantic (never a Continental) framework. The country's accession to the European Free Trade Association (EFTA) best exemplifies this strategy.[15] Third, there was the constant effort to forge extra-Peninsular alliances other than those adopted by Spain. Portugal was always where Spain was not – in the Atlantic context, Portugal acceded to NATO while Spain did not; and in the European context, Portugal joined EFTA which Spain did not. Finally, despite increasingly interdependent international relations and the progressive multilateralization of diplomacy, there persisted the bilateral diplomacy based on the Lisbon–Madrid–maritime power triangle.

The Portuguese process of democratization altered national foreign policy entirely. However, it did more than that: the transition to and consolidation of democracy in Portugal and Spain on the one hand and changes in the international arena on the other led to the disappearance in only twelve years (1974–1986) of Portugal's five-century-old historical position in the international system. Some things remained constant, but the Portuguese process of democratization also wrought changes in the country's foreign policy. The first and most important of these changes was Europeanization, which itself altered the national model of insertion into the international system.

The international dimensions of democratization

With the demise of authoritarianism and the transition to democracy initiated on 25 April 1974, there was a profound redefinition of Portuguese foreign policy in the spirit of the programme of the Armed Forces Movement (AFM). In short-hand, the latter was based on the formula "democratization, decolonization, development." Although the AFM programme claimed to guarantee compliance with all of Portugal's ongoing international commitments, democratization and decolonization clearly required a reinterpretation of old commitments and an overhauling of the foreign policy orientation of the Portuguese state. Decolo-nization negotiations began in 1974, and became the first major foreign policy challenge faced by the new regime.[16] There were various contrasting ideological positions about decolonization: one, based on General Spínola's proposal as out-lined in his book *Portugal and the Future*, was federalist; another, inspired by Melo Antunes, advocated the creation of a neutral, non-aligned and Third World axis; and yet another, propounded by Vasco Gonçalves, was pro-Soviet. The various ideological nuances can be divided into two distinct political positions: the proponents of one argued that self-determination did not mean automatic independence, and were intransigent about Portuguese sovereignty until such a time as a referendum determined the fate of the colonies; proponents of the second view argued that self-determination did involve immediate independence and that there should be an immediate transfer of power to the national libera-tion movements as legitimate representatives of the former colonial peoples. This latter view won the day after what was a complex struggle with a not insignificant impact on domestic politics. A ceasefire was implemented in the field, and diplomatic negotiations initiated. Guiné-Bissau, which had declared independence unilaterally in 1973, was the first country to be recognized as a sovereign state by its former colonial power in August 1974. Between that date and January 1975, similar processes of transfer of power to national liberation movements – albeit with case-dependent variations – took place in all the former colonies.

With decolonization still under way, diplomatic relations were established with the Soviet Union, the countries of Eastern Europe and Third World nations, with the exception of Albania and China (the difficulties experienced with these countries were only resolved in 1979). However, decolonization, diplomatic opening and the end of international isolation were not the be all and end all of the new democracy's new foreign policy orientation. In fact, as the noisy strug-gles that were part of the domestic process of democratization were waged, another, silent, struggle went on over the future goals and strategic options of Portugal's foreign policy. Between April 1974 and January 1986, the country's foreign policy oscillated between two basic paths that also marked two distinct phases: that of the transition to democracy or of the pre-constitutional period dominated by the revolutionary process; and that of the consolidation of demo-cracy, corresponding to the constitutional period, or the institutionalization and stabilization of the democratic regime.[17]

The pre-constitutional period was marked by the struggle between various political forces over the foreign policy options available to Portugal. This was still the era of the Cold War, so the Western, Soviet and neutral or Third World models vied for supremacy, as a result of which there was no clear definition of goals and means: parallel diplomatic efforts were made and foreign policy remained undefined. The next phase, initiated with the first constitutional government, was marked by the clarification of Portuguese foreign policy and an unequivocal positioning of Portugal in the international arena. The country wholly embraced its position as a Western country, with simultaneously a European and an Atlantic dimension. These, then, were the two fundamental aspects and true strategic options adopted by democratic Portugal, to which must be added a third: post-colonial relations with the new Portuguese-speaking countries.

For Portugal, the Atlantic dimension was the most enduring historical feature of national foreign policy – one which also played an important role in stabilizing domestic politics. Bilaterally, Portuguese "Atlanticism" was expressed through diplomatic relations with the US and the renovation of the Lajes Agreement in 1979 and 1983. With these agreements, Portugal granted so-called "facilities" to the US on its Azores bases until 1991 in exchange for economic and military "assistance."[18] At the multilateral level, the Atlantic dimension involved the maintenance and reinforcement of Portuguese participation in the Atlantic Alliance, and in the redefinition and renovation of Portuguese commitments to NATO military efforts, which it had been forced to abandon from the 1960s onwards because of the war in Africa. For the army, this reinforcement meant the constitution of a Mixed Independent Brigade (later renamed the Airborne Brigade), which replaced and reactivated the old Independent Army Division and still operates essentially according to its old goals when engaged in NATO missions on the southern flank of the Alliance. Navy and Air Force patrol missions were reinforced within IBERLAND, and the IBERLAND command was upgraded to the category of Commander-in-Chief (CINCIBERLAND) and placed under the command of a Portuguese officer.[19]

The "European option" was the most notable foreign policy innovation of the post-25 April era; it was also the single greatest external challenge faced by democratic Portugal. Once anti-European resistance had been vanquished in 1976 (the African "option" of the authoritarian regime and then the Third World "temptation" of the revolutionary period laid to rest), Portugal clearly opted for Europe. This time, however, Europe was not regarded simply from an economic (as it had been with the association agreements signed in 1972) but also from a political perspective.

The Portuguese rapprochement with European integration started in 1976 with accession to the Council of Europe and the signature of the Additional Protocols to the 1972 Agreement (itself seen as a preliminary negotiation for full accession). After a successful round of negotiations in various European capitals between September 1976 and February 1977, in March 1977 the first constitutional government formally requested accession to the European Community, signalling the end of all hesitation over the best formula for Portuguese integration (regarding pre-accession status, or the so-called "special association"). Thus, the "European option" had become a reality. It was a strategic choice that decisively marked Portugal's future, and a centrepiece of the international dimension of the country's democratic consolidation.[20]

Two goals motivated the Portuguese government and justified that strategic option: first, the consolidation of democracy, which was ensured by Portuguese membership of the Community; and second, economic modernization and development, which were enhanced by the Community. Both goals – the first in particular – reveal the importance of the international context in the Portuguese process of democratization, if not during the transition phase then certainly during the process of consolidation of democracy.

The request for accession was followed by a long and complex negotiation process lasting for nearly a decade. The culminating point of that process took place in June 1985 with the signature of the Treaty of Accession to the EC. From 1 January 1986, Portugal became a full member of the European Community.[21]

The third foreign policy strategic dimension under democracy was the development of post-colonial relations. From 1976, Portugal's governments and presidents made unstinting efforts to re-establish and reinforce relations of friendship and cooperation with the new countries emerging after decolonization. From the early 1990s onwards, there was a normalization of relations between Portugal and the Portuguese-speaking African countries. The solidity of those relations and the international credibility of Portugal were important factors contributing to Portugal's mediating role in the Angolan and Mozambican peace processes. Brazil too became a foreign policy priority, and the 1980s were also the decade during which the Luso-Brazilian summit process was inaugurated.

At first, post-colonial relations evolved separately and exclusively at a bilateral level, but over time they also evolved multilaterally, with the establishment of the Community of Portuguese Speaking Countries (*Comunidade dos Países Língua Portuguesa*, CPLP) in 1996.[22] Africa and Brazil thus became active features of Portugal's foreign policy, which also gained a new meaning in the context of the European Union. Democratization may not have changed Portugal's place in the international system, but it did change the country's strategic priorities. Historically, Portugal had thought of itself as an Atlantic country and a colonial power, and when the balance shifted too far seaward, it sought to restore equilibrium through Europe. By contrast, Portugal is now a European country that seeks to gain advantages from its position in the Atlantic and relations with its former colonies.

Democratization and foreign policy

The Portuguese process of democratization had an international dimension and an impact on the country's foreign policy. How did regime change affect foreign policy, and what characterizes foreign policy under democracy? Let us begin by addressing the two questions posed in the introduction.

First, as regards the temporal dimension of democratization, did the external and domestic dimensions of the transition to and consolidation of democracy coincide in chronological terms? During the transition there was simultaneity, but the same cannot be said of the period of consolidation. In the first instance, the end of the transition and the beginning of the constitutional period went hand in hand with the clarification of Portugal's international position as a Western nation that was both Atlantic and European. In the second instance, the end of the process of consolidation did not coincide with the consolidation of Portugal's position in the international arena: whereas the domestic process had ended by 1982 with the constitutional revision and the promulgation of the national defence and armed forces law, consolidation of Portugal's new international position only occurred in 1986, when the country acceded to the European Community.

As regards the issue of continuity or rupture in Portugal's foreign policy before and after democracy, what changed and what remained unchanged? The elements of continuity all result from structural and geopolitical elements and enduring areas of strategic interest: the Atlantic, Europe, post-colonial relations and, later, the Mediterranean. There have been at least four changes which are clearly a product of regime change. The first was the end of the antinomic Europe–Atlantic logic – it makes no sense today, as its terms are complementary rather than contradictory. Portuguese foreign policy has gained value within Europe because of the country's transatlantic relations, and its participation in European integration gives it greater power in the context of Atlantic relations. This is true not only for North Atlantic relations with the US and NATO, but also for South Atlantic relations with Brazil and the former African colonies.

Second, although the geopolitical equation remained European–Atlantic, there was an inversion of strategic priorities: in the past, Portugal had prioritized the Atlantic and the colonies, and a continental "compensation" had come into play only when the maritime dimension gained too much prominence. Now the reverse is true: the priority is Europe and the European Union, and Portugal seeks to boost its Atlantic position and post-colonial relations to strengthen its position within Europe.

Third, as a result of the arrival of democracy in Portugal and Spain, both peninsular states have moved towards increasingly similar international positions. Between 1974 and 1975, Portugal underwent decolonization. In 1979, Spain got closer to EFTA, and it joined NATO's political structures in 1982. In 1986, Portugal and Spain both acceded to the European Community, and in 1990 they acceded to the Western European Union (WEU). In 1997, Spain joined the NATO military structure. Not only did Portugal's geo-economic apparatus "turn continental" with accession to the European Community, but Portugal's and Spain's strategic diplomatic apparata moved closer together to the point of coincidence. Succinctly, Portugal and Spain have the same extra-Peninsular alliances (the EU and NATO) for the first time ever in their histories.

Fourth, and finally, as a result of increasingly interdependent international relations and ever more intense multilateral activity, Portuguese diplomacy has become increasingly multilateral, which means that the country has a growing presence in the multilateral organizations working on its areas of strategic interest – the EU in Europe, NATO in the Atlantic, and the CPSC covering post-colonial relations.

These, then, are the changes wrought by democratization – changes that decisively and in some instances radically altered Portugal's foreign policy. Over the short term, these changes characterize the general orientation of foreign policy under democracy. However, from a long-term perspective, their reach is greater: they are changes that forever altered the country's historical place in the international system, and signalled the beginning of a new model of international insertion based on democratization and Europeanization.

Notes

1 Juan J. Linz and Alfred Stepan, *The Breakdown of Democratic Regimes*. Baltimore, MD: Johns Hopkins University Press, 1978; Philippe Schmitter, Guillermo O'Donnell and Laurence Whitehead (eds), *Transitions from Authoritarian Rule: Prospects to Democracy*. Baltimore, MD: Johns Hopkins University Press, 1986.

2 Laurence Whitehead, "Democratization with the Benefit of Hindsight: The Changing International Components," in: Plenary Session "What Have We Learnt from Thirty Years of Transitions from Authoritarian Rule?" *XIX World Congress of International Political Science Association*, Durban, South Africa, 30 June–4 July 2003.

3 Samuel P. Huntington, *The Third Wave*. Oklahoma, OH: University of Oklahoma Press, 1991; Geoffrey Pridham, *Encouraging Democracy. The International Context of Regime Transition in Southern Europe*. Leicester, Leicester University Press, 1991; Geoffrey Pridham, Eric Herring and George Sanford (eds), *Building Democracy? The International Dimension of Democratization in Eastern Europe*. Leicester, Leicester University Press, 1997; Geoffrey Pridham, "The International Dimensions of Democratization," Chapter 9 in *The Dynamics of Democratization: A Comparative Approach*. London: Continuum, 2000; Laurence Whitehead, *The International Dimension of Democratization: Europe and Americas*. Oxford: Oxford University Press, 1996; Philippe Schmitter, "O contexto internacional da democratização contemporânea," Chapter 8 in *Portugal: do Autoritarismo à Democracia*. Lisbon: Imprensa de Ciências Sociais, 1999; Jean Grugel, *Democratization: A Critical Introduction*. New York, NY: Palgrave/Macmillan, 2002, Chapter 6.

4 Laurence Whitehead, "Democratization with the Benefit of Hindsight," op. cit.

5 See Chapter 1, by Laurence Whitehead, in this volume.

6 See Chapter 5, by Juan Carlos Pereira, in this volume.

7 Carlos Gaspar, "The International Dimensions of the Portuguese Transition," paper presented at the conference "The Transition to Democracy in Spain, Portugal and Greece: Thirty Years After," Konstantinos G. Karamanlis Foundation, Athens, Greece, 2005.

8 J. B. de Macedo, *História Diplomática Portuguesa Constantes e Linhas de Força*. Lisbon: Tribuna da História, 2006 (2nd edtion).

9 Nuno Severiano Teixeira, "Between Africa and Europe: Portuguese Foreign Policy 1890–1986," in: António Costa Pinto (ed.), *Contemporary Portugal*. New York: Columbia University Press, 2003.

10 I. Delgado, *Portugal e a Guerra Civil de Espanha*. Lisbon: Publicações Europa-América, 1981; C. Oliveira, *Salazar e a Guerra Civil de Espanha*. Lisbon: O Jornal, 1987; Fernando Rosas (ed.) *Portugal e a Guerra Civil de Espanha*. Lisbon: Edições Colibri, 1998.

11 G. Stone, *The Oldest Ally: Britain and Portuguese Connection*. London: Boydell, 1994; A. Telo, *Portugal na Segunda Guerra*. Lisbon: Perspectivas e Realidades, 1987; A. Telo, *Portugal na Segunda Guerra*, Volumes I and II. Lisbon: Veja, 1991; A. J. Telo, A Neutralidade *Portuguesa e o Ouro Nazi*. Lisbon: Quetzal, 2000; M. Car-

rilho *et al.*, *Portugal na Segunda Guerra Mundial*. Lisbon: D. Quixote, 1989; Fernando Rosas, *Portugal entre a Paz e a Guerra*. Lisbon: Editorial Estampa, 1990.

12 Nuno Severiano Teixeira, *From Neutrality to Alignment: Portugal and the Foundation of the Atlantic Pact*. Florence, Italy: European University Institute, 1991; A. J. Telo, *Portugal e a NATO: O reencontro da tradição atlântica*. Lisbon: Cosmos, 1996.

13 F. Rolo, *Portugal e o Plano Marshall*. Lisbon: Editorial Estampa, 1994; J. M. T. Castilho, *A ideia de Europa no Marcelismo 1968–1974*. Lisbon: Edições Afrontamento, 2000; António Costa Pinto and Nuno Severiano Teixeira, "Portugal e a unificação europeia," *Penélope* 18, Lisbon, 1998; Pedro Cantinho Pereira, *Portugal e o início da construção europeia 1947–1953*. Lisbon: Instituto Diplomático, 2006.

14 Nuno S. Teixeira, "Portugal e as guerras da descolonização," in: M. T. Barata and N. S. Teixeira (eds), *Nova história militar*. Volume IV. Lisbon: Círculo de Leitores, 2004; W. W. Schneidman, *Engaging Africa: Washington and the Fall of Portugal's Empire*. New York/Oxford: University Press of America, 2004; L. N. Rodrigues, *Salazar e Kennedy: A crise e uma aliança*. Lisbon: Editorial Notícias, 2002; F. Martins, "A política externa do Estado Novo, o ultramar e a ONU," *Penélope* 18 (Lisbon), 1998; A. E. D. Silva, "O litígio entre Portugal e a ONU," *Análise Social* 30 (Lisbon), 1995.

15 R. Griffiths and B. Lie, "Portugal e a EFTA 1969–1973," in: *Portugal e a Europa 50 anos de integração*. Lisbon: Centro de Informação Jacques Delors, 1995; Elsa Santos Alípio, *Salazar e a Europa: história da adesão à EFTA*. Lisbon: Livros Horizonte, 2006; N. A. Leitão, "O convidado inesperado: Portugal e a fundação da EFTA 1956–1960," *Análise Social* 171 (Lisbon), 2004.

16 António Costa Pinto, *O fim do império português*. Lisbon: Livros Horizonte, 2001; P. P. Correia, "Descolonização," in: J. M. B. Brito (ed.), *Do Marcelismo ao fim do Império*. Lisbon: Círculo dos Leitores, 1999; J. S. Cevelló, *El último império occidental: la descolonización portuguesa*. Mérida, Spain: UNED, 1998; N. MacQueen, *The Portuguese Decolonization: Metropolitan Revolution and the Dissolution of Empire*. London/New York: Longman, 1997.

17 A. Dulphy and Y. Léonard (eds), *De la dictature à lá démocratie: voies ibériques*. Brussels: Peter-Lang, 2003; A. J. Telo, "As relações internacionais da transição," in: J. M. B. Brito (ed.), *Do marcelismo ao fim do império*. Lisboa: Círculo dos Leitores, 1999; A. J. Telo, "A Revolução e a posição de Portugal no mundo," in: Fernando Rosas (ed.), *Portugal e a transição para a democracia*. Lisboa: Edições Colibri, 1999.

18 T. M. Sá, *Os americanos na revolução portuguesa (1974–1976)*. Lisbon: Notícias Editorial, 2004; B. F. Pereira, "Continuidade na mudança: As relações entre Portugal e os Estados Unidos," *Política Internacional* 2 (Lisbon), 1990; J. C. Magalhães, "Portugal e os Estados Unidos: Relações no domínio da defesa," *Estratégia* 4 (Lisbon), 1988.

19 N. S. Teixeira, "Portugal na NATO 1949–1999," *Nação e Defesa* 89 (Lisbon), 1999; A. Telo, "Portugal e a Nato (1949–1976)," *Nação e Defesa* 89 (Lisbon), 1999; Vasco Rato, "A Aliança Atlântica e a consolidação da democracia," in: J. M. Ferreira, *Política externa e política de defesa do Portugal democrático*. Lisbon: Edições Colibri, 2001.

20 A. C. Pinto and N. S. Teixeira, "From Atlantic Past to European Destiny," in: W. Kaiser and J. Elvert (eds), *European Union Enlargement: A Comparative History*. London/New York: Routledge, 2004; A. C. Pinto and N. S. Teixeira, "From Africa to Europe: Portugal and European Integration," in: A. C. Pinto and N. S. Teixeira (eds), *Southern Europe and the Making of the European Union*. New York: Columbia University Press, 2002; J. M. Ferreira, "A estratégia para a adesão de Portugal às Instituições Europeias," in: M. M. T. Ribeiro, A. M. B. de Melo and M. C. L. Porto (eds), *Portugal e a construção europeia*. Coimbra: Almedina, 2003; M. M. T. Ribeiro, "Le

Portugal et le nouveau défi européen," in: *Fédérations ou Nations*. Paris: Éditions Sedes, 1999.

21 J. M. Magone, *The Developing Place of Portugal in the European Union*. New Brunswick, NJ: Transaction Publishers, 2004; E. R. Lopes, "O processo de integração de Portugal nas Comunidades Europeias: Uma avaliação geral década e meia depois," in: M. M. T. Ribeiro, A. M. B. de Melo and M. C. L. Porto (eds), *Portugal e a construção europeia*. Coimbra: Almedina, 2003; António Barreto, "Portugal: Democracy through Europe," in: J. J. Anderson (ed.), *Regional Integration and Democracy*. New York/Oxford: Rowman & Littlefeld, 1999; J. S. Lopes, *Portugal and EC Membership Evaluated*. London/New York: Pinter Publishers, 1993.

22 M. R. Marchueta, *A CPLP e o seu enquadramento*. Lisbon: Ministry of Foreign Affairs, 2003; J. Lamego, "A emergência da CPLP e as suas consequências," in: J. M. Ferreira (ed.), *Política externa e política de defesa do Portugal democrático*. Lisbon: Edições Colibri, 2001; Y. Léonard, *La lusophonie dans le monde*. Paris: La Documentation Française, 1988; A. Enders, *Histoire de l'Afrique lusophone*. Paris: Editions Chandeigne, 1994; "Géopolitques des Mondes Lusophones," *Lusotopie* 1–2 (Paris), 1994.

5   The international dimension of the Spanish transition

Juan Carlos Pereira

Introduction

At the opening ceremony of the Congress celebrating the Spanish transition in Madrid in 1995, Professor Juan José Linz began his speech thus:

> [This is] an encounter between history and historians: the transition is already history, it is not something under debate or politically contested nowadays, it is a academic object today, and there is the risk that those who did not witness it will ignore it, consider it obvious, as something that was unproblematic. Those of us who experienced it can remember the uncertainties, the risks, the difficulties that accompanied it as well as the excitement and hopes it generated.[1]

These words, proffered by one of the leading world experts on transitions, whose work on the nature of the Franco regime published after 1964 had a great influence on Spanish historians, influenced my attitude and research on the Spanish transition and foreign affairs as well. Ramón Cotarelo, a leading Spanish expert in the field, expressed a similar idea when he stated that "the transition itself, as an already *historical* political phenomenon, cannot be interpreted unilaterally."[2] The Spanish transition to democracy is, indeed, part of Spanish contemporary history. It is a history characterized by permanent political and constitutional uncertainty, the near absence of a democratic regime, slow economic modernization, a rigid social structure, and a foreign policy that oscillated between isolation and forced neutrality. This is why Spain has been characterized frequently as "different," or "unsuccessful," or "pre-modern."[3]

The death of General Francisco Franco on 20 November 1975 doubtless opened a new chapter in that traumatic history. The dictator had led an authoritarian regime from 1939 that distanced itself from Europe and the wave of democratization of the post-war period. In 1969, Franco named the then Prince Juan Carlos of Bourbon as his successor. When the latter was proclaimed King on 22 November 1975, a new period of hope and doubt regarding his political objectives began. It is evident today that, with determination (if not with a specific plan), the clear aim of the King was to make Spain a democratic, modern country and to open it up to Europe and the world. Some key figures of the Franco regime and of the opposition also played a key role in this. What is now known is that the political transition took place between the demise of the Franco regime and the emergence of democratic Spain.

In 1997, the Spanish Centre of Sociological Investigations (CIS) undertook a survey on the "Memory of the Spanish Transition," in which respondents emphasized three points: that Spanish society had changed greatly since 1975; that the changes were generally quite positive; and that all Spaniards should be proud of how those changes had been brought about during the transition. In 2000, the twenty-fifth anniversary of the coronation of King Juan Carlos, the level of satisfaction in Spanish society remained very high, which confirms the view that this is one of very few historical periods about which Spaniards feel proud and satisfied. Respondents also highlighted that the country's international image had changed significantly since 1975. The historical relationship between Spain and violence, instability, war and backwardness ended with the peaceful transition to democracy from an almost forty-year-long authoritarian regime. Many foreign and Spanish specialists and observers alike, including those who experienced the "pacted rupture" with expectation and anguish, have wondered how Spaniards were able to make that transition in such a short space of time without violence. The fact that transitologists such as Pridham and di Palma have described the Spanish transition as "paradigmatic," "exemplary" or "ideal" is notable. Indeed, the Spanish transition has been the object of special attention of various foreign specialists, mostly political scientists, and there are many juridical, economic, ideological, political and memory-based studies in Spain on the subject, which is covered significantly more than any other period of the country's history.[4]

Three conclusions can be extracted from these works. First, the Spanish transition is no longer the object of attention of leading social scientists, as it has become a historical matter and part of the recent past. Second, Spanish historians began to study the transition only rather belatedly and somewhat haphazardly, with the first works appearing between 1979 and 1990. More were produced between 1991 and 1996, and with the change in the political cycle such works became more selective in focus. Third, the literature indicates repeatedly that international influence on the transition was very limited, although the international context was favourable. It also notes that only some details or very specific foreign policy aims changed with the transition (which explains the lack of work on the international or foreign policy dimensions of the transition). A review of studies on the transition shows there is widespread consensus that the international context was favourable from the beginning in the Spanish transition, that its influence was not in any way decisive, and that foreign policy was not a key issue, with the exception of the impact of accession to the European Economic Community (EEC) and the polemic caused by hurried accession to the North Atlantic Treaty Organization (NATO).

What explains this consensus? In 1990, political scientist Roberto Mesa stated that it existed for institutional academic reasons (namely, the shortage of international relations and foreign policy specialists in Spain), and because of the relegation to the background of foreign policy studies given the primacy of domestic politics during the transition, the lack of reliable documents and memoirs, and parliamentary indifference to international topics.[5] The argument made here is that the lack of focus on international factors was the result of three factors. First there was the acceptance almost without discussion of the positions of the main specialists on transition processes,[6] which posited that domestic actors were the key and thus rendered it seemingly unnecessary to study the international influence on liberalization and transition.[7] This was reiterated later, as exemplified by Schmitter's view that "the transitions from authoritarianism and the immediate perspectives of political democracy should be explained in function of national forces and calculations," and that "external actors spread to play an indirect and generally marginal part, with the obvious exception of those cases in which a foreign power is present."[8] Such interpretations have fortunately changed radically over the last few years, but they have had a great impact on various interpretations of Spanish transition, and on the tendency to place domestic factors above all others.

Second, there is the oft reiterated notion that the transition was influenced by a favourable international context. The journalist Justino Sinova, among others, insists on the "normality" of the process of Spanish international insertion, notably NATO membership and accession to the EEC, which made Spain immediately comparable "to the oldest democracies and [allowed it] to find a place in Europe and in the world that it was denied during Francoism."[9] But was insertion really that easy? This is the impression one gets from reading the earlier works on the transition by historian Carlos Seco Serrano: the positive "military and economic understanding with United States was not only 'tightly tied' after the death of Franco, but also reinforced until full NATO membership," and as a result of this Spanish–US "alliance" between 1953 and 1982, "the transition evolved peacefully and Spain integrated with the world."[10] Such statements are not as persuasive today.

Third, the lack of attention to international and foreign policy topics owes much to the traditional indifference to these subjects among Spanish social scientists – despite the significant changes in Spain's international position after 1975, and the decisive influence of the international context in domestic matters (suffice it to mention the examples of accession to the EEC in 1986, and the influence of international factors on issues as varied as agricultural politics or university study plans), and despite the huge public interest in international topics in what is a globalized and media-dominated society.

This panorama has changed, however. Spanish political scientists such as Gil Calvo have observed that when specialists say that the transition was imposed from above or forged from below, it is forgotten that

> part of the new game rules were indeed granted from above, but they could only be applied thanks to the explicit consent of the "anti-Franco" opposition, which first took them on board (accepted them) and then approved

them (ratified them). Further, from the outset, the opposition maintained the power of veto, since it monopolized the recognition of the outside world (given by international and European bodies), on which the ex-post facto legitimacy of the transition depended as a sine qua non condition. Thus, forces on both sides were tied, each monopolizing their respective de facto powers.[11]

Roberto Mesa mentions that it is not enough to provide a census of the more or less important Spanish actors when speaking about the people who shaped the transition; it is necessary to mention "foreign personalities," and importance of the "material support" given by French and German governments, parties and unions, and even by "agents that were well placed and better connected in Spain."[12] At the same time, the revolutionary process in Eastern Europe after 1989, in which the so-called "popular democracies" disappeared and were replaced by more or less consolidated democracies, also opened up a new stage of research and reflection.

Indeed, the international context that permitted this process of historical change was so decisive and the influence of the international factors in each transition process so outstanding that transitologists were soon forced to change their position. German sociologist Claus Offe initiated the debate, and was followed by specialists such as Pridham, Schmitter, Tovias and Whitehead, who reassessed the influence of international factors in the transition processes,[13] including in previous transitions, among them those of Portugal, Greece and Spain. More recently, Grugel has presented a reinterpretation of the relationships between the international system, the international context and transition processes.[14] She argues that there are three main factors explaining the growing influence of international factors:

1   the development of a global economy from 1944 with the globalization of production, trade and finance that has led to growing interdependence, a loss of economic sovereignty, a convergence between the political and economic spheres, a process of regional integration and the development of a strategy of global liberalization among various countries;
2   that increasing democratization has been accompanied by more global governance, which diminishes the autonomy of the state in a new called "post-Westphalian" order, as exemplified by the power of organizations such as the International Monetary Fund (IMF), the World Bank (WB), the United Nations (UN), or the Organization for Economic Cooperation and Development (OECD), which are promoting democracy globally according to a "Western" paradigm; and
3   a progressive diffusion of democratic values as a result of the emergence of global communications, technological advances and the mass media. In the words of Giddens, there are no longer national cultures but global cultures in an interconnected world, and their common language is democracy.[15]

The research project I direct at the Complutense University of Madrid is part of this shift in focus, and this chapter is based on the results of work undertaken in the context of that project. Its focus is on international factors in transitions to democracy and, more specifically, the Spanish transition, and the impact of those factors on internal political change, including foreign policy. International factors are seen from two perspectives: from the "outside in" (the impact of the international context on domestic actors, their behaviour and its results) and from the "inside out" (foreign policy changes mirroring domestic political changes, and the shift to a democratic foreign policy). The project consists of a revision of the information and ideas in political science and international relations literature in Spain and abroad.

The result of that work has been the elaboration of six hypotheses as follows:

1   that international factors play a role in the origins, development and final results of transition processes;
2   that they vary according to geo-historical area (European transitions processes are broadly similarly conditioned);
3   that if the transition is from authoritarianism to democracy and culminates in the establishment of a democratic state, a foreign policy transition also occurs concurrently;
4   that a foreign police transition should take place in the same way;
5   that in the Spanish transition the international context was extremely important, particularly in the development stage and in terms of results, but also during the phase of consolidation, conditioning the process of political change and integration in the international arena, and in European political-defence structures in particular;
6   that there was also a transition in foreign policy in Spain, from Francoist authoritarianism to democracy, which culminated in the formulation of a democratic foreign policy.

It should be noted that the research project develops a perspective that has not been very relevant in Spanish historiography, so it has been necessary to work with a broad theoretical, conceptual and methodological framework and to resort to political science and international relations theory. The priority has been to select the most relevant contributions from among the immense existing bibliography on transitions, and the Spanish transition in particular. Given the absence of established and agreed models regarding the influence of international factors on transition processes and the cycle of transition on foreign policy, it was necessary to elaborate models for both to apply to the Spanish case. Because of the absence of a definition of a "democratic foreign policy," a model had to be developed for that as well. The selection and prioritization of primary and secondary sources that might be useful for the project in Spain and abroad were deemed crucially important. Finally, the methodology and approach adopted had to reflect the requirements of historical study, as well as the study of contemporary world history and recent history, understood as periods of still-living generations.

The international context and the Spanish transition

As noted above, events in Central and Eastern Europe after 1989 radically changed views about the international context in transition processes. Analysts realized that such processes could not be explained from a domestic standpoint alone, even from a functional, genetic or integrative point of view, and that international factors and the relationship between domestic political change and foreign change (the theory of a linkage) had been undervalued. The issue commanded greater attention because it not only applied to the "third wave" democracies, as they were called by Huntington and of which the Spanish was a part, but also to previous and subsequent waves. Transitologists began to develop conceptual schemes, precise methodologies and a comparative perspective to attempt to explain how, why or when international factors influenced transition processes. The same specialists also realized that transitions were not simply about political change in a specific state (from authoritarianism or totalitarianism to democracy), but also involved social, economic, institutional-organizational and decision-making changes, as well as changes in actors, power relationships, and even mentalities and behaviours. In this context, transitologists began to talk about *transitions* rather than *transition*.

As regards Spain, two difficult questions stood out: given the nature of international society from 1945 onwards, the geo-strategic position of Spain and the specific interests of some states, how was it possible for external actors not to intervene in the Spanish transition process? This question called for a precise answer, not least because, as various authors have shown, the left-wing revolutionary experience of Portugal after 1974 had forced some actors such as the US, NATO, the EEC itself to intervene, influence or control the process of transition. And, if a democratizing political change had altered laws, institutions and behaviours in Spain, should not the decisions and behaviour of the domestic actors who led the establishment of democratic state also have produced a change in foreign policy so as to adapt it to the demands of a democratic state? In connection with the first point, it was necessary to develop an interpretation and a model to evaluate the impact of the international context on transition processes. This led to the consideration of seven topics.

First, there are the characteristics of the international system in which concrete transition processes evolve. The influence of the international context is not only affected by the international system in which transition processes occur, but also by the geo-historical area in which states are inserted when the transition takes place. Observation of differences in the transitions in Europe, Latin America or Asia highlighted the importance of Europe as a whole, and of the EEC and "European identity," in the "third wave." Since 1950 the EEC has been an outstanding actor, both on the continent and internationally, as a global model of coexistence and democracy. Because of this, it is impossible to disregard the impact of the ECC on the European transition processes.

Second, there are the international actors with the capacity or the power to intervene in, coerce or influence countries – namely states, international governmental actors, international non-governmental actors, non-central governmental actors and some outstanding individuals. There are relatively few works on the subject (with the oft-cited exceptions of Pridham, Schmitter, Whitehead and, more recently, Tovias and Grugel). All these authors have developed concepts to help explain external influences on the processes of democratization, such as diffusion, infection, penetration, effect demonstration, emulation, reaction, control, incorporation, interdependence and conditionality. All suggest there is some form of active and passive influence, and include some autonomous socio-economic or cultural transnational influences. A further aspect examined concerns the reasons why international actors intervene, among which the following stand out.

During the Cold War and the global bipolar confrontation, any intervention to promote the progressive democratization of the world by Western powers had to favour world security – hence the 1961 US Foreign Assistance Act to help deeply anti-communist individuals and parties. In the 1970s, economic pressures and, later, demands for respect for human rights were used to condition aid. The EEC also sought to promote democracy as part of its "European identity," even outside its frontiers, as exemplified by the Fourth Lomé Programme. Further, the superpowers or key powers with a special relationship with regions where countries are undergoing a transition are obliged to defend their strategic and security interests, even to the detriment of democracy promotion. Moreover, international intervention may be encouraged in cases where there is uncertainty when dictators are ousted and when there is an internal power vacuum motivated by a war or, especially, defeat in a war. This is demonstrated by the Portuguese, Greek and Argentine cases, where one observes the failure of authoritarian governments to project military power beyond national borders. External support may also be necessary when there is a crisis of a hegemonic power in a region – like that of the USSR after 1989 – that once imposed its power and influence to establish authoritarian regimes. Weakness or a fracture within a dominant power can also accelerate the liberalization of states that are a part of its zone of influence. The historical process of decolonization, particularly linked with events after the Second World War, and most particularly after 1960, also encouraged the diffusion of democratic models (India post-1947, for instance), and encouraged international organizations to support post-colonial democratizations. Also to be taken into account is pressure from international financial organizations (such as the IMF, the WB or the European Bank of Reconstruction and Development (EBRD)) to promote not only economic liberalization but also political reform as a condition for offering material assistance. Regional organizations can also shape the course of domestic events in states because of their influence or role as models, using a wide variety of resources, and always with the prospect of possible inclusion if democratization requirements are met (the Council of Europe (CoE) and now the EU are paradigmatic cases).

Third, there is the issue of how actors intervene, influence or coerce. Among them, the following should be emphasized, following Whitehead: initially there is *contagion*, which requires an understanding of neither states nor actors but only of the context in which groups of states carry out a transition process in any given period, and their geographical distribution. There can be "infection by vicinity," as in Central and East Europe after 1989, or Spain and Portugal in 1974–1975, or Africa between 1990 and 1994. Since 1974, there have been approximately forty democratizations of this kind. Next, there is *control*, whereby powers control the internal situations of states, in which case democratization acts like a "vaccine" against authoritarianism or anti-communism, as in some US interventions in Latin America or Great Britain after decolonization. Approximately two-thirds of existing democracies in 1990 at least partly originated as a result of deliberate imposition or intervention. This calls for an analysis of the role of foreign powers in such processes. There are the cases of Britain in the Commonwealth in 1945, or the two sub-systems or the crisis of the USSR in the context of the Cold War. Finally, there is *consent*, which refers to the attitude of domestic groups in states where a very direct relationship is established between domestic politics and foreign policy, or what Pridham refers to as "linkage politics."

It is open to debate "whether the appropriate perspective for studying a given issue is contagion, control, or consent," and "it may be artificial to dichotomize the analysis into domestic and international elements. Although there will always be some purely domestic and some exclusively international factors involved, most of the analysis will contain a tangle of both elements."[16] In reference to Whitehead, Schmitter asks the following question: "perhaps, it is time to reconsider the impact of the international context upon regime change. Without seeking to elevate it to the status of prime mover, could it not be more significant than was originally thought?"[17] He adds two further forms of external influence to the above list: *conditionality*, or deliberate coercion through the institutions or multilateral organizations (like the IMF, the EEC, the CE, the EBRD and, less obviously, the OAS or the Commonwealth); and *interdependence*, based on an "inverted Kantianism" or paradigm of "perpetual peace," which promotes a broad range of exchanges that can lead to national institutional democratization, and which upturns Marxist dependency theory. The role of the EEC in the new democracies of Southern Europe, including Spain, where the Community had an initially marginal influence but deep repercussions on institutions and politics after regime consolidation, notably on the networks of public and private exchange that connected each state with the Community, is a case in point. To this list of factors, Grugel adds the extension of citizenship and transnational activities by non-governmental organizations, international political organizations, government institutions, or political organizations, which transmit solidarity, technical support or political advice to promote democratization. Of course, alongside these peaceful means there are other non-peaceful methods, such as invasion, occupation, control or even war (such as the recent example of Iraq, and the historical cases of Germany, Japan, Italy and Austria).

Fourth, there is the timing of the intervention process. For some authors, timing varies according to circumstances, but international actors generally intervene at any one of three points: the *inaugural or initial phase*, when the first decisions are adopted to change a regime and adopt a democratic structure (in this phase external influences can be important or decisive, especially to avoid the failure of initial reforms); the *constituent phase*, when the main task is the formulation of a constitution, accompanied by other decisions that help to define the form of democracy or the rule of law (in this phase external influence usually diminishes); or during the *termination phase* when, once defined, the system begins to acquire defined political contours, among them the elaboration of a new foreign policy, which is also shaped by external influence. Pridham distinguishes between what he calls *transition-development* (in which international influence is general and continuous) and *transition-event* (in which external influence is felt at a crucial moment or through specific acts). Others argue that international influence will be greater if it occurs during consolidation rather than the transition phase, partly because of the structure of opportunities, as the initial phase of improvisation or uncertainty does not allow for decisive influence, or influence may not be well received. With consolidation the situation becomes clearer, the number of domestic actors decreases, identities and territorial limits are fixed, and external actors are able to intervene more deliberately and selectively, and even to penetrate civil society. This is the moment for conditionality through multilateral diplomacy or international organizations, when it becomes possible for politicians to blame "external conditionality" for unpopular reforms implemented at home. Military alliances may also soften behaviour, as in the case of Portugal and NATO, limiting uncertainty or the influence of "enemy powers." This tendency can arise as a result of interdependence and internationalization.

Fifth, there is the speed of the transition process. A quick transition may leave little time for international influence, while a lingering and controversial process can generate greater opportunities external intervention.

Sixth, there are conditioning factors or operational limitations (as some authors term them), which include: *conditioning variables*, such as international commitments (treaties, alliances) that remain in effect after authoritarianism, and new alliances established as a result of the transition process; *external limitations of national actors*, such as relationships with economic, political, military, religious or cultural external groups, with the attitudes of the former varying according to their points of view and interests; the *broad domestic setting*, including the role of public opinion and the mass media, as well as the degree of fragmentation or consent over international issues in particular; and the *geostrategic context*, which can influence democratic regimes very specifically, encouraging them to emulate and become part of the dominant system or, if the context is non-democratic, can hinder transitions and new regime stability.

Finally, there are the results of intervention of different actors. International influence depends on aims, and varies according to the way in which the regime is consolidated after a transition. The international context can have a negative or dissuasive effect on a democracy, or hinder the transition, as it can "overload" governments when these are busy with the priority task of building a new democracy. Equally, some external events can destabilize a fragile system that is being constructed. History has shown that there are also transitions from demo-cracy to authoritarianism (Italy in 1922, Portugal in 1926, Spain in 1939 and Greece in 1967, for instance) or from democracy to totalitarianism (Germany in 1933), or what Huntington calls "democratic counter-waves."

How does all this apply to the Spanish case? The basic hypothesis proposed here is that a wide range of international actors intervened during the whole of the Spanish transition period (*transition-development*), at different levels, with specific results that affected or conditioned the process of political change. The level of international influence should not be underestimated, but the influence was not always positive or favourable, and many more actors than those men-tioned by the literature intervened. The research undertaken for the project on which this chapter is based confirms the above hypotheses. There was a group of states (particularly France, the Federal Republic of Germany, the USSR, Portugal and Italy in Europe, and the US, which had a permanent role even during the period of consolidation, though they did not intervene directly. These had two precise objectives: to avoid a second "Portuguese transition" and, in the case of the US, to preserve US defence interests. Further, there were three organizations and international institutions: the EEC, towards which national actors looked constantly and consensually, seeking the paradigms of "Europeanization," "modernization," and "democratization;" the CoE, which clearly bet on democratization and incorporated Spain in November 1977 before it had a Constitution (a fact without precedent); and NATO, which permanently influenced national actors and even determined the participation, for the first time in the history of the Spanish people in a referendum on an international matter. Third, there were international NGOs – in this instance, the political party Internationals and the trade unions, especially the Socialist International, the German parties and trade unions, and private foundations (mostly Catholic and German, with the Vatican playing a key role, given its relevance in Spanish society). Finally, there were various individuals, such as Brandt, Schmidt, Kohl, Palme, Giscard d'Estaing, Mitterrand and Kissinger, as well as various foreign correspondents, all of whom played a decisive role in the transition on different occasions.

All these actors intervened for various reasons, in some cases because of guilt for having abandoned or betrayed the Spaniards at the end of the Second War and allowing the Franco dictatorship to survive, in other cases because of a desire to guide the transition, to establish close ties with national actors and the new democracy, and to promote democracy among a people not accustomed to it. The methods of intervention varied – they were fundamentally economic, but included political pressure – and their impact was felt throughout the transition process and beyond, on both domestic and foreign policy. The combined result was the establishment of a stable, modern and consolidated democratic state that was able to confront serious threats such as the *coup d'état* on 23 February 1981 and face the challenge of economic transformation that led to European acces-sion, all in the absence of violence and civil conflict, and in a climate of consen-sus that is admired by other countries undergoing transitions.[18]

The transition from an authoritarian to a democratic foreign policy

As noted above, the second question posed by our research project regards changes in foreign policy concomitant with domestic social and political change, which has been largely ignored by the Spanish political scientists and historiography. What was Spain's international position when Franco died, and what is the position of democratic Spain? After 1973, Spain underwent a period of intense global crisis, following the ETA murder of President Luis Carrero Blanco. This is why Francoism ended as it began – sunk in isolation and surrounded by international condemnation, which included the recall of ambassadors, and the suspension of relationships and even flights by some countries. After 1974, Franco was the only remaining dictator in Western Europe. The new President, Arias Navarro, only carried out one official visit in the whole of 1975, and only one significant foreign visitor, Maltese Dom Mintoff, came to Spain. The Minister of Foreign Affairs made just six official trips, to countries of little import. The only Head of State that made an official visit was US President Gerald Ford, against the advice of his own ambassador and of the Spanish democratic opposition. Mexico officially requested the expulsion of Spain from the UN, and negotiations with the EEC were suspended. The CoE issued a tough declaration against Spain, and the words and aims proclaimed by the Spanish President, Carlos Arias, during his visit to Helsinki for the European Security and Cooperation Conference meeting were not confirmed by the decisions of the Spanish government. Franco died on 20 November 1975 in an atmosphere of isolation and international criticism, as demonstrated by the level of seniority of the international officials that attended his funeral. On 22 November 1975 Juan Carlos inaugurated his monarchy. Significantly, this was attended by the presidents of France, the Federal Republic of Germany, and Ireland, by princes of various royal houses, including Prince Philip from Britain, by representatives of international organizations, and by a large number of foreign delegations. There were all the signs of international trust in the new Head of the State and in the desire for a speedy process of democratization.

Obviously, foreign policy played a role in the process of democratization. The argument here is that the new foreign policy had to fulfil three aims: first, to help "present" the new Spain, its main actors and people to international society (foreign policy as a resource); second, to contribute to the consolidation and democratic approval of Spain (foreign policy as an end); and third, to become more democratic, with an abandonment of past authoritarian positions based on the theory of external power, to gain broad public support, and become open to democratic debate among political parties (foreign policy as a factor of modernization).

Foreign policy was not a priority in the political debate during the transition, as energies were focused on the elaboration of the Constitution and on building a strong democratic state with social backing. In that context, external factors were conditioned, as Roberto Mesa points out,[19] by the evolution of the constitutional project. Similarly, the mechanics of domestic consensus-building affected external action between 1976 and 1980, leading Spain to ignore the most polemic international questions (integration into NATO, and the problem of the Western Sahara, for example) and to avoid introducing divisive topics to ensure the climate of understanding necessary to approve the Constitution. As noted by Celestino del Arenal, "the consensus impeded the accurate and clear definition of key foreign policy guidelines, with the exception of its European dimension."[20] Foreign policy was conditioned by the nature of the dominant political forces (the heterogeneity of the government party, the UCD, which had simple parliamentary majorities, and the ideologically cohesive Socialist Party, PSOE, which had absolute majorities in the Parliament most of the time it was in power), progressive public involvement in international issues (such as NATO membership), and the precepts of the 1978 Constitution on foreign policy (the deficiencies of which have already been noted). Between November 1975 and the formation of the first Suárez government on 6 July 1976, in which Marcelino Oreja occupied the Ministry of Foreign Affairs, time and resources were lost, and it was June–July of 1976 before the Spanish foreign policy transition began, when it became possible to change foreign policy in accordance with a programme that included objectives and an inspiring philosophy of clear democratic content, and to attain the first international achievements (the end of the debt that stood in the way of external normalization).

Foreign policy was regarded as one among many elements of the democratic system, and so it was subjected to the same rules and elaboration and control mechanisms found in other Western democracies. As the product of the active participation of society through representative institutions, foreign policy also came to include the democratic parliament. In a talk at the 1977 Conference at the Spanish Diplomatic School, Minister Marcelino Oreja stated the new aims of the democratic government; these involved "popular representation, and consequently, the involvement of the whole population of the country in the creation, carrying out and control of the foreign policy." Oreja also outlined policy more specifically. Spain was seen as a medium power that could play an important part in its geopolitical sphere. In this context, the focus was on Western Europe (accession to the EEC and improved bilateral relations with surrounding countries), and Latin America and the Arab world. To this was added the never questioned maintenance of and willingness to deepen relations with the US, the definition of security and defence issues, and a cordial and balanced relationship with the Vatican. The role of King Juan Carlos in the foreign policy process was momentous, not only as Head of the State or "first ambassador from the new Spain," but also because of the political power he inherited from Franco and maintained until the approval of the Constitution in December 1978. The King's first official trip in May–June 1976 was to the Dominican Republic and the US, where he gave a key speech that can be said to have signalled the beginning of the foreign policy transition.

What is the main focus of a transition in foreign policy? The key aim is to create and apply a democratic foreign policy. Four things must be kept in mind here: that foreign policy is a political activity that is the exclusive competency of states; that it is related to the concept of state and political systems; that there is a growing link between domestic and foreign policy; and that a democratic state must have a democratic foreign policy. Further, although there is no clear academic consensus regarding what defines it, it is necessary to bear in mind the nature of the formal cycle (formulation, decision-making, execution and control), goals, decision-making actors, and the administrative machine that must be established or reformed to execute established policy goals. For a state to have and carry out a foreign policy, it must have its own recognizable style, develop a precise strategy, establish a certain calendar and gain proportionate resources, defend interests and pursue goals in a continuous way, respect commitments and existing alliances, and adopt decisions in a manner coherent with general state policy.

Preliminary research results suggest that the period of transition in foreign policy did not coincide with internal transition. It extended from the summer of 1976 (May–July) until the end of 1986, by which time foreign policy had become fully democratized. It was necessary to elaborate a model of transition from the authoritarian foreign policy that characterized the Franco regime to a democratic foreign one. There were few studies on the topic, in Spain and abroad, and after extended debate among the research team a chronology was established as follows: authoritarian Franco regime (1939–75) – authoritarian foreign policy and theory of external power; crisis-collapse of the authoritarian regime (1973–5) – foreign policy crisis (1973–5); beginning of the transition in foreign policy (May–June 1976); search for the international legitimization of the new regime and national actors (1976–7); democratization of structures, decision-making processes and execution organs; new cycle in foreign policy (1978–82); normalization vis-à-vis domestic policy of the matter of foreign policy; approval of surrounding states (1982–6); consolidation of foreign policy (1986); democratic state democratic foreign policy (thereafter). Thus, by 1986 foreign policy democratization had been fully achieved in accordance with the above scheme. It is important to bear in mind the position of the main actors that intervened in and led that process: the prevalence of the King; the various presidents who progressively gained ultimate powers of decision; the foreign ministers (who had varying roles and degrees of influence); and the political parties, which exercised their role responsibly, preferring consensus rather than confrontation. A similar analysis has been undertaken of changes in the formal policy cycle and the renewal of foreign policy goals. All of the above allows one to affirm (as the main people involved have stated in interviews) that, after a long period of transition, in 1986 "Spain found its place, for the first time in its history."

What, then, defines a democratic foreign policy? The view here is that it must be based on, or fulfil, the following requirements: it must be state and not only government policy; as state policy it must be subjected permanently to democratic scrutiny by parliament; the public must play a role in controlling and influencing the formal policy cycle; in a pluralistic regime and a complex society, the political parties must also play a central role; and state policy must be executed by a democratic, modern, effective, professionalized, responsible and autonomous administration. Finally, foreign policy goals must become universal in two ways: by opting to broaden diplomatic relations with all those states that respect the principles of the international law and the shared values on which the international community is based; and by becoming fully integrated into international society, the latter through membership of international organizations, by acting with committed internationalism so that the principles and norms of international law are applied domestically to ensure international legitimacy, by recognising the nature of the political regime and incorporation of social actors into the international democratic community, and, as a result of all this, by applying and constantly defending a democratic peace, or ensuring that domestic democracy becomes an essential element in peaceful relationships among states.

Notes

This chapter is part of the Research Project BHA 2002–01909, directed by myself and financed by the Spanish Ministry of Science and Technology, entitled *La transición y consolidación democrática en España y la formulación del modelo de política exterior democrática.*

1 Juan José Linz, "La transición española en perspectiva comparada," in: Javier Tusell and Álvaro Soto (eds), *Historia de la transición, 1975–1986.* Madrid: Alianza, 1986, p. 21.
2 See: Ramón Cotarelo, "Visiones de la transición," *Revista del Centro de Estudios Constitucionales* 18, 1994: 9–78 (author italics).
3 See, for example, studies such as: Juan Pablo Fusi and Jordi Palafox, *España 1808–1996 el desafío de la modernidad.* Madrid: Espasa, 1997; David Ringrose, *España 1700–1900. El mito del fracaso.* Madrid: Alianza, 1997; Santos Julia, "Anomalía, dolor y fracaso de España," *Claves* 66, 1996: 10–22; and Juan Carlos Pereira, "Europeización de España/Españolización de Europa: el dilema histórico resuelto," *Documentación Social* 111, 1998: 39–58.
4 There is a large bibliography on the Spanish transition. Recent useful bibliographies are: José Casas Pardo, Joaquín Martín Cubas and Carlos Flores Juberías, "Una selección bibliográfica para el estudio de la transición española," *Cuadernos Constitucionales de la Cátedra Fadrique Furió Ceriol* 18–19, 1997: 205–73; P. Fernández-Miranda, "Bibliografía sobre la transición política española," *Revista de Derecho Político* (Madrid) 30, 1997.
5 Roberto Mesa, "La normalización exterior de España," in: Ramón Cotarelo (ed.), *Transición política y consolidación democrática. España (1975–1986).* Madrid: CIS, 1992, pp. 137–8.
6 Guillermo O'Donnell, Philippe C. Schmitter and Laurence Whitehead (eds), *Transiciones desde un gobierno autoritario.* Buenos Aires: Paidós, 1988.
7 Ibid., Vol. 4, p. 35.
8 Philippe C. Schmitter, "An Introduction to Southern European Transitions from Authoritarian Rule: Italy, Greece, Portugal, Spain," in: Guillermo O'Donnell, Philippe C. Schmitter and Laurence Whitehead (eds), *Transitions from Authoritarian Rule.* Baltimore, MD: Johns Hopkins University Press, 1986.
9 See: Justino Sinova, "XXV aniversario de un éxito incompleto," *La Aventura de la Historia* 26, 2000: 29.

10 Carlos Seco Serrano, "La transición a la democracia, 1975–1982," in: A. Domínguez Ortíz (ed.), *Historia de España*, Vol. 12. Barcelona: Planeta, 1991.

11 Enrique Gil Calvo, "Crítica de la transición," *Claves* 107, 2000: 10.

12 Roberto Mesa, "De nuevo la transición," *Sistema* 160, 2001: 3–14.

13 See, among others: Claus Offe, "Capitalism by Democratic Design? Democratic Theory Facing the Triple Transition in East Central Europe," *Social Research* 58 (4), 1991: 868–72; Geoffrey Pridham (ed.), *Encouraging Democracy: The International Context of Regime Transition in Southern Europe*. Leicester: Leicester University Press, 1991; Laurence Whitehead (ed.), *The International Dimensions of Democratization: Europe and the Americas*. Oxford: Oxford University Press, 1996.

14 Jean Grugel, *Democratization: A Critical Introduction*. New York, NY: Palgrave, 2002, particularly chapter 6.

15 See: Anthony Giddens, *The Consequences of Modernity*. Cambridge: Polity Press, 1990.

16 Laurence Whitehead, op. cit., p. 24.

17 Philippe C. Schmitter, "The Influence of the International Context upon the Choice of National Institutions and Policies in Neo-Democracies," in: Laurence Whitehead (ed.), *The International Dimensions of Democratization*, op. cit., pp. 27–8.

18 More detailed treatment of this topic can be found in: Juan Carlos Pereira, "Transición y política exterior: el nuevo reto de la historiografía española," *Ayer: Asociación de historia contemporanea* 42, 2001: 97–123; (ed.), *La política exterior de España, 1800–2003*. Barcelona: Ariel, 2003; and, "El factor internacional en la transición española: la influencia del contexto internacional y el papel de las potencias centrales," *Studia Storica-Historia Contemporánea* 22, 2004: 185–224, both by the same author.

19 Roberto Mesa, *Democracia y política exterior*. Madrid: Eudema, 1988; and José María Armero, *Política Exterior de España en Democracia*. Madrid: Espasa, 1989.

20 Celestino del Arenal, "Democracia y política exterior: el largo camino hacia el cambio," in: J. Vidal (ed.), *España a debate: La política*. Madrid: Tecnos, 1991.

6 The international dimensions of democratization
The case of Argentina

Andrés Malamud

Introduction

Argentine politics are usually described as eccentric, or at least unconventional, for a number of reasons. Economically, Argentina was a rich country that went from wealth to bankruptcy over a period of about seventy years, between 1930 and 2001. Socially, it has always had the most developed middle class and the most educated population in Latin America – a region where strong middle classes and universal education are extremely rare. Politically, it saw the emergence and predominance of rather autochthonous political movements, which included the most relevant and elusive example of Peronism. Internationally, it was the country in the western hemisphere that (apart from Cuba) most frequently opposed American foreign policies, although it never sided openly with either Nazi Germany or the Soviet Union. Argentina has been one of the most economically developed and one of the least politically stable countries in Latin America, a paradox first explained by Guillermo O'Donnell in the 1970s.[1] In spite of all these particularities, the cycles of Argentine politics since 1930 matched with international developments taking place at the time. This chapter argues that both the frequent democratic breakdowns and processes of re-democratization that followed were linked to international factors.

The chapter proceeds as follows. First, it describes the cycles of political instability in Argentina from 1930 to the present, tracing their relations with the international context. Second, it analyses the democratization process that took place during the 1980s in order to single out the international factors that had an influence upon it. Third, it examines the ways in which Argentina's renewed democracy has affected its international environment, focusing especially on the region where it is embedded – the Southern Cone of Latin America.

International context and political cycles in Argentina

There were six *coups d'état* in Argentina between 1930 and 1976. The literature usually interprets them as the outcome of internal rifts that pitted rival civil–military alliances against one another. To be sure, none of the coups was the result of direct intervention by a foreign power, as was frequently the case in

Central America; neither did they entail an indirect but strong involvement of external actors, such as US support for the ousting of Chilean president, Salvador Allende. And yet the cycles of regime instability in Argentina can hardly be understood without reference to the international context: the sequence and substance of the coups closely followed world – and, more clearly, regional – events of the time.

The first two coups were rooted in nationalistic, proto-fascistic movements. In 1930, the leaders of the takeover espoused an anti-liberal, corporatist organization of state and society, much as Benito Mussolini did for Italy and Getúlio Vargas would for Brazil some years later. The military officers that took power in 1943 were likewise rebelling against the alleged pro-Allied stance of the governing coalition and its presidential candidate, Robustiano Patrón Costas. The aftermath of both coups was unexpected: in the first instance, the nationalists were quickly overridden by the liberal rebel wing, which governed until 1943 under the guise of constitutional government but through electoral fraud; in the second case, the revolution was swallowed by its own son. Juan Domingo Perón, the man initially chosen to garner mass support for the dictatorship, became a popular leader and the founder of one of the most enduring political movements in Latin America. These later developments notwithstanding, the timing of the democratic breakdowns paralleled the global decline of liberal democracy and the rise of nationalistic movements that characterized the interwar period.

The next two coups were of a different nature. They were both oriented against Peronism – by then the new hegemonic movement – and both legitimated themselves as the forces that would combat the tyranny of Perón to restore full constitutional authority. In both cases, the military were divided and internal struggles prevented them from accomplishing their plans. In 1955, the president that ousted Perón and forced him into exile was displaced after only two months in power, given his allegedly soft stance against Peronism; and the 1962 putsch failed even before it was consummated – internal divisions and lack of coordination left the leaders of the coup out in the cold, as the constitutional succession was cleverly managed after the resignation of the civilian president and before his would-be military successor was able to take the oath of office. Both these coups were justified according to a liberal rhetoric, and held up by the United States and its Latin American foreign policy as the beacon of anti-authoritarianism, both globally and in Argentina.

Finally, the latter coups were again very different. This time, both aimed not to restore traditional society or a desecrated Constitution but rather to uproot past political practices and sectoral groups, and to transform Argentine society into a new authoritarian polity. Although they were within the "Western" fold, the ensuing military governments were not Western in their lack of attachment to human rights and the rule of law. The overthrowing of two constitutional governments – first in 1966 and then in 1976 – was part of a regional wave of bureaucratic-authoritarian coups. The first had taken place in Brazil in 1964, putting an end to a convulsive period of democratic rule, and the other two took place in 1973, when the democratic presidents of Chile and Uruguay were ousted from power. The timeframe and various key policies implemented by the new authoritarian rulers of all these countries were similar. As a result of the ideological proximity of Southern Cone military forces, these dictatorships implemented similar economic policies and developed similar plans to combat terrorism, and its allegedly subversive communist source in particular. The details of *Operation Condor*, the name given to this regionally coordinated repressive plan, have yet fully to come to light because of its clandestine nature; however, its very existence shows that regime change in the region was not an isolated, exclusively domestic, phenomenon; on the contrary, there was clearly a mechanism of contagion at work, and cooperation among members and supporters of these authoritarian regimes made these new Latin American dictatorships resemble a connected archipelago rather than independent islands.

The similarities noted above should not lead one to conclude that the dictatorships of the Southern Cone were all allies: they were rivals as much as friends. Nationalistic political traditions, old-fashioned military education and training, historical territorial disputes and economic tensions frequently obscured common authoritarian goals and gave rise to serious conflicts that sometimes verged on open war. This was the case of the Argentine–Chilean conflict over the Beagle Channel, which led to the deployment and amassing of troops on both sides of the southern border separating the two countries. In December 1978, only the intervention of Cardinal Samoré, the papal envoy, prevented hostilities from breaking out. This "schizophrenic" relationship between the dictatorships in the sub-region can be understood in two ways: on the one hand, military governments regarded national interests as being in conflict, at least in foreign policy terms; on the other hand, they also perceived a common threat to the stability of their regimes and were thus eager to cooperate in the sphere of internal security. So, while foreign policy drove them apart, domestic policy (regime preservation) brought them together. Awareness of a shared political destiny in terms of regime was transmitted from dictatorial rulers to their democratic successors in the Southern Cone.[2] While all six countries of the sub-region lived under authoritarian rule in 1980, by 1990 they were all democracies – or at least well on the way to being democratic.

International factors supporting democratization

The Argentine path from military rule towards free elections can be divided into three phases. The first began in mid-1981, when President Roberto Viola decided to soften restrictions prohibiting political party activity and took steps – albeit minor ones – to liberalize the regime. The second occurred between the ousting of Viola by hardliner Leopoldo Galtieri (who intended to halt liberalization) in December 1981, and the military defeat at the hands of the British in the Malvinas-Falklands War on 14 June 1982. The last phase was presided over by General Reynaldo Bignone, and consisted of an accelerated process lasting a year and a half, starting with modest liberalization, continued with the convocation of national elections and a free electoral campaign, and culminating in the victory of the party most inimical to the dictatorship and the inauguration of a democratically elected president. Generally, the influence of international factors is only acknowledged for the intermediate period of the transition process, but there are reasons to believe that the other two were also influenced by the international context and the intervention of foreign actors.

During the first phase, as early as 1977 and even before initial liberalization, there was well-documented pressure by top US administration officials and the US Congress itself on the military government regarding human rights.[3] What is less well known is the significance of international human rights networks in preserving the life of top political activists. They did this by raising the public international visibility of potential victims of repression and thus the cost of government decisions to incarcerate or abduct key figures. Difficult to gauge as this factor is, the fact is that this "international protective umbrella" shaped the behaviour of the actors involved, giving them some limited but greater room to manoeuvre than they would have had otherwise.[4] More importantly, it may have saved their lives.

The second phase was triggered by an indisputable international phenomenon, and unfolded according to its evolution: the Falklands War. Sovereignty over the southern islands had been disputed by the British and Spanish (and the Argentines, following independence in 1816) for over two centuries, but they had been in British hands since 1833 after the seizure of an Argentine military garrison. Argentina had renewed its diplomatic claim to the islands in 1964 at the United Nations (UN), but had failed to move the British, who continued to claim sovereign rights over the territory. A violent showdown had never been considered seriously by any of the parties. This changed after the ousting of General Viola. In early 1982, as the government faced growing unrest due to deep economic troubles (soaring inflation, declining output and plummeting wages[5]), as the unions gathered support against government economic policy and as street revolts spiralled out of control, the military Junta decided to seize the islands in order to deflect public anger onto a foreign enemy and gain domestic support. Grasping at a minor excuse, Argentine troops invaded the islands on 2 April 1982. Initially, the plan seemed to work: the invasion was almost bloodless, and the Argentine people rallied behind the government. The Junta strategy was based on two main assumptions: that the United States would not interfere in a quarrel between two allies, and that the British would opt not to go to war over such an unimportant and distant territory.[6] This mistake was soon compounded by others, including a defective combat strategy, poor military training and successive diplomatic blunders. Thus, on 14 June, just 72 days after the invasion, the Argentine field commander was forced to sign an "unnegotiated ceasefire," a euphemism for unconditional surrender. More than 600 Argentines died in the conflict, and the days of the regime that had sent them to their deaths were numbered.

The consequences of defeat for the Argentine dictatorship are now clear, but are twofold rather than linear: on the one hand, the ignominious outcome helped to bring down the regime by definitely weakening the hardliners and igniting a palace crisis, as a consequence of which the three military branches split, with the Army running the government and then managing the transition in isolation; on the other hand, the military adventure provoked the withdrawal of support for the regime from both the US government and Argentines at home. This implies the presence of two factors, acknowledged in the literature as favourable to democratization: control and consent, in the words of Laurence Whitehead.[7] The former refers to the fact that the dominant power in the western hemisphere no longer backed an unreliable dictatorship that had attacked its most loyal ally, which sent an encouraging signal to democratic forces; the latter refers to the fact that domestic support for the government was no longer there after what were parallel economic and military catastrophes. The regime was doomed; democracy, however, had yet to emerge.

After a first phase of failed liberalization and a second phase of aborted authoritarian re-emergence, the third phase of the transition paved the way for a proper democratization process. In this period international influence was not always evident, but it nonetheless manifested itself in two ways. There was mounting international and particularly Western pressure on the military government to hold prompt, free and fair elections as a condition for Argentina to overcome its semi-pariah status; and opposition forces were influenced positively by the example of the transitions to democracy a decade earlier in Southern Europe. Particularly inspiring for soon-to-be-democratic leaders was the trial of the Greek colonels, as well as the Spanish "Moncloa Pact."[8]

During 1983, the weakness of the government increased proportionally to the popularity of the presidential candidate of the Radical Civic Union (*Unión Cívica Radical*, UCR), Raúl Alfonsín. The UCR was a traditional party, proud of its autochthonous origins and idealistic philosophy, with some leaders who even took pride in never having been abroad. Alfonsín, by contrast, was pragmatic and open-minded, and considered himself and his party as natural members of the international family of social democratic parties. He was well connected with foreign leaders, both politicians and human rights activists, and was regarded by them as a modern, democratic leader. But he was not expected to win: Italo Luder, the candidate of the Peronist Party (*Partido Justicialista*, PJ) – the party that had won every fair election since its foundation in the 1940s – was considered the frontrunner by most observers. He was close to traditional nationalistic positions and to the outgoing government in particular, as evidenced by his refusal to abolish the preventive amnesty decreed by Bignone covering all military personnel. Alfonsín rejected the self-amnesty and went a step further, denouncing a secret pact between the military and the labour unions, the latter closely linked to the PJ. Finally, on 30 October 1983, the elections were held under close international scrutiny. Alfonsín garnered 52 per cent of the vote, and Luder peaked at 40 per cent. The unambiguousness of the result and the lack of authority of the government sped up the transfer of power, and on 10 December 1983 Alfonsín inaugurated the current democratic period – which has been the longest in Argentine history.

Although Alfonsín was sworn into office without controversy, and even though he enjoyed both constitutional legitimacy and broad popular support, the democratic transition was not yet over. Alfonsín himself was well aware of this, openly calling his administration "a transition government."[9] The new regime owed its existence to the power vacuum caused by the military collapse in the Falklands, and not to victory over former regime forces. It had to build its strength against the encroachment of many antagonists, many of them military officers, who were simply waiting for an opportunity to manifest their hostility openly. The new democracy was tested by a series of putsches between 1987 and 1990, and in order to survive it needed to avoid international isolation, which would certainly ensue with a successful coup.

The first uprising, in the Easter week of 1987, saw a group of military rebels led by Lieutenant Colonel Aldo Rico taking control of a series of barracks in protest against the prosecution of military officers for human rights crimes. The rebellion was formally driven by a sectoral claim (protecting the lower ranks from prosecution in accordance with the principle of due obedience), but yielding to the demand would have had consequences familiar to anyone with a modicum of awareness of Argentine history: every administration that had previously acquiesced to military claims had faced successive, incremental demands culminating in a coup. In this instance, the military officers declaring their loyalty to the new civilian government were unwilling to open fire against their comrades, which meant that the constitutional authorities had to garner non-violent domestic and international backing. The rebellion was finally put down, but the government was obliged to make concessions for which the incumbent party would pay a significant price.

Taking advantage of lenient house-arrest conditions, Aldo Rico led a second rebellion in 1988. Again unable to persuade loyal military forces to repress the rebels, the government had to seek a negotiated agreement to end the mutiny. Rico was again confined, but by then the general impression was that the government was incapable of keeping the armed forces under control. This was confirmed by the Villa Martelli revolt of December 1998, led by the charismatic Colonel Mohamed Seineldín. Once again, the administration quelled the rebellion without resorting (and unable to resort) to force. While it was clear that the military rebels had neither domestic nor international support, it was also evident that the democratic authorities were unable to discipline the armed forces, and it was only two years later, with the electoral victory of Carlos Menem and the PJ in 1989, that a fourth and final revolt was violently crushed by loyal officers on 3 December 1990. The latter event marked the end of the transition, as the rules of the game were now definitely constitutional and democratic, and there was no room for uncertainty regarding the state's monopoly on violence. After sixty years of regime instability, two factors had helped to consolidate democracy: the unity of domestic democratic political forces, and the unrestricted support of foreign powers, particularly regional neighbours and the US.

The international effects of democratization

Argentina still faced either unsolved conflicts or grave tensions with three countries – Chile, Brazil and the United Kingdom – after the 1983 transition. Further, it badly needed to regain an honourable international reputation, which meant restoring friendly ties with the US. The new administration understood that peaceful international reinsertion was not just an end in itself, but also a means to downplay the significance and influence of the military at home. Alfonsín's strategy was based on three main pillars: bilateral peace with Chile, regional integration with Brazil, and multilateral international diplomacy. This section explores these issues.

Chile

Relations with Chile were strained for three main reasons: human rights, the pro-British position adopted by the Pinochet regime during the Falklands dispute, and the persistence of the Beagle Conflict.[10] As the former was a domestic matter and the latter the indirect consequence of a problem involving a third country, it was the Beagle Conflict that became the hottest issue on the bilateral agenda. Alfonsín went as far as to define it the "number one priority" of his administration.[11] The first step to solve the conflict was the signature of a Declaration of Peace and Friendship at the Vatican on 23 January 1984 (barely two months after the inauguration of democratic rule), which expressed the intention to reach a fair and honourable solution through exclusively peaceful means. The treaty had detractors on both sides of the Andes, but the political context differed in each country: whereas nobody doubted the capacity of Pinochet to enforce the agreement, Alfonsín faced the hostility of the PJ, the main opposition party, which was only one senator short of holding a majority in the upper chamber – the body with constitutional responsibility for approving international treaties.

In an attempt to overcome the nationalist obstruction, Alfonsín and Foreign Minister Dante Caputo resorted to a popular consultation (usually called a referendum, but not actually binding for the executive or the Senate). The administration hoped to project the image of a reasonable government, respectful of international agreements.[12] Besides making a clear break with the wretched impression left by the dictatorship, this image was considered as an asset in any later global disarmament initiatives and negotiations over the Falklands. Certainly, the rationale was that the Argentine people would vote positively and that, in the absence of such explicit support, the agreement would have been defeated in the Senate. As this complex scenario shows, Alfonsín resorted to a domestic policy (the call for a referendum) to gain support for a foreign policy initiative that would, in turn, reinforce his position vis-à-vis other domestic and international actors. And, as Alfonsín saw it (quite correctly), in those troubled times the strengthening of his administration was directly related to the consolidation of democracy. The referendum was held on 25 November 1984, and turnout exceeded 70 per cent for what was a non-mandatory election, which is unusual in Argentina. The votes in favour of the agreement outnumbered those against it by more than four to one. Two-and-a-half years after having massively supported the attack on the Falklands, the Argentines were ready to support democracy and the peaceful resolution of international conflicts. On 29 November 1984, the foreign ministers returned to the Vatican to sign the Treaty, as foreseen by the Declaration ten months earlier. The agreement fixed territorial limits in the disputed zone, and established procedures for the resolution of future disagreements. A commission was also created to foster economic cooperation and develop projects of physical integration. After heated debate, the Treaty was approved by the senate with just one vote of difference. Notwithstanding the close result, the mutual ratification of the Treaty in May 1985 signalled the end of a historical rivalry dating back to the nineteenth century. Since the Chilean return to democracy later in 1990, the bilateral relations have become ever stronger, and minor skirmishes have diminished over time.

Brazil

In contrast with Chile, historical relations with Brazil have been distant rather than hostile. While there have been two occasions on which there could have been open war with Chile over the last 150 years (in 1898 and in 1978), the last war with Brazil dates back to 1828.[13] Reciprocal mistrust between the two countries was expressed in a "pretended" mutual ignorance. The shared border was as clearly delimited as it was politically neglected, physical connections were mostly absent, and trade and investment interdependence were virtually nonexistent. The advent of democracy in both countries permanently changed the nature of the bilateral relations. Indeed, the Argentine–Brazilian axis became the core of what was later the most successful process of regional integration ever in Latin America: the Common Market of the South (MERCOSUR). The process that led to its foundation was launched in the mid-1980s with the transitions to democracy. Democracy hence became a key goal and an indispensable condition for regional agreements.

The first steps towards regional cooperation had been taken in 1979, under the Videla and João Figueiredo military presidencies. That year, both countries, together with General Ströessner's Paraguay, signed a trilateral agreement on the Paraná Basin, which settled various disputes over water resources, including the inconvenience and perceived threat to Argentina of the construction of the giant Itaipú Dam.[14] A second crucial phase was ushered in by the Falklands War: it boosted confidence-building and the emergence of a shared perception of world politics.[15] Despite its reluctance to support the use of force, Brazil explicitly endorsed Argentina's right to the islands. This coincided with the position of most of Latin America (excluding Chile), but it was particularly significant because Brazil was not only the mightiest Latin American power but also Argentina's traditional rival. However, it was only in the mid-1980s that the new democratic leaders initiated the third stage, which ultimately gave rise to lasting cooperation covering issues ranging from economic matters to the sensitive question of nuclear power. Elected in 1983 and 1985 respectively, Alfonsín and José Sarney engaged in a process that would have been unlikely to succeed without their strong commitment. In 1985 they signed the Declaration of Foz de Iguazú, which laid the bases for future integration, and created a High Level Bilateral Commission to foster that process. The crucial Argentine–Brazilian Integration Act was endorsed in July 1986 in Buenos Aires, and set in motion the Argentine–Brazilian Integration and Cooperation Programme (PICAB). As was later broadly acknowledged, the latter constituted a turning point in the history of bilateral relations, and was the embryo of the MERCOSUR. Within the framework of these treaties, between 1984 and 1989 both countries signed twenty-four bilateral protocols to promote bilateral trade. There were agreements that even included military cooperation and the mutual inspection of their nuclear installations.[16] This historical shift occurred largely as a result of the newly appointed democratic presidents and their decision to adopt a new regional policy. Arguably, neither the pressures of globalization nor democratization by themselves would have sufficed to overcome a history of mutual distrust. A further Treaty on Integration, Cooperation and Development was signed in 1988. Seen as the culmination of the process of mutual recognition and confidence-building, it became just another step towards ever closer ties. At the end of 1990, Argentina and Brazil signed an Agreement on Economic Cooperation that systematized and deepened pre-existing trade agreements. That same year, representatives of both countries met with Uruguayan and Paraguayan authorities, which also wanted to participate in the integration process. The result was an agreement to establish the four-nation MERCOSUR with the 26 March 1991 Treaty of Asunción. Although not inexorable, this was the outcome of the regional process of democratization.

Excursus *on how democracy paved the way for regional integration*

The rapprochement between Argentina and Brazil was not automatic. There were few incentives to change the traditional pattern of mutual indifference. To account for regional cooperation, therefore, it is necessary to understand the new democratic context, the institutional resources and the personal preferences that drove and shaped the process.[17] The first bilateral agreements were based on political rather than economic reasons, although economic cooperation was the main instrument.[18] The primary goal was to protect the new democracies and diminish the domestic role of the military, which led to the attempt to limit external threats. The private sector had little influence during the first stages of integration, and trade agreements were simply political instruments to bring the neighbours closer together and discourage rivalry. Carlos Márcio Cozendey, former Director of the Itamaraty MERCOSUR Division, supported this view: "the process initiated in 1985–1986 had a clear political motivation that was apparent in the direct intervention of the presidents; but the instruments used to accomplish the political goals were commercial."[19]

Despite widespread consensus regarding the aims of early initiatives, there is some disagreement over what kept the process going. On the one hand, a key protagonist, Dante Caputo, affirms that Brazil always saw the MERCOSUR as a platform for enhanced insertion into the political and international arena, while Argentina tended to have a double standard, seeking ties with Brazil for trade reasons but aligning with the US on political and military issues.[20] On the other hand, an equally crucial actor, Brazil's former undersecretary of regional integration José Graça Lima, presents a more tempered view of the divergence, stating that "the reasons for the rapprochement between the two countries was mainly political [given the] level of confrontation [that existed] a short time before."[21] Regardless of the divergence over the goals of association, the main protagonists acknowledge the primacy of democratic politics. Alfonsín recalls that "when President Sarney and I launched the process of integration together, the political meaning of the project was very clear."[22] The view that the economy was instrumental was also clear:

> President Sarney liked Argentina, understood its needs and was ready to make significant gestures [...] His first measure as president, in 1985, was precisely to import 1.3 million tons of wheat in order to reduce the trade deficit that Argentina had with Brazil.[23]

In part because of the subjectivity of the actors, who tend to magnify the significance of their personal role, it is hard to establish the origins of the idea of strengthening ties between the two countries. Peña believes it is possible that the talks between the newly elected presidents began with Alfonsín and Tancredo Neves, before the inauguration of Sarney.[24] Unfortunately, Neves died before he would express his view of regional integration, but his attitude towards good neighbourly relations with Argentina was clear. Unlike other Brazilian scholars, Mónica Hirst says that the initiative "was Argentine rather than Brazilian, but Sarney rapidly became enthusiastic about it."[25] She believes that some objective conditions fostered the process, but emphasizes political issues (i.e. democracy), timing, and personal disposition rather than economic criteria. She notes that the initial economic conditions were terrible for integration, and that it is not surprising that the first moves were in the foreign policy sphere. This shaped the integration process for a long time, as it has remained highly politicized and dependent upon presidential will ever since.[26] Julio Sanguinetti, the first post-authoritarian Uruguayan president, also underlines the importance of regime change: "the democratization process of the 1980s generated an atmosphere of proximity among countries, and of solidarity among the democratic leaders that emerged after the period of military rule."[27] Strengthening ties between the Southern Cone countries was also a historical and personal challenge. Sanguinetti expresses pride in the fact that, for him, "integration, as a concept, is the homily of a lifetime." His claim cannot be overlooked, as his regional vocation is widely recognized as a significant element in the push towards increasing cooperation in the Plata Basin region. As Alfonsín acknowledged, "the accession of Uruguay to the MERCOSUR was an outcome of the intelligent impetus of President Julio Sanguinetti."[28]

The sense of supporting a common cause among the presidents was crucial. Sanguinetti recalls that

> there was a natural empathy [with Alfonsín] that existed from when we first met at the time of the struggle against the dictatorships; and later we found Sarney, with whom we had no previous relationship but who soon pleasantly surprised us.[29]

He also notes that Sarney won the respect of his peers

> because he made a great effort to understand the culture of the Río de la Plata, to learn and give his speeches in Spanish when he visited our countries, and because he was a man of culture with a remarkable knowledge of history and an open mind.[30]

Under Sanguinetti's leadership, Uruguay played a key role in the Argentine–Brazilian relationship. In his words, it served "to articulate [the relationship], like a hinge of sorts." This "hinge" or buffer state mediated and moderated tensions as they arose. He understood "the presence of Uruguay as a catalyst, something that gave negotiations between Argentina and Brazil a multilateral character." The trilateralization of the negotiating process was acknowledged with the presidential Declaration of Alvorada of April 1988, which established the conditions for the incorporation of Uruguay. With the ousting of General Stroessner in 1989 and the rise to the presidency of military officer Andrés Rodriguez, Paraguay finally also began its transition to democracy, which set the stage for the closure of ancient rivalries and opened the door to lasting regional cooperation.

The United States and the United Kingdom

In addition to settling regional disputes and launching an ambitious process of regional integration, democratic Argentina needed to seek a reconciliation with the two world powers with which it had had strained relations during the last years of dictatorship: the United States and the United Kingdom. Reconciliation can be divided into two stages: the first under Alfonsín in 1983 signalled the end of any attempt to use violence to reach political goals. At this stage, however, relations with the US remained cordial but distant, and there were no diplomatic relations with Britain, as the British refused to discuss the sovereignty issue; the second stage began under Menem in 1989, and was characterized by much closer relations with both countries, eventually leading to close alignment with the US and restoration of diplomatic relations with Britain.

In 1983, the new democracy was at a crossroads. No matter how much progress it made in any given area of domestic or international politics, to "reposition the nation in the world arena" the administration had to define its relations with the US.[31] Alfonsín and Caputo aimed to restore the relations with the hemispheric power damaged by the Falklands War and international drift, but they also wanted to maintain an independent stand to allow for the development of a foreign policy based on universal principles rather than national interests. This produced intermittent confrontational postures vis-à-vis the United States. An eloquent example of the search for a principled autonomy was the creation of the Group of Six (G6) in 1984, an awkward amalgamation bringing together countries as dissimilar as Argentina, Greece, India, Mexico, Sweden and Tanzania. The Group aimed to campaign in favour of disarmament and against nuclear proliferation, advocating the transfer of military resources to social development. However, the fact that not all the members of the Group were wholly democratic was never frankly addressed, and this limited the moral impact of the endeavour. Further, the international arena is not dominated by newly-born domestic regimes but by national states with historical continuity, so Alfonsín's best intentions and outstanding prestige were never sufficient to overcome the burden of Argentina's past, including its long authoritarian history and changing alignments.

In 1989, the new administration made a dramatic turnabout. Menem, seconded in the foreign ministry by Domingo Cavallo and then Guido Di Tella, decided to put an end to all remaining disagreements with the US and adopt a "realist" policy (one of "capitulation," according to the opposition). In the words of a specialist,

> whereas the Alfonsín government sought to distance itself from the United States to prove itself independent and autonomous, the Menem government [...] attempted the reverse: to prove itself to be in league with the United States, its fate linked to that of the US.[32]

This policy was rhetorical and involved concrete concessions as well, two of the latter particularly remarkable: the deactivation of the project to develop a missile, *Condor II*, and the decision to send two naval vessels to join the blockade of Iraq in 1991. Argentina thus dissociated itself from neighbouring Brazil and Chile, which not only carried on with their missile projects based on domestic technology but also refused to send troops to the Gulf. In fact, Argentina was the only Latin American country to do so, and the decision was taken without even consulting Congress. After 1999, when Menem left the presidency, Argentine foreign policy continued to twist and turn with every passing president. Although democracy is firmly in place and war seems impracticable, the country has yet to define a steady policy towards the US and, by extension, in world affairs.

Somewhat surprisingly, relations with Britain have not been as changeable as those with the US, although this is due more to the inflexible stance of the British rather than to a stable, bipartisan Argentine policy. In fact, the official position over the Falklands changed greatly between the Alfonsín and Menem presidencies, but British rigidity meant that this change made little difference. It was a rigidity that was tough for the new democracy: as Tulchin suggests,[33] the failure of the Alfonsín administration to shift the British position reduced the political manoeuvrability of the government. The Falklands issue was a constant thorn, feeding the claims of nationalists on the left and right and arguably emboldening the rebels in the Easter rebellion of 1987. Notwithstanding the later "make nice" strategy promoted by di Tella towards the islanders, the British have never accepted discussion of sovereignty. This intransigence was somewhat sidelined by the Menem administration when it accepted the restoration of diplomatic relations and the negotiation of all other issues while freezing the sovereignty debate. In this way, the democratic regime was able to deal with the bitterest and most sensitive issue of its foreign agenda without risking its stability and public legitimacy. If "democratic consolidation" means anything, it certainly applies to a country in which a democratic regime manages to overcome several putsches, endure multiple government turnovers and accept dramatic reversals of its most sensitive foreign policy issues.

Conclusion

In the two decades following the start of the most recent process of democratization, the Southern Cone has undergone two historical changes: first, at the domestic level, its larger countries enjoy a degree of democratic stability never attained before; second, at the international level, they have developed such strong ties with each other that the likelihood of a military conflict in the region seems to have been completely eradicated. Regional integration is an unfinished process, but there is a security community in place for the first time in history.[34] Did democracy foster peace and cooperation, or was it the other way around? As argued above, the answer is that they reinforced each other. The shift from rivalry to cooperation was an outcome of policies undertaken by democratic governments, whose stability was, in turn, supported by the peaceful transformations of the intra-regional relations. Hence, the MERCOSUR can be understood as a creature of democracy as well as a creator – or at least protector – of democracy.

The international context shaped the Argentine transition in many ways. The four main factors acknowledged in the democratization literature (i.e. control, contagion, consent and conditionality) played a role, although not all of them developed simultaneously or with the same degree of influence. The end of dictatorship was provoked, if not by the direct *control* of a foreign power, by a disrupting *event* brought about by defeat in an international war.[35] *Contagion* was also evident, as signalled by the simultaneity with which most countries in the region turned to democracy and by the processes of cooperation and mutual democratic reinforcement they engaged in. Complementarily, domestic *consent* and popular support for democracy was widespread for the first time since 1930, encompassing the UCR and the PJ, elites and masses, domestic entrepreneurs and foreign investors. This consensus was the consequence of the twin military and economic catastrophes produced by the dictatorship, which fed the perception that authoritarian governments were ill-suited to rebuild the country. Finally, *conditionality* was a constant, if less marked, presence, particularly in the critical moments of military rebellion. By making it clear that Argentina would become an international pariah if an authoritarian reversal took place, international actors such as foreign governments, businesses and NGOs contributed greatly to shifting the domestic relation of forces in favour of democratic players.

The effects of Argentine democratization on the international context through a renewed foreign policy were equally important: its most relevant outcomes were the pacification of relations with Chile and the solution of all remaining border disputes; the rapprochement with Brazil and the establishment of the MERCOSUR; the restoration of diplomatic relations with Britain; the improvement of relations with the US; and the solid entry into the Western, democratic, and capitalist international camp. Argentina still faces daunting challenges today, particularly economic reconstruction and social reparation, but, in contrast with most of the last century, democracy is seen as a condition and not an obstacle to tackle those challenges.

Notes

1 Guillermo O'Donnell, *Modernization and Bureaucratic-Authoritarianism*. Berkeley, CA: Institute of International Studies, University of California, 1972.
2 The Southern Cone includes Argentina, Brazil, Chile, Paraguay, Uruguay, and – if politics rather than geography is the criterion – Bolivia.
3 Cynthia Brown (ed.), *With Friends like These: The Americas Watch Report on Human Rights and US Policy in Latin America*. New York, NY: Pantheon Books, 1985, pp. 99–100.
4 In particular, human right activists believed that this was the reason why Alfonsín had been spared by the dictatorship. Author interview (AI) with Aldo Etchegoyen, Bishop of the Evangelical Methodist Church of Argentina and human rights activist, in 1982.
5 David Rock, *Argentina, 1516–1982: From Spanish Colonization to the Falklands War*. London: IB Tauris, 1987.
6 For more detailed accounts of the Falklands War, see: Max Hastings and Simon Jenkins, *The Battle for the Falklands*. New York, NY: Norton, 1983; and Óscar Raúl Cardoso, Ricardo Kirschbaum and Eduardo Van der Kooy, *Malvinas, la trama secreta*. Buenos Aires: Editorial Sudamericana-Planeta, 1983.
7 Laurence Whitehead, *Democratization: Theory and Experience*. Oxford: Oxford University Press, 2002.
8 Raúl Alfonsín, *Memoria política. Transición a la democracia*. Buenos Aires: Fondo de Cultura Económica, 2004.
9 Ibid.
10 Carlos Escudé and Andrés Cisneros, *Historia general de las relaciones exteriores de la República Argentina*. Buenos Aires: GEL, 2000.
11 Bruno Passarelli, *El delirio armado. Argentina-Chile: La guerra que evitó el Papa*. Buenos Aires: Sudamericana, 1998, p. 241.
12 Roberto Russell, *Política exterior y toma de decisiones en América Latina*. Buenos Aires: GEL, 1990, pp. 54–5.
13 Argentina and Brazil fought another war later, only as allies: together with Uruguay, they attacked and defeated Paraguay in the Triple Alliance War that ended in 1870.

14 Celso Lafer, "Relações Brasil-Argentina: alcance e significado de uma parceria estratégica," *Contexto Internacional* 19 (2), 1997: 249–65.
15 Ibid. See also: Andrea Oelsner, "Two Sides of the Same Coin: Mutual Perceptions and Security Community in the Case of Argentina and Brazil," in: Finn Larsen (ed.), *Comparative Regional Integration: Theoretical Perspectives*. Aldershot: Ashgate, 2003; and Félix Peña, *Momentos y perspectivas: La Argentina en el mundo y en América Latina*. Buenos Aires: Editorial UNTREF, 2003.
16 Along with the main Treaty, the presidents signed a Joint Declaration on Nuclear Policy. For more details on nuclear cooperation, see: Mónica Hirst and Héctor E. Bocco, "Cooperação nuclear e integração Brasil-Argentina," *Contexto Internacional* 5 (9), 1989: 63–78.
17 The following account on relations with Brazil and the MERCOSUR draws on Andrés Malamud, *Presidential Democracies and Regional Integration: An Institutional Approach to Mercosur, 1985–2000*, unpublished PhD dissertation, European University Institute in Florence, 2003. The citations in this chapter with no references to sources are author interviews (AI) conducted between 2000 and 2001. Full references are provided in the above-mentioned thesis.
18 Luiz Olavo Baptista, "Mercosul: Instituições, linhas mestras, rumos," in: *O novo multilateralismo. Perspectiva da União Europeia e do Mercosul*, Forum Euro-Latino-Americano. Instituto de Estudos Estratégicos e Internacionais. Lisboa: Principia, 2001.
19 Author Interview (AI) with Carlos Márcio, in Andrés Malamud, *Presidential Democracies*, op. cit.
20 AI with Dante Caputo, in ibid.
21 José Alfredo Graça Lima, in ibid.
22 Raúl Alfonsín, "La Integración Sudamericana: Una Cuestión Política," *Síntesis FUALI* 9 (24), 2001: 3.
23 Ibid., p. 4.
24 AI with Félix Peña, in Andrés Malamud, op. cit.
25 AI with Monica Hirst, in ibid.
26 Andrés Malamud, "Presidential Diplomacy and the Institutional Underpinnings of Mercosur. An Empirical Examination," *Latin American Research Review* 40 (1), 2005: 138–64.
27 AI with Julio María Sanguinetti, in Andrés Malamud, op. cit.
28 Raúl Alfonsín, op. cit., p. 3.
29 Julio María Sanguinetti, op. cit.
30 Ibid.
31 Joseph S. Tulchin, "Continuity and Change in Argentine Foreign Policy," *Latin American Nations in World Politics*. Boulder, CO: Westview Press, 1996, p. 169.
32 Ibid., p. 169.
33 Ibid., p. 180.
34 Andrea Oelsner, op. cit.
35 Philippe C. Schmitter, "The Influence of the International Context upon the Choice of National Institutions and Policies in Neo-Democracies," in: Laurence Whitehead (ed.), *The International Dimensions of Democratization: Europe and the Americas*. Oxford: Oxford University Press, 2001, p. 35.

7 International dimensions of democratization

Brazil

Alexandra Barahona de Brito

Introduction: democratization and the international dimension

The international dimension of democratization or the contribution of international actors to processes of domestic political transformation is tremendously varied in scope and effect,[1] but it is hard to establish causality with any degree of accuracy. First, the nature of their role depends on the particular combination of internal and external economic, social and political factors at play, the foreign actors involved, the mode of intervention or policies that are adopted, the relationship between foreign and domestic players, and on the ideological and normative climate of the times. Second, interventions of any kind, ranging from sanctions to quiet diplomacy, are fraught with pitfalls, and success often depends on the qualities of leadership and other unpredictable factors. Third, it is equally hard to say, in hindsight, which variables were fundamental catalysts for change. And finally, it is increasingly difficult to separate the domestic from the external given economic internationalization and the "transnationalization" of domestic actors (or "domestic-ization" of international actors). As Milner notes, "international politics and foreign policy become part of the domestic struggle for power and the search for internal compromise."[2]

The conventional wisdom is that international actors play a secondary and supportive role at best, and that domestic players are dominant. However, as various socio-political and economic trends promote increasing interdependence and increasingly interweave domestic and foreign dimensions, this affirmation is likely to shift and change over time. Older, structural theories, such as modernization theory and its critical riposte – neo-Marxist dependence theory – posited a much stronger causal relationship between international economic conditions and domestic political outcomes. Although ideologically very different, the idea was that international economic conditions and structures shaped overwhelmingly "pre-requisites for democracy." This approach was challenged by more political analyses, focused on actors, political systems, laws and institutions, and the ideologies that "surround" and shape the actions of different actors. Rather than emphasizing "inevitability," the latter give wider berth to choice, affirming the relative autonomy of the political sphere.[3]

Given the myriad variables that go into making up a process of regime change, and the essential uniqueness of processes in each country, one of the features of attempts to categorize "transition types" or "paths to democratization" is that they often create less a typology than an immense list of possible dynamics for political change. Transitions occur in any number of ways and involve a variety of factors and actors, and multiple causalities. Hence the highly abstract approach, like that adopted by Dahl, who summarizes the problem thus: "the more the costs of suppression exceed the costs of toleration, the greater the chance for a competitive regime."[4]

Among the factors that may lead a regime to determine that the costs are too high is a change in the international context or the changed attitudes and action of international actors. As far as *states or governments* are concerned, the general consensus is that their role in effecting political change abroad can range from being limited to extremely relevant. On the "positive" side, there is now greater acceptance of "interventionism" by foreign states, particularly where human rights and democracy are concerned, than there was in the Cold War past. Thus, domestic opposition forces may opt to ally themselves with external actors to achieve certain results in a way that in more nationalistic and non-interventionist times would have immediately disqualified them as being legitimately able to represent "the people." Various "openings" can be taken advantage of by committed "foreign democrats" – the "politics of outrage" with gross violations is an example. Sometimes the financing of a single action can make all the difference, acting as a catalyst for change.[5] Other times,

> local perceptions as to what the reaction of an external actor might be can have an even stronger impact than a specific action *per se*. Thus, the symbolic aspects of the language and practices of international politics become particularly important.[6]

External actors "may affect the development of internal political and economic conditions either by specific actions or by *omission*."[7] Indeed, states can often shift the balance of power just by ceasing to give support to authoritarian regimes.[8]

On the "negative" side, even in a case of great asymmetry of power – as between the US and the Central American republics – "in almost all cases the democratic or civilianizing trend was the result of internal factors; it was not the result of external factors such as US policy."[9] The rule of thumb is that there is *not* much of a rule of thumb: the success or failure of foreign intervention depends on myriad local factors that may be unpredictable, not only for the outsider but also for those directly engaged in reform processes at home. As Carothers argues, states should assume they have relatively little influence, and conflicting policy goals may render policy ineffective or even produce more violence and instability. Further, while democratic development is a slow, precarious process, riddled with setbacks and uncertainties, requiring consistency, and sustained attention and financing, long-term, steady implementation and funding is rarely a feature of US foreign policy for a variety of reasons, including the tendency for new administrations to try to re-invent the foreign policy wheel and the short attention span of the US government and the US public.[10]

The US does not have a monopoly on this failing, which is shared by all potential and current "democracy promoting" states.[11] The same kinds of lessons apply to political or democratic conditionality applied by states, whereby aid and other assistance are conditional upon respect for democratic governance and human rights standards. As noted in one study:

> sustaining democracy [...] is neither a quick nor cheap endeavour. The role that conditions attached to aid plays is at most quite modest. However, aid that provides support and is accompanied by information and advise based on relevant expertise and experience can make a contribution [...][12]

Another category of actor in democracy promotion is the *non-governmental organization* (NGO), or transnational civil society actors. Analysts studying such organizations or actors have come up with the designation "transnational actors" to denote any persons or groups participating in international relations outside their own country and autonomously from their government.[13] In fact, the number of NGOs dedicated to the promotion of democracy and other democracy-reinforcing activities abroad, such as human rights, peace mediation, development, humanitarian relief, women's and children's rights, labour rights, sustainable development, poverty and many others, has increased dramatically over the last two decades in particular. Never before has "civil society" been so involved in contributing to change and the reshaping of the political destinies of far-off polities as today. Activists in transnational networks use symbolic politics (as when organizing protest against the celebrations of the 500th anniversary of Columbus's "discovery" of America), moral and material leverage politics (as when voting in international organizations, when money or other goods are conditioned or when there is a "mobilization of shame" by submitting certain states to special scrutiny), and accountability politics (one good example is the use that human rights NGOs made of the human rights chapter in the 1975 Helsinki Accords to press for accountability in the former Iron Curtain countries). The influence of these actors is felt at various stages, starting with issue creation and agenda setting, influencing the discursive position of states or international organizations, contributing to or shaping institutional procedures, influencing policy of target countries or actors such as like multinationals or the World Bank (WB), or shaping the behaviour of states.

It is difficult to determine the net impact of the efforts of such groups on democratization. The extremely varied origins, nature, modus operandi, objectives, financing and legitimacy of these organizations makes it difficult to make blanket judgements. As Keck notes, "because the networks *are not the only reform minded actors engaged*, exact attributions of influence are difficult." Indeed, evaluating the influence of networks is similar to evaluating the influence of sanctions, about which there has been considerable study and much disagreement. As in the sanctions literature, we must look at characteristics of the "target" and of the "sender" or "source," and at relations between the two.

Further, because "a network as a sender is not a single actor like a state, but a multiple actor, its influences is even more difficult to trace." In short, it is difficult to establish causalities and therefore hard to pin down exact contributions. And it is also important to note that "for almost all transnational campaigns, how the issue of *nationalism* is engaged is crucial to achieving issue resonance." Thus, how open a "target" country is, and whether it has what can be called a "defensive nationalist" attitude, are crucial. As with states and all other international actors, the success of outside intervention depends on how the latter works itself into the changing fabric of domestic dynamics, values and structures. Such networks are also most effective in these various areas and at these different stages when the issues at stake are normative, and when they are able to create a "causal story," which establishes victims and guilty parties: the clearer the causal chain, the more powerful the public response.[14] This leads one to conclude that such networks are not ideal to promote democracy, as this is a complex process with unclear "innocent" or "guilty" parties. They are better suited to press for specific changes, like ending a policy of systematic torture. However, it is also true that it is often a symbolic case of injustice that triggers broader domestic reforms or liberalization movements. Insofar as this is true, advocacy networks can act as triggers for change. In sum, there are indications that transnational activism works in some instances: as will be shown below, in the case of Brazil, it had an impact on environmental and human rights policies of democratic governments.

International organizations can also play a positive role in promoting democratization. The recent experience of the UN in "nation-building" in East Timor is a case in point. However, the contribution of institutions made up of states is often too ambiguous for a clear judgement to be made: for every East Timor there is a Somalia. A good example is the OAS democracy defence regime, which responded to anti-democratic manoeuvres in Haiti (1991), Peru (1992), Guatemala (1993) and Paraguay (1996). Despite early optimism regarding the strength and power its democracy-protecting mechanisms, the results achieved by the OAS were not very encouraging: as noted by one observer,

> it seems that national democratic elites have not yet fully understood to what extent their future is linked to the protection and promotion of democracy in other countries. As a result, the OAS expresses a vision of national interests that limits its potential.[15]

The more recent struggle of the OAS with Venezuela suggests that the system works best when unpopular *golpistas* threaten democracies; when anti-democratic forces are popular or when civil societies lack the will or means to resist them, the OAS is not in a position to become a substitute actor. In other, more modest, ways the OAS has been useful. One example is the work of its Unit for the Promotion of Democracy (UPD), established in 1990, which has facilitated the expanding role of organization in electoral monitoring programmes.

Thus far, the focus has been on different kinds of actors. However, it is hard to separate the action of individual actors like states and NGOs, say, and the general international climate or *zeitgeist*. The permeation of a climate of values, and the influence or diffusion of models, ideologies and political attitudes are as – if not more – powerful as individual interventionist acts by specific actors. It can be said that "the most important external factor in a democratic transition is an international context that requires competitive, representative, and participatory democracy as the basis for [a] country's participation in the international system."[16] All three categories of international actors cited above have shaped and been shaped by an international climate that is more propitious for domestic democratization efforts than it was a couple of decades ago, at least until September 11, 2001. Although a *zeitgeist* is not measurable and therefore difficult to insert into causal models, it cannot be underestimated. It is perhaps the single greatest contributor to empowering the international dimension of democratization.

Perhaps the most important "climate change" was the collapse of the communist bloc. The end of the Cold War led to a waning of ideological support by the US for "friendly" authoritarian regimes, helped to reduce anti-communist fears in many countries, and opened up prospects for liberalization and democratization. The weakening of domestic Communist parties with the "divine surprise"[17] of the fall of the Berlin Wall and its salutary effects on the democratic inclinations of the right was clear in various Latin American countries, for example. But this climate change was not just negative (the absence of the communist threat) but also positive: in the ten years following the fall of the Berlin Wall, the international climate was changed by the values and practices of five main, interdependent, forces: a shift in values, a communications and technology revolution, economic globalization, the emergence of a global civil society, and wide-ranging institutional transformations. All of these trends were in place before the fall of the Berlin Wall, but they gained new power and visibility thereafter.

The values shift has expressed itself in the spread of a human rights discourse, which "narrowed the gaps between state and society, and between state and world, by providing a common normative currency that is exchanged by government, international institutions and civil society,"[18] and in the spread of human rights law, norms and institutions, and of democratic values and practice in various regions. Democracy creates space for civil society organizations to establish themselves and link up with international actors; it also allows the media to raise the profile of otherwise "invisible" non-state actors.[19] Another shift concerns our concepts of sovereignty. Human rights and humanitarian considerations have become increasingly legitimate concerns of the international community, breaking down previously stricter sovereign boundaries. The ratification of human rights treaties and regional democracy-protecting regimes are other forms of concession of sovereignty (to treat one's citizens as one pleases), as is the emergence and reinforcement of regimes of conditionality. Conditioning development by respect for human rights and democratic governance constitute sovereignty-limiting mechanisms in inter-state relations, and an admission by states that sovereignty cannot be absolute, particularly where human well-being and core values are concerned. One already cited example is the growing panoply of Latin American "defence of democracy" instruments.[20]

Changing views of sovereignty have been shaped by the second change: economic internationalization or globalization. The implications for sovereignty of global free trade are profound. It challenges the idea that states can act in isolation. Global trade and investment calls for a degree of stability and predictability that demands the establishment of common "game rules." This has entailed a "quiet revolution" affecting national sovereignty at every turn. Such rules create obligations that limit the scope for ad hoc sovereign decisions by national governments. Once it is a participant in global trade and investment networks, a government will pay a potentially high price if it violates the rules of those networks. The interlocking effects of economic and financial globalization have been complemented and reinforced by regional integration, which is itself largely a response to the competitive challenges posed by that phenomenon. In the EU, for instance, the attempt to remain competitive has even entailed the abandonment of control over exchange rate policy – one of the key manifestations of economic sovereignty – and has led to the substitution of centuries old national currencies for a new "supranational" one.

The third aspect of climate change is related to the emergence of the international activist networks working in many diverse areas, including poverty, the environment, corruption, drug and people trafficking, weapons of mass destruction, human rights, culture, education, professional associations, and religious ecumenism. These networks have emerged not only because there are "free civil societies" on a global scale never witnessed before, but also because there are international norms to which they can appeal. There are many examples of the powerful roles played by such coalitions in prosecuting human rights violators, promoting the rights of women, protecting the environment, fighting poor labour conditions within multinational companies, and working towards the banning of landmines, all across borders.[21] These efforts have been immensely assisted by a fourth change: the revolution in communications technology. It has been both a generator and facilitator of a global civil society committed to right and democracy. It means that conditions in once remote countries can be immediately brought to light for an immense global public, and human rights or other kinds of campaigns thus become immediately accessible to that public. One can sit in an office in Cascais, Portugal, and just by surfing the net find out what is happening in a jail in the Sudan and take action to help change the situation of a particular inmate. The power of the immediacy of this kind of information is immense.

Finally, there have been institutional changes that reflect all or some of the above shifts. The 1990s also saw the first attempt since 1945 to bring grave human rights crimes to justice, with the International Criminal Tribunals for the Former Yugoslavia (ICTFY) and Rwanda (ICTR). A permanent international criminal Court was established in 2003, indicating a clear and permanent rather than just ad hoc concern of the international community with gross violations. The Generally Agreement on Trade and Tariffs (GATT) was transformed into the World Trade Organization (WTO), which projects the global ambition to create global rules and regulations for trade and even for social and environmental issues that are affected by trade patterns and conditions. And the UN has shifted from a peacekeeping role to undertaking more ambitious settlements and nation-building activities, as in Angola, the Western Sahara, Cambodia, Rwanda, Mozambique and El Salvador, and in humanitarian and peace enforcement in the former Yugoslavia, Haiti, Somalia, East Timor and Afghanistan.

All of the above indicate that there is a nascent – albeit hotly contested – universal jurisdiction in place, and it is now considered more legitimate for the international community to intervene to establish peace or to seek justice. This makes us look differently at the links between international action and the nation state: "as the clarity of statism recedes in an era of globalization, the essential character of sovereignty becomes more and more elusive and subject to re-negotiation by the play of political forces, moral attitudes and prevailing perceptions."[22] This climate change means that national political contexts are much more permeable to the influence of outsiders, most particularly when it comes to normative issues, including the establishment and deepening of democracy.[23] Clearly, the international climate has changed substantially since September 11, 2001, the invasion of Iraq, and the war between the Hezbollah and Israel, with the Lebanese people caught in the crossfire. The optimism of the 1990s about "democracy promotion" has declined as the rhetoric of anti-terrorist democracy promotion has increased in intensity, not only as a result of the dubious effects of the Iraq experiment but also because of growing suspicions about the motivations and values of the most active democracy-promoting states.

Despite the setbacks of the last five years, it has become clear that international actors can play an important role in transitional processes: they can create a positive climate for change, and they can act as catalysts for change. The instruments at the disposal of the international community are well-known quiet diplomacy and more aggressive diplomatic pressure, conditionality regimes (which include not only conditioned development or military assistance, but also the "positive" conditionality that the EU imposes on states aspiring to membership of that community) – targeted assistance for elections or civil society groups, for example; normative advocacy, or the "politics of shame," an expression coined by Brazilian human rights activist, Paulo Sérgio Pinheiro, which includes denunciations of torture, imprisonment or disappearance; military interventions; and sanctions and various kinds of economic, financial or political carrots, such as loans and membership of international institutions, among others. The evidence suggests that, all things being equal, the kinds of interventions that are the most likely to be successful are those that combine pressures from all sources: interventions that are multilateral (involving various states) and multidimensional (involving various levels of action). As Palmer says about Peru, a

> *combination* of human rights organization lobbying and US government initiatives may well have contributed to the sharp reduction in Peruvian government abuses in 1993 and to the Fujimori regime's growing willingness to investigate past violations by its military and police forces.[24]

Multilateral interventions allow the international community to draw on a wealth of expertise and experience and are generally perceived as the most legitimate (multinationality of forces has been crucial for the perception of neutrality of UN peacekeeping forces, for example). The evidence also suggests that pressure works best when there is already an endogenous movement and desire to liberalize or democratize: "the assistance of external players has seemed most significant when it has come in response to a domestically inspired effort at political transformation."[25]

Finally, whether a process of democratization is influenced – positively – by international actors, or has a strong international dimension, depends a lot on the international climate in place. The *zeitgeist*, which is more than the sum of the parts, more than the combined action of all kinds of actors, counts a great deal. It may become "internalized" and part of the thinking of new governments. Indeed, while it is safe to say that international actors play a secondary role in domestic processes of political change – that individual states, policies, or NGOs or international multilateral agencies are essentially secondary players – it is harder to affirm this when one takes the whole set of international activities and, particularly, the wider international setting and *zeitgeist*. This is certainly the case in Brazil, where climate and conditions play a much greater role than individual policies or interventionist acts.

The Brazilian transition and democratization process

Brazil underwent one of the most protracted transitions to democracy on record. It began as early as 1974, and ended in 1990, with the direct election of President Fernando Collor de Mello. The reasons for the military leaving power were varied, but two stand out in particular. First, there was the perception that institutional survival required an exit from power (though the establishment of a sympathetic civilian regime). Thus, in 1974, the then new president, General Ernesto Geisel, began to seek out civilian allies to "check the growing autonomy of the security community, which [he] considered dangerous for the military-as-institution and unnecessary because all guerrilla movements from the left had been destroyed."[26] Second, there was the loss of support from the elites and the middle classes, as the so-called "economic miracle" came to an end:

the Brazilian military were no longer sailing with the economic winds, as in 1968–1972, but instead, by 1981–1982, against a gale of economic adversity. Worse, they appeared to have no clear strategy as to how to surmount the most severe economic crisis in the country's history.[27]

Thus, in addition to institutional survival, there was the perceived need to "widen the base of support" for the regime in the aftermath of the "miracle."[28]

It should be said that decisions were also influenced by outside references, or regional comparison: the Argentine defeat in the Falklands (1981–1983) and the civil–military negotiations in Uruguay for a transition pact following a military defeat in a plebiscite proposing a prolongation of military rule (1980–1984) encouraged the Brazilian military to believe that continued resistance to civilian rule was inadvisable. In sum, the "triggers" for transition were endogenous (military considerations and internal opposition pressures) and – only secondarily – exogenous (a change in the national economic environment, which was at least partly caused by changing international conditions, and negative neighbourhood examples). Perhaps even more important was the powerful influence of the Portuguese and, particularly, the Spanish transitions from authoritarian rule, the first taking place in 1974 and the latter a year later. The desire to avoid a Portuguese-style transition, where the old regime practically collapsed by inadvisedly clinging to unsustainable domestic and foreign policies and was followed by a period of intense left-wing radicalization, and the more positive example of the Spanish transition, were certainly "internalized" by military actors in their calculations about how best to proceed with Brazilian liberalization.

It is important here to distinguish between the international *zeitgeist* described above, which has "global dimensions," and a more area- or region-specific *zeitgeist*, which may differ somewhat in the message it sends domestic actors. In the case of Brazil, the examples of Portugal and Spain may have been more relevant than those of Argentina and Uruguay: they showed for the first time how the only alternative to authoritarianism was not a Castroite revolution, and thus opened the way for liberalization. With liberalization taking place in the midst of what was then still a particularly raw period of the Cold War, this "micro-climate" may have been more influential than that at the global level, at least when the initial decision to liberalize – and how to go about it – was debated and adopted. In other words, it is important to distinguish between international dimensions that are global and those that are regional in scope.[29]

Despite these external influences, and if one discounts the obvious relevance and very powerful influence of economic conditions in shaping political decision-making, comparatively speaking the international dimension was relatively "anonymous" in Brazil (compared, say, to Chile). Why was this so? First, there is the unfailingly cited continental dimension of the country, which has the tenth largest economy in the world. There is the self-perception of greatness (both symbolically and more literally in terms of sheer size), and the unfettered self-sustaining Comtean notions of *ordem e progresso* that permeate the national culture and its behaviour not only on the wider global stage but also in the immediate neighbourhood (although this sense has produced different policy choices towards the latter: back-turning and competition in the first instance, and cooperation with constructive leadership in the second).[30] The explanatory power of the historical–cultural factor is weak in causal terms, but strong in the sense that self-perceptions create a disposition which colours and gives "attitude" to politics. Brazil is "immanent" in this sense, a paler version of the US, and like the US it can afford to "ignore" the world rather more than other countries of the region can.[31] This is not to say that Brazil is isolationist, but rather that it has such an immense and unique "sense of self" that this can often make the experiences of its immediate neighbourhood in particular seem distant – hence the mitigated impact of the so-called contagion effect.

A second reason for this relative anonymity has to do with the nature of the party system. This comes across quite well if one compares Brazil with Chile. A fundamental reason for the immense importance of Chile for the international community – and if there is any example of a transition in which the domestic and external dimensions are almost incestuous it is the Chilean[32] – is the fact that Chile's main political parties belong to larger political families: the Socialist International and the Christian Democratic International. By contrast, none of Brazil's parties, with the exception of the silenced Communist Party, were thus connected. This isolation from international "brotherhood" meant that political parties were more self-referential (in national terms) and, concomitantly, that international party political actors were less inclined to get involved with Brazil.[33] Indeed, the problem is not just one of lack of links to the outside, but the fragmented and fragile nature of the party system as a whole, and the virtually wholesale disappearance of pre-1964 parties during military rule and their replacement by new electoral vehicles.[34]

The third explanation also comes to life when placed in a comparative perspective: Brazil's civil society organizations were much less "internationally connected" than some of their counterparts in other national contexts. Further, with the exception of the business and economic elite (which includes more inward-looking import-substitution industrialization (ISI) beneficiaries as well as business interests linked with multinational and exporting interests, which are more outward looking) and the unions (repressed under military rule and linked to a *sui generis* Workers Party (*Partido dos Trabalhadores*, PT) with no international affiliations), civil society organizations were few and far between. The case of human rights illustrates this. In contrast with Chile, where human rights organizations emerged simultaneously with repression, in Brazil repression began in 1964 and the first organizations only appeared in 1972.[35] Further, when they did emerge, none were as well known abroad as organizations such as the Vicariate of Solidarity (*Vicaría de la Solidaridad*) in Chile, or the Mothers (*Madres*) of the Plaza de Mayo in Argentina. They lived in relative international isolation.[36] In contrast with the present situation, in which NGOs have a great deal of influence in certain public policy arenas and in which the links between domestic and foreign NGOs are extensive and intense, during the period of liberalization and early democratization the NGOs' influence on the political process as a whole was negligible.[37]

Furthermore, Brazil never became an international "cause célèbre" like Israel, or Argentina, Chile and South Africa were for the nascent human rights monitoring institutions of the United Nations in the late 1960s and particularly the 1970s and 1980s (although Amnesty International (AI) reported on torture and other violations from the outset). This is a result of factors such as the comparatively low level of repression compared with all of the above-mentioned countries, and the success of the Brazilian diplomatic corps in deflecting any attempts to bring the country under official scrutiny. In a sense, Brazil was the rule rather than the exception in this regard. Most authoritarian regimes where violations were taking place did not become internationally notorious like South Africa or Chile.

Finally, the military were very successful at controlling what was a gradual process of exit from power: the "*abertura* entailed a dialectic between regime concession and societal conquest in which the architects of the initial opening attempted to define the content and delimit the boundaries of liberalization."[38] There was mass civil society mobilization in 1984 in favour of direct elections for new civilian authorities, but the military preference for indirect elections prevailed, and José Sarney, a member of the pro-regime party, the National Renovating Alliance (*Aliança Renovadora Nacional*, ARENA), became the first civilian president of the new democracy.[39] Sarney meant continuity and economic, political and social disarray, a "hyperactive paralysis" in the words of Bolívar Lamounier.[40] The economic crisis (with the debt crisis and the failure of economic heterodoxy) and lack of popular legitimacy of a government intent on failed economic experiments made it impossible to establish the bases for more stable, routine forms of power mediation and for deeper democracy. The passage of the 1988 Constitution marks the beginning of what was to be a break with this period and of greater openness to outside influences under Collor de Mello.[41]

The situation began to change after 1989, when the influence of external factors becomes more apparent. It is somewhat artificial to make such a break, as the seeds of an external presence were there before 1989. Nonetheless, it is possible to say that the transition and early democratic period contrast with the subsequent period of "democratization" proper in terms of the level of international influence over key domestic themes. It is quite clear that with the coming to office of Fernando Collor de Mello, Brazil seemed to enter into the new *zeitgeist* or post-Berlin Wall international climate and become more open to outside influences.

It is useful here to examine the country's changing foreign policy under democracy, as this is very revealing regarding the "internalization" of the new normative climate, albeit with a Brazilian twist. Fernando Collor de Mello took office as the Berlin Wall fell, and his new policy marked a break with the past: an abandonment of protectionism and the promotion of economic liberalization; a commitment to "international insertion"[42] and a desire to avoid marginalization;[43] greater acceptance of the US; greater efforts to integrate with, participate in and influence multilateral institutions such as the UN, the GATT or WTO and the OAS; and the adoption of a more open attitude towards sovereignty. Also, while a critique and insistence on fairer rules and distribution was maintained, it was now argued within the framework of acceptance of existing global rules and from a more cooperative standpoint.[44]

The Cardoso presidency consolidated this shift. Under Cardoso's administration there was full recognition of the new paradigm – democracy and economic liberalism – as well as of a new international environment that attached greater importance (at least nominally) to norms, rules and the internationalization of power. This was the judgement of then Foreign Minister Lampreia at the UN in 1995:

> the current configuration of international relations converges towards the two concepts that have inspired the revolution of the 90s: democracy and economic liberty with social justice. This is the main characteristic that will shape the century that approaches us and will assure liberty and prosperity for all of us.[45]

This shift was backed by the new constitutional order:

> Brazil's return to democracy ... had a positive impact on its foreign policy, especially given the international order that [emerged]. The constitution of 1988 makes democracy the driving idea and accelerates the constitutionalization of foreign relations. Brazil's highest law establishes as principles human rights, the defence of peace, the solution of conflict and the repudiation of terrorism and racism.[46]

Under the Cardoso presidency, Celso Lafer, Gelson Fonseca, Hélio Jaguaribe and others developed an intellectually elaborate vision of the meaning of multilateralism in international relations, both in political and economic forums, and there were great debates about the relative merits of multipolarity and multilateralism.[47] Central themes for the "new multilateralism" were greater distribution of power internationally, and the normative issues of human rights, democracy and, last but not least, sustainable development; the aim was to strike a balance between the acceptance of a growing web of international norms and conditionalities and the protection of state sovereignty.

The impact of this shift in outlook is apparent in a number of issue areas. One is that of greater openness about proliferation.[48] In 1987 the government acknowledged its nuclear programme; the 1988 Constitution stated that nuclear development can only be undertaken for peaceful purposes; in 1991 Brazil allowed the International Atomic Energy Agency (IAEA) to inspect its once secret nuclear facilities and signed the Mendoza Declaration with Argentina against the use of chemical and biological weapons to which Bolivia, Ecuador, Paraguay and Uruguay acceded later; in 1994 it adhered to the Tlatelolco Treaty; in 1995 it joined the Nuclear Suppliers Group that oversees export controls to prevent proliferation and the Convention on Certain Conventional Weapons and supported the ban on anti-personnel land mines; and in 1998 it acceded to the

Nuclear Non-Proliferation Treaty and, as a member of Southern Common Market (MERCOSUR), declared the sub-region, including Chile and Bolivia, a "zone of peace."

Another key shift regards relations with Argentina. Historical competition (first nuclear and, more recently, hydroelectric power) turned to cooperation after 1985, when military and civilian contacts led to the establishment of mutual nuclear inspections and confidence-building measures thereafter, and a 1991 agreement with the IAEA – the same year that both created the Argentine–Brazilian Agency for Accounting and Control of Nuclear Materials and, last but not least, saw the establishment of the MERCOSUR. There is still tension, but it is now over trade and tariffs, a common currency and the speed and intensity of integration, and differing approaches to relations with the US, rather than over military issues. Indeed, one of the hallmarks of democratic foreign policy has been a move towards more involvement and cooperation in Latin America, particularly though the MERCOSUR and Amazonian cooperation initiatives.[49]

Where the environment is concerned, there was a shift from a defensive posture under Sarney to openness (although there were domestic policies adopted as much for internal consumption as *para inglês ver* (for foreign consumption), such as lower incentives for cattle raising, and monitoring of land burning). Collor de Mello brought in the issue of "sustainable development," hosted the 1992 Rio Conference and participated in other international environmental instruments. A similar opening was apparent in the human rights arena, marked by the 1992 ratification of the American Convention on Human Rights, and two UN Conventions; the prominent role played at the UN Vienna Conference on Human Rights; the acceptance of the jurisdiction of the American Court in 1997; and the promotion of UN-assisted national human rights programmes – with Brazil being one of the first countries to adopt one in 1995.[50]

Where international security and relations with the US are concerned, the record is more mixed.[51] In the realm of security, there has been a greater willingness to participate in international decision-making as part of national security; support for sanctions (as against the National Union for the Total Independence of Angola (*União Nacional para a Independência Total de Angola*, UNITA) in Angola in 1992); accepting a wider remit for UN operations (nation building) and the UNSC (non-proliferation and disarmament functions supported); and intensified participation in peacekeeping.[52] However, there has also been a resistance to a more militarized, interventionist ethos (non-participation in the Gulf War in 1991, and lack of support for intervention in Somalia and Rwanda and (until very recently) the use of force in Haiti, are cases in point). The same ambiguity was apparent where the OAS is concerned: there has been acceptance of the OAS democracy protection regime, including the 2001 Democracy Charter, but continued suspicion of the OAS as a military rather than a diplomatic instrument, given the view that it is essentially used by the US to maintain its hegemony in the region.

Relations with the US have always been ambiguous – generally friendly, but never *carnales*, as the Argentines would have them at one point. The peak of friendly relations occurred in the 1960s during the early years of military rule. In the mid-1970s, Brazil made greater efforts to diversify foreign, trade and arms relations, partly as a result of its decision to develop its own military industrial complex. This, and primarily trade-related issues such as intellectual property and technology access, but also debt and the environment, were bones of contentions in bilateral relations from then on. There was a shift in the 1990s with the acceptance of the democracy-liberal economic creed by Brazil, although differences have remained regarding how to organize and distribute power in the international system (with the US being more unilateral and opportunistically multilateral, and Brazil being – from necessity and interest, perhaps, rather than innate virtue – a more principled multilateralist country and favouring a more multipolar order), the way in which liberalization should occur (the Free Trade of the Americas Agreement (FTAA) vs the "deep integration" of the MERCO-SUR and, less plausibly, SAFTA), and visions of democracy (with the US focusing on civil and political liberties and Brazil focusing on a more holistic vision of sustainable development). Another point of tension is over the issue of drugs and security. However, relations have never been openly antagonistic and, given the failure of the European Union (EU) to provide a truly credible alternative to the US, the emphasis has always been on cooperation and high-level relations.

The international dimension of environmental and human rights politics in democratic Brazil

What we see with the Brazilian case is that the international dimension which has been most important is not the work of states, but rather the "internalization" of new, more liberal and less defensive values. As a result of this, there has been a permeability to the critical opinion of non-governmental actors working on normative issues. This is apparent in the field of environmental politics and human rights.

In her study of rainforest advocacy campaigns, Keck shows how networks were able to change the discourse and policy of major multilateral institutions, and even domestic policy. The story she tells shows that concern and the formation of what Peter Haas calls an epistemic community around the issue of deforestation began in the 1970s, with unease over the decision of the military regime to increase the rate of colonization and developments projects in the Amazon. Early pressures, however, "quickly foundered under president Reagan, and several of the most important tropical forest countries (including Brazil [which]) refused to participate in United Nations Environmental Programme UNEP meetings on the subject."[53] A campaign by activists to change the policy of lending institutions, particularly the WB, towards the financing of project with negative environmental impacts was more successful, and had an impact on Brazil. The WB loan to the Polonoreste Programme, a project to rationalize colonization in the Brazilian northeast, was temporarily suspended in 1985 due to transnational activist pressures. The capacity of the network to have an impact on WB policy, and consequently on Brazilian government policy (the successor to Polonoroeste was Planafloro in the early 1990s, a much more environmentally friendly project), was tied up with the fact that the campaign coincided with the first period of democracy:

> The timing – the project began in 1981 – placed it just on the cusp of Brazil's democratization process; the first free gubernatorial elections took place in 1982, and Brazil's first civilian president since the 1964 coup took office in 1985. Democratization stimulated political and social organization and greater circulation of information.[54]

Thus, while democratic opening favoured closer connections between local and outside activists, this in turn allowed outsiders to shape the politics of demo-cracy – in this case regarding the environment, a crucial issue for Brazil. Also relevant is that high levels of international attention provided incentives for locals to organize:

> incentives for local groups to become organized were high. With foreign attention focused on the Amazon and the approach of the 1992 Earth Summit in Rio de Janeiro, money and media attention were available as never before. Conflicts among NGOs in the region [Rondônia] were smoothed over, and in 1991 the Rondônia NGO Forum was created. This forum became the formal NGO interlocutor from Rondônia for the Planafloro project and another large environmental project, the Amazon Project, sponsored by the Group of Seven (G-7).[55]

The point here is that international actors, through the formation of transnational activist networks, help local civil societies to organize themselves and mobilize. In this sense, it can be said that international actors can make a crucial contribu-tion to one important aspect of democratization: the fortification of civil society.

A further effect is the increasing legitimacy of NGOs as partners for govern-ment and policy elaboration and implementation. As noted in an analysis of NGOs and the environment, the United Nations Conference on Environment and Development (UNCED) demonstrated "the importance of civil society [...] Rio will be remembered for showing that governments alone cannot address the environmental crisis. Politicians are beginning to accept they cannot have a decision-making monopoly on these issues."[56]

The international dimension of the struggle for human rights in Brazil has also been increasingly apparent, both in the process leading up to the adoption of a national human rights plan, and in more circumscribed issue areas such as indigenous rights and the rights of street children and the prison population. Reforms in all these areas have been undertaken in large measure as a result of pressures from local NGOs allied with international groups, forming powerful, opinion-shaping, transnational activist networks.

After 1985 the profile of human rights issues was gradually raised, and governments acknowledged the country's human rights problems with increasing openness, engaging in a dialogue with international and domestic human rights organizations and promoting initiatives to stem human rights abuses. Federal authorities and the executive in particular progressed slowly but surely away from the "politics of shame" towards a more proactive attitude. Successive efforts to implement specific policies culminated in the National Programme for Human Rights (*Programa Nacional de Direitos Humanos*, PNDR), launched by President Cardoso in May 1996 – the first of its kind in Latin America, and the third worldwide.[57] The role of transnational networks in bringing about this change was important, although it only became more apparent under Collor de Mello. The Sarney administration was still largely beholden to the military and defensive where human rights issues were concerned, and maintained an attachment to the values of a defensive nationalism. After 1989, however, human rights issues acquired a new prominence, not least because of two hard-hitting AI reports on torture and the plight of street children. The first of these led Collor to make a nationally televised speech in June 1990, stating that his country would never again be "cited as violent in reports by Amnesty International" and that the "new Brazil" would no longer "accept any form of disrespect for human rights."[58] A second report in September 1990 on the torture and killing of street children by police officers and death squads led Collor to call for a federal investigation of all the cases featured in the publication. This constituted a departure from previous policy, whereby federal authorities would refuse to investigate human rights violations on the grounds that it was the responsibility of state and local authorities to do so. Thus, reports ceased to be denied, ignored or silenced, and human rights became an explicit part of the presidential political agenda.

A nationalist rather than a modernizer, President Franco's initial reaction to reports by international organizations on human rights violations in Brazil was ambiguous. However, a combination of internal and external events encouraged the presidency to adopt a more positive attitude towards the issue. The murder of eight street children in July 1993 in Candelaria, Rio de Janeiro, allegedly by off-duty policemen; the killing of twenty-one people by over thirty hooded armed men later identified as police officers in the shanty town of Vigário Geral in Rio de Janeiro in August 1993, reportedly in revenge for the killing of four military police officers allegedly murdered by drug-traffickers based in the shanty town; and the massacre of approximately sixteen Yanomami Indians near the Brazilian–Venezuelan border shocked public opinion and provoked widespread protest from both domestic and international human rights organizations.[59] In response to the outcry, the Franco administration promised a prompt investigation of the Candelaria massacre, calling for the involvement of the federal government to ensure an expeditious trial;[60] it also placed itself within the discursive field of the defenders of human rights, sending thousands of letters in response to those demanding an investigation of the murders, acknowledging the existence of violence against children and expressing the president's personal commitment to the investigations. Further action on the human rights front was undertaken between July and October 1993, in the aftermath of the Vienna Conference on Human Rights in 1993. The Ministry of Justice promoted a series of meetings between ministers, members of parliament, civil servants, police and military officers, as well as representatives of approximately thirty non-governmental organizations (NGOs) to discuss ways of improving mechanisms for the protection of human rights. This resulted in the presentation in December 1993 of the National Programme for the Promotion of Citizenship and to Combat Violence.

Human rights featured frequently in President Cardoso's public addresses. In what has been considered his most significant speech on the issue, his address to the nation on the anniversary of Brazil's independence, on 7 September 1995, stated that human rights was "the new name of the struggle for freedom and democracy" and emphasized "the willingness of the Brazilian people not just to speak about human rights but to work for their protection." The president subsequently called on the Congress to pass laws to re-structure the CNDH, to typify torture as a criminal offence and to institute a witness protection programme. He also announced the creation of an annual Human Rights prize, awardable to an agency, non-governmental organization or individual distinguished in the defence of human rights, and the drawing up of the PNDH as recommended by the 1993 Vienna Declaration. The PNDH was elaborated with key Brazilian NGOs[61] and debated by the National Human Rights Movement and at the first National Human Rights Conference, organized by the Human Rights Commission of the Federal Chamber of Deputies established in 1995. In April 1996, a National Human Rights Secretariat was set up within the Ministry of Justice to promote the PNDH and to liaise with social organizations. The NPHR was launched on 13 May 1996. It consisted of 226 proposals covering a wide spectrum of rights, but concentrates primarily on the protection of the right to life. Because of its comprehensive nature and because it has actively sought the promotion of the involvement of both state and society in its elaboration and implementation, the Plan has been seen as a positive "framework to ensure the fulfilment of the rule of law and of a partnership between the State and civil society."[62]

As this summary shows, first, international pressures bring about states' responses, as the impact of the AI reports and international public protest against Candelaria indicates; and second, international actors strengthen and provide incentives for local actors to organize, empowering them, and vica versa. This is very clear in the case of the defence of the rights of street children and of indigenous groups, where local, foreign and international NGOs work with other civil society groups, church organizations, political parties and official organizations, both national and international, to promote policy change.[63] Thus "international human rights pressures can lead to changes in human rights practices, helping to transform understandings about the nature of a state's sovereign authority over its citizens."[64] Given the nature of the issue, moreover, the contribution to democratization is wider than just stimulating civil society; it has led the government to reform key institutions that have an impact on the quality of democracy.[65] It is also important to note that, in this case as well, the nature of the impact of outside intervention is shaped by what exists at home: "domestic political structures, political cultures and coalition behaviour are important factors" in determining success or failure of transnational activist pressure.[66]

There is actually a mutually reinforcing dynamic at work. During a transition, a fluid and uncertain situation, governments and civil society and transnational activists may use international commitments to "lock in" domestic preferences. Citing a study of the creation of a human rights framework in post-war Europe:

> international institutional commitments, like domestic institutional commitments, are self-interested means of "locking in" certain preferred domestic policies – at home and abroad – in the face of future political uncertainty [...] by placing interpretation in the hands of independent authorities managed in part by foreign governments – in other words, by alienating sovereignty to an international body – governments seek to establish reliable judicial constraints on future non-democratic governments or on democratically elected governments that may seek ... to subvert democracy from within. In the language of international relations theory, this "two-level" commitment "ties the hands" of future governments, thereby enhancing the credibility of current domestic policies and institutions.[67]

Conclusions

As this chapter has attempted to show, while the international dimension was not, comparatively, very relevant in the early years of the transition to democracy in Brazil, it did acquire some prominence after 1989, not only due to the work of transnational networks of activists shaping key issue areas with an direct and indirect impact on the process of deepening democracy, but also because the values permeating the international order of the post-Cold War period became internalized and part of the new Brazilian political scenario.

At this point it is worth qualifying what may appear to be an unquestioning attitude towards the positive impact of an organized civil society and the national and transnational NGO world. Regarding the first, it is important to take on board that civil society is not always an obvious democratizing force. Indeed, it has not always been seen in the heroic light in which it tends to be regarded today, as Nancy Bermeo says:

> The portrait of civil society [in scholarly works] from the 1960s and the 1970s is very different from the portrait we see most frequently today. Rather than associating civil society with the stabilization of democracy, or with good and efficient government, these earlier works emphasize an association with *ineffective* policy-making and *instability* instead.

Social groups can place unbearable pressure on democratic systems by making impossible distributive demands of them.[68] It is therefore important to adopt a balanced approach where civil society is concerned. As regards the more circumscribed world of issue-specific NGOs, the "heroic view" must be tempered by an awareness of what is often a lack of accountability, the tendency for issue areas to become "industries," and the fact that NGOs may spend a lot of money without actually making much difference at all.[69]

Finally, it would be remiss not to reiterate that the more optimistic view of the post-Cold War period is now somewhat misplaced, given the overwhelming shifts in discourse and practice since the felling of the Twin Towers in New York. Although the subject of external dimensions of democratization is very much on the international political agenda, talk of democratization is now more than ever restricted to countries where Al-Qaeda is thought to be operative, or to so-called "failed" or "rogue" states, and peaceful means to promote democratic change are under fire from a unilateralist US administration that has militarized democracy promotion.[70] It is also important to note that, under the guise of anti-terrorism, governments around the globe have increased the internal repression of political dissidence and engaged in hair-raising policies that during the "liberal internationalist" 1990s would have not passed unnoticed.[71]

This new context has contributed to changes in domestic and foreign policy under Lula. The election of Lula owed much to dissatisfaction with the economic and social policies of the previous government, particularly after the recovery, prompted by the 1994 stabilization plan, began to wane. Lula's platform spoke of change and the need for greater social justice and, in the foreign policy field, a commitment to a stronger sovereignty stance and refocusing on the immediate neighbourhood. Foreign policy was to be about increasing the living standards of and providing jobs for Brazilians. Although this has meant a higher degree of economic orthodoxy at home than might have been expected from campaign speeches, in the international sphere there has been an effort to engage in "alternative" diplomacy, though participation in The World Socialist and World Economic Forums[72] and forging of closer ties with "alternative" power centres, including China, India, Russia and South Africa. The vision behind this posture is summed up by Foreign Minister Amorim:

> In Latin America we have been suffering for some time now the social consequences of policies unsuited to our circumstances. The emerging consensus is that globalization has not lived up to its promise. It has failed to improve the livelihood of most people in the developing world. In many quarters it has made social problems more acute. We must review some of the neo-liberal assumptions and prescriptions about minimizing the role of the state and a blind faith in the ability of market mechanisms to produce the changes needed to make the world socially fairer and politically more stable.[73]

This critical vision results from an ideological outlook that differs from that of preceding administrations, but it has also been reinforced by the post-September 11 international context. There is greater divergence now with the

US over how the international system should be organized, as the US has acted in a rampantly unilateral way and Brazil continues to favour a more multilateral and multipolar vision of the world. Brazil has also shown itself more willing to adopt a more open leadership stance, both regionally and internationally. One can consider this the mature behaviour of a democracy: if the first step is to allow the outside in, the second is to project the inside out, as Western democracies do.[74] One example of this, which contrasts starkly with a previous resistance to accepting a peacekeeping delegation by the UN to the OAS, is the dispatch of 1,200 troops to Haiti – "the country's biggest foreign military deployment since the Second World War." Indeed, Brazil commanded a 6,700-strong force of mostly Latin American troops and 1,600 police officers, taking over from US and French forces. The justification offered by Foreign Minister Celso Amorim is that these kinds of action promote a "more balanced world."[75] The message, therefore, is not one of confrontation, but that "we do things our own way." Clearly, then, the international environment, or *zeitgeist*, continues to shape domestic and national foreign policy responses. They are likely to intensify if increasing interdependence trends continue to prevail. And in the absence of such leadership from *o camarada Bush* up North, the greatest service that Lula's Brazil could render the international democracy-promoting ethos is to continue to support the values of lowered sovereign barriers, as it has increasingly done since 1990, and to argue for a multilateral ethos in international relations. Right now, the peaceful international dimension of national regime change and political transformation badly needs this kind of boost.

Notes

1 One of the first such studies was undertaken by one of the inaugural speakers of this conference, Laurence Whitehead, in his essay "International Aspects of Democratization," in: Guillermo O'Donnell, Philippe C. Schmitter and Laurence Whitehead (eds), *Transitions from Authoritarian Rule: Comparative Perspectives*. Baltimore, MD: Johns Hopkins University Press, 1986, pp. 3–46. For a fuller treatment of the literature on the issue of democracy promotion, see my "Direitos humanos, democratização e actores internacionais," *Revista de Estudos Internacionais* 9 (13), 2006.

2 Helen V. Milner, *Interests, Institutions, and Information*. Princeton, NJ: Princeton University Press, 1997, p. 11.

3 Cases in point are early studies by Juan José Linz and the groundbreaking volume by O'Donnell, Schmitter and Whitehead, *Transitions from Authoritarian Rule*. Baltimore, MD: Johns Hopkins University Press, 1987.

4 Robert Dahl, *Polyarchy: Participation and Opposition*. New Haven, CT: Yale University Press, 1972, p. 15.

5 The best example I can think of is the National Endowment for Democracy (NED) financed electoral monitoring of the Chilean plebiscite in 1989. It is widely believed that had the results not been available to external monitors, and had not Air Force General Matthei declared the opposition win on the basis of those monitored results, Pinochet was prepared to declare himself the winner. That defeat was the beginning of the end of the regime.

6 Alicia Frohmann, "Chile: External Actors and the Transition to Democracy," in: Tom Farer (ed.), *Beyond Sovereignty: Collectively Defending Democracy in the Americas*. Baltimore, MD: Johns Hopkins University Press, 1996, p. 248.

7 Ibid., p. 248.
8 Sara Steinmetz, *Democratic Transition and Human Rights: Perspectives on US Foreign Policy*. New York, NY: State University of New York Press, 1994. This volume surveys the impact of US policy on human rights in Iran, Nicaragua and the Philippines.
9 Thomas Carothers, *In the Name of Democracy: US Policy toward Latin America in the Reagan Years*. Berkeley, CA: University of California Press, 1991, p. 250.
10 Ibid., pp. 258–9.
11 Although he cautions against policy inconsistency, Diamond has a more sanguine view of the capacity of the US and international actors to defend or promote democracy. Larry Diamond, "Promoting Democracy," *Foreign Policy* 87, 1992: 25–46. In his view, the most important way that states can contribute to democracy is by bolstering economic reform with special aid, loans and even debt forgiveness. Larry Diamond, "Democracy in Latin America: Degrees, Illusions, and Directions for Consolidation," in: Tom Farer, op. cit., pp. 102–3.
12 Joan M. Nelson and Stephanie J. Eglinton, "The International Donor Community: Conditioned Aid and the Promotion and Defence of Democracy," in: Tom Farer, op. cit., p. 186. For a full analysis of political conditionality as applied by the EU and its democracy and human rights promoting instruments, see my "A União Europeia e o MERCO-SUL: A promoção da democracia e dos direitos humanos," in: A B. Brito *et al.*, *Além do comércio: As relações entre a União Europeia e o MERCOSUL*. Lisbon: IEEI, 1997.
13 See Robert O. Keohane and Joseph S. Nye (eds), *Transnational Relations and World Politics*. Cambridge, MA: Harvard University Press, 1970; Peter Willetts (ed.), *Pressure Groups in the Global System: The Transnational Relations of Issue-Orientated Non-Governmental Organizations*. London: Pinter, 1982; Margaret E. Keck and Kathryn Sikkink, *Activists beyond Borders: Advocacy Networks in International Politics*. Ithaca, NY: Cornell University Press, 1998.
14 Margaret Keck and Kathryn Sikkink, op. cit., in order of appearance: pp. 22–4; 25; p. 161 (my emphasis); pp. 202–3; p. 203; p. 202 (my italics); and p. 27.
15 Domingo E. Acevedo and Claudio Grossman, "The Organization of American States and the Protection of Democracy," in: Tom Farer, op. cit., p. 149.
16 Alicia Frohmann, "Chile," op. cit., p. 256. George Joffé makes a similar point when he refers to the importance of "habits of mind," a Tocquevillean phrase, and political culture, as this must contain the intellectual and cultural conviction necessary for democracy to take root. George Joffé, "Democracy and the Muslim World," Chapter 10 in this volume.
17 This is Schmitter's happy turn of phrase, in his contribution to this volume.
18 Richard Falk, *Human Rights Horizons: The Pursuit of Justice in a Globalising World*. London: Routledge, 2000, p. 54.
19 In 1974, forty-one of the then 150 existing states were democracies; since then, half of the remaining 109 have become democratic. Three-quarters of the forty-five new states created since 1974 have become democratic. Most of these democracies have remained so; in fourteen of the 125 democracy broke down, but was later restored in nine. As for freedom, according to the Freedom House index, in 1973 there were sixty-three non-free, forty-three free and thirty-eight partly free countries; in 2001–2, 121 out of 192 governments were electoral democracies, and forty-eight non-free; comparable figures for 1987–88 were that sixty-six of 164 countries were electoral democracies. See: www.freedomhouse.org.
20 In addition to the defence of democracy regime of the OAS, there is the "democratic clause" of the MERCOSUR 1996, North America Free Trade Agreement (NAFTA)-related human rights hearings on Mexico in the US Congress 1990, for the first time, the FTAA link between democracy and respect for human rights with free trade, and the democracy clause of the Rio Group which led to the suspension of membership of Panama and Peru.

21 Naomi Roht-Arriaza, "The Role of International Actors in National Accountability Processes," in: Alexandra Barahona de Brito *et al.* (eds), *The Politics of Memory: Transitional Justice in Democratising Societies.* Oxford: Oxford University Press, 2001, pp. 40–64.
22 Richard Falk, op. cit., p. 70.
23 This section of the chapter is drawn from previous work, namely *Setting Global Rules: A Report of the V Euro-Latin American Forum.* Lisbon: IEEI, 1998, co-written with Álvaro de Vasconcelos; and on "The Pinochet Case and the Changing Boundaries of Democracy" in: Madeleine Davis (ed.), *The Pinochet Case.* London: ILAS, 2003.
24 David Scott Palmer, "Peru: Collectively Defending Democracy in the Western Hemisphere," in: Tom Farer, op. cit., p. 275 (my italics).
25 Anita Isaacs, in Tom Farer, op. cit., p. 278.
26 Juan José Linz and Alfred Stepan, "Crises of Efficacy, Legitimacy, and Democratic State 'Presence': Brazil," in: Juan José Linz and Alfred Stepan (eds), *Problems of Democratic Transition and Consolidation: Southern Europe, South America and Post-Communist Europe.* Baltimore, MD: Johns Hopkins University Press 1996, p. 168.
27 Ibid., p. 56–7.
28 Thomas Bruneau, "Brazil's Political Transition," in: John Higley and Richard Gunther (eds), *Elites and Democratic Consolidation in Latin America and Southern Europe.* Cambridge: Cambridge University Press 1992, p. 260. See also Luciano Martins, "The Liberalization of Authoritarian Rule in Brasil," in: Guillermo O'Donnell, Philippe Schmitter and Laurence Whitehead (eds), *Transitions from Authoritarian Rule: Latin America.* Baltimore, MD: Johns Hopkins University Press 1986, pp. 72–94.
29 I owe this insight to comments made at the IPRI Óbidos conference by Laurence Whitehead.
30 Brazil also sees itself as a "whale," with the heft and appetite to act on its own. Mr Amorim's answer is that, in a world likely to be dominated by blocs, Brazil's best option is to cooperate as much as possible with its neighbours and other developing countries. Whales, he notes, "are gregarious animals." "A Giant Stirs," *The Economist,* 10 June 2004.
31 On the immanence of the US, see the forthcoming book edited by R. Lieberman, Desmond King and Laurence Whitehead on US democracy.
32 In Chile, "influence from abroad seldom took the form of direct political or economic pressure [...] however, historically the Chilean political system was strongly influenced by external policy models and many international trends." Alicia Frohmann, in: Tom Farer, op. cit., pp. 238–9.
33 For an examination of the influence of political party internationals, see: Laurence Whitehead, "International Aspects of Democratization," in: Guillermo O'Donnell, Philippe Schmitter and Laurence Whitehead (eds), *Transitions from Authoritarian Rule: Comparative Perspectives,* op. cit., pp. 25–31.
34 Scott Mainwaring, "Brazil: Weak Parties, Feckless Democracy," in: Scott Mainwaring and Timothy R. Scully (eds), *Building Democratic Institutions: Party Systems in Latin America.* Stanford, CA: Stanford University Press, 1995, p. 354. For Brazil's political system and parties, see also: Frances Hagopian, *Traditional Politics and Regime Change in Brazil.* New York, NY: Cambridge University Press, 1996.
35 Brazil is not alone in this, and in a sense Chile is the exception to the rule. However, this is one of the explanations for the lack of international influence over the Brazilian transition. For these dates, see: Edward Cleary, *The Struggle for Human Rights in Latin America.* Westport, CT: Praeger, 1997, p. 66.
36 The exception to this general rule is the extraordinary story of the compilation of the *Nunca Mais* report, which involved national and international church organizations,

chronicled in Lawrence Weschler, *A Miracle a Universe: Settling Accounts with Past Torturers*. New York, NY: Pantheon Books, 1990; and my "Truth, Justice, Memory and Democratization in the Southern Cone," in: Alexandra Barahona de Brito *et al.* (eds), op. cit.

37 According to the Brazilian magazine *Veja*, by the end of 1993 "social-cause NGOs had doubled" in two years, to 5,000. These organizations, working on a variety of social causes, were then receiving an estimated US$700 million per year, of which an estimated US$400 million came from abroad. See: *Veja* 1326, 9 February 1994: 70–77, cited in Edward Cleary, op. cit., pp. 67–8 and 82.

38 Alfred Stepan, *Rethinking Military Politics: Brazil and the Southern Cone*. Princeton, NJ: Princeton University Press, 1988, p. 45.

39 Tancredo Neves actually won the elections, but he died before taking office. For more information about the Brazilian transition process, see: Alfred Stepan (ed.), *Democratising Brazil: Problems of Transition and Consolidation*. New York, NY: Oxford University Press, 1989.

40 See Bolívar Lamounier, "Brazil: The Hyperactive Paralysis Syndrome," in Jorge I. Dominguez and Abraham R. Lowenthal (eds), *Constructing Democratic Governance: South America in the 1990s*. Baltimore, MD: Johns Hopkins University Press, 1996, pp. 170–71.

41 Although it must be said that the inflexible and extremely detailed constitution has created as many difficulties for democratization and rational government spending as it has offered a structure within which to govern under democracy.

42 Celso Lafer and Gelson Fonseca, "Questões para a diplomacia no contexto internacional das polaridades indefinidas," in: Gelson Fonseca and Sérgio Henrique Nabuco de Castro (eds), *Temas de política externa brasileira II*. Rio de Janeiro: Paz e Terra, 1994, pp. 31–46.

43 See Roberto Abdenur, "A política externa brasileira e o 'sentimento de exclusão'," in ibid., pp. 31–46.

44 Monica Hirst and Letícia Pinheiro, "A política exterior do Brasil," *Revista Brasileira de Política Internacional* 38 (1), 1995: 5–23.

45 See Fundação Alexandre de Gusmão, *A palavra do Brasil nas Nações Unidas 1946–1995*. Rio de Janeiro: FUNAG, 1995.

46 Celso Lafer, "Brazil in a New World," in: Abraham F. Lowenthal and Gregory F. Treverton (eds), *Latin America in a New World*. Boulder, CO: Westview Press, 1994, p. 224.

47 Celso Luís Nunes Amorim, "Entre o desequilíbrio unipolar e a multipolaridade: o Conselho de Segurança da ONU no período pós-Guerra Fria," in: Gilberto Dupas and Tullo Vigevani (eds), *O Brasil e as novas dimensões da segurança internacional*, São Paulo: Alfa Omega, 1999, p. 98. Gelson Fonseca, *A legitimidade e outras questões internacionais*. Rio de Janeiro: Paz Terra, 1999; Celso Lafer and Gelson Fonseca, op. cit., 49–76. See also various publications of the Euro-Latin American Forum, published by the IEEI in Lisbon, to which these and other Brazilian authors have contributed (at: www.iee.pt).

48 See: Celso Lafer, "As novas dimensões do desarmamento: os regimes de controle das armas de destruição em massa e as perspectivas para a eliminação das armas nucleares," in: Gilberto Dupas and Tullo Vigevani, op. cit.; and Paulo S. Wrobel, "Brazil and the NPT: Resistance to Change?," *Security Dialogue* 27 (3), 1996: 337–47.

49 Cooperation has been the response to Amazonian concerns with drugs, insurgency, and illegal activities such as mining, logging, and smuggling, with the creation of Plano Cobra between Colombia and Brazil to reinforce border policing and greater efforts to integrate with the other Amazonian countries of the region. Examples are the Andean Community–MERCOSUR negotiations, the Brazilian–Bolivian gas pipeline and the Manaus-Boa Vista-Caracas highway, as well as the negotiations to

establish a permanent secretariat for the Amazon Cooperation Treaty in Brasília in 1995 and the creation of a tripartite command for the triple frontier in 1996 between Brazil, Argentina and Paraguay to police what is widely seen as an area of terrorist activity.

50 Antonio Augusto Cançado Trindade, "A protecção internacional dos direitos humanos no limiar do novo século e as perspectivas brasileiras," in: Lafer and Fonseca, op. cit., pp. 168–87.

51 Celso Amorim, "O Brasil e o Conselho de Segurança da ONU," *Política Externa* 3, 1995; and by the same author, "A reforma da ONU," *Estudos Avançados* 43, São Paulo, 1996.

52 Brazil has sent soldiers, doctors, police and election specialists to Africa particularly Angola and Mozambique, Central America Esquipulas II, the UN Mission in El Salvador (ONU.S.AL), and the UN Mission in Guatemala (MINUGUA), Asia, Cambodia, East Timor and UN missions in the Balkans, Croatia and Macedonia, and it is a member of the Special Committee on Peace Operations of the General Assembly.

53 Keck and Sikkink, op. cit., p. 134.

54 Ibid., p. 137.

55 Ibid., p. 143. It should also be noted that rubber tapper Chico Mendes, a leader of the local element of this network, was murdered in 1988, an event which made the front page of *The New York Times*.

56 Ian H. Rowlands, "Environment and Development: The Post-UNCED Agenda," *Millennium* 21 (2), 1992: 220, cited in Sally Morphet, "NGOs and the Environment," in: Peter Willetts (ed.), *The Influence of Non-Governmental Organization in the UN System: The Conscience of the World*. Washington, DC: Brookings Institution, 1996, pp. 116–46.

57 This section of the chapter is drawn from the article co-authored with Francisco Panizza, "The Politics of Human Rights in Democratic Brazil: '*A Lei Não Pega*'," *Journal of Democratization*, 5 (4), 1998: 20–51. See also, by the same authors, "A política doméstica e internacional dos direitos humanos no Brasil: "Glasnost sem Perestroika"," *Política Internacional*, 17 (2), 1988. Paulo Sérgio Pinheiro, "O passado não esta morto, nem ainda é passado," in: Gilberto Dimenstein (ed.), *Democracia em pedaços: as violações de direitos humanos no Brasil*. São Paulo: Companhia das Letras, 1996, pp. 7–8.; *Programa Nacional de Direitos Humanos*. Brasília: Ministério de Justiça, 1996; Paulo Sérgio Pinheiro and Paulo de Mesquita Neto, "Programa Nacional de Direitos Humanos: Avaliação do primeiro ano e perspectivas," *Estudos Avançados*, 11 (30), 1997: p. 117.

58 For this speech, see: Amnesty International, *Brazil Report*. London: AI, 1991, p. 49; for actual report, see: AI, *Torture and Extra-judicial Executions in Urban Brazil*. London: AI, 1990.

59 See: AI, *Beyond Despair. An Agenda for Human Rights in Brazil*. London: AI, 1994.

60 See: AI, *The Candelaria Trial: A Small Wedge in the Fortress of Impunity*. London: AI, 1996.

61 Paulo de Mesquita Neto, "Programa Nacional de Direitos Humanos: continuidade ou mudança no tratamento dos direitos humanos no Brasil," *Revista CEJ* 1 1, April 1997 on the elaboration of the programme.

62 Paulo Sergio Pinheiro and Paulo de Mesquita Neto, op. cit., p. 120.

63 For an account of the movement for street children, see: Edward Cleary, op. cit., pp. 69–81; on indigenous rights, see: S. James Anaya, *Indigenous People in International Law*. Oxford: Oxford University Press, 2000.

64 Sikkink on Mexico and Argentina, in Keck and Sikkink, op. cit., p. 116.

65 On the very negative impact of unreformed mentalities, practices and law and order institutions on the quality of democracy, see: Juan E. Méndez, Guillermo O'Donnell and Paulo Sérgio Pinheiro (eds), *The (Un) Rule of Law and the Underprivileged in*

Latin America. Notre Dame, NC: Notre Dame University Press, 1999, particularly the introductory chapter by Pinheiro, pp. 1–24.

66 Ibid., p. 162 and p. 228.

67 Ibid., p. 228.

68 Nancy Bermeo, *Ordinary People in Extraordinary Times: The Citizenry and the Breakdown of Democracy.* Princeton, NJ: Princeton University Press, 2003. Bermeo cites a number of examples: Juan J. Linz, *Crisis Breakdown and Re-equilibration*; Samuel P. Huntington, *Political Order in Changing Societies*; the "mass praetorianism" of Guillermo O'Donnell in *Modernization and Bureaucratic Authoritarianism*; and Albert Hirschman, *Exit, Voice and Loyalty.* See also: Douglas Chalmers, "The Politicized State in Latin America," in: James Malloy (ed.), *Authoritarianism and Corporatism in Latin America.* Pittsburgh: Pittsburgh University Press, 1977, pp. 23–46.

69 Cleary refers to the criticism of the children's rights movement in Brazil, which some say has become an "industry," given the large amount of foreign aid and attention given to its activities. He cites an interviewee:

> A certain pathology takes over. Foremost, organizations should be turned outward, to the benefit of their clients. Instead some become more interested in their own functioning and welfare. They spend much time justifying their activities before foreign funding agencies. They have to compete for funding with other groups. So attention goes on winning grants. Further, foreign benefactors mostly European of various nationalities have their own agendas to which Brazilians have to conform. Sometimes these agendas are out of touch with the Brazilian situation.
>
> Edward Cleary, op. cit., pp. 79–81.

70 Laurence Whitehead makes similar points in his contribution to this volume. Indeed, were President Bush able to read, he would now recognize his plight in the following words by Machiavelli: "In seizing a new principality,

> you have as enemies all those whom you have offended in seizing that principality, and you cannot keep as friends those who have put you there because you cannot satisfy them in the mode they had presumed and because you cannot use strong medicines against them, since you are obligated to them.
>
> See: Niccolò Machiavelli, *The Prince.* New York: Bantam Classics, 1984
> ("Of Mixed Principalities", III).

71 See: Human Rights Watch, *Opportunism in the Face of Tragedy: Repression in the Name of Anti-Terrorism.* New York, NY: HRW, 20 January 2002; HRW, *Anti Terror Campaign Cloaking Human Rights Abuse.* New York, NY: HRW, 16 January 2002. As HRW shows, this is happening not only in authoritarian or fragile democratic contexts, but also in countries like the UK, Australia and the US

72 One example is the adoption of a critical stance at the Cancun WTO meeting in 2003 through G-20 membership. Brazil was a founder of the poor man's club that aims to force open agricultural trade with wealthy countries.

73 Celso Amorim, "Building our Latin American 'Community of Nations'," from a speech at the London School of Economics, 6 April 2004.

74 The first Lula-"Comrade Bush" meeting was a public relations success, but Lula has been critical of US policy towards the Middle East, and there are persistent tensions over trade and intellectual property, and, more recently, because of Brazilian ambiguity regarding its nuclear intentions it refused to allow international inspections of its uranium enriching centrifuges and has indicated it intends to reactivate its nuclear programme.

75 "A Giant Stirs," *Economist*, op. cit. The same article also reports that Lula has adopted a more proactive stance towards Bolivia and Colombia.

8 Redefining Eastern Europe

Democratization in Central and South-Eastern Europe

Lawrence S. Graham

Introduction

In the midst of all the changes that have swept across Europe at the end of the twentieth century and the beginning of the twenty-first, two dates stand out in the reconfiguration of a region which for forty-five years was defined as Eastern Europe: 1989 and 2004. The former marks the ending of Soviet domination of that part of Europe where Russia was hegemonic as a consequence of the outcomes of the Second World War, while 2004 best captures the reconfiguration that has been going on in Europe at large over the last decade with the expansion of the European Union (EU) from fifteen to twenty-five member governments. In this regard, 2004 calls attention to the need, more so now than ever before, to differentiate among the countries to the east of the original core of the EU.

The impact of 1989

Fifteen years after the momentous events which took place in 1989, it is amazing how quickly the impact of the Cold War on Eastern Europe has receded into the background and been consigned to a history these countries are determined not to see repeated. Yet 1989 began uneventfully, with the same constraints in place that had operated in the region since the Second World War. Despite a political opening within the Soviet Union and a serious attempt to restructure the economy, the outlook for Eastern Europe was largely the same: continued Soviet domination of the region, backed up by a military presence, and economic and political stagnation in the various republics. Then, suddenly, the military government of General Wojciech Jaruzelski in Poland signed an accord with the leaders of the Solidarity Movement in which they agreed to hold elections in June – elections which the opponents of the regime won. This was followed immediately by the formation of a non-Communist government which took power in September.

Rather than trigger Soviet intervention, what transpired was Moscow's acquiescence and acceptance of the changes in Poland as inevitable. This, in turn, led to an upheaval throughout Eastern Europe. The Hungarian government accelerated its economic and political reforms, announcing in October the reorganization of its Communist Party as the Hungarian Socialist party and its acceptance of political pluralism. Unable to suppress mass exodus, the East German regime ended its restrictions on travel and emigration in November, and likewise reorganized its party. Overnight, reunification became unavoidable and the German Democratic Republic (*Deutsches Demokratische Republik*, DDR) collapsed. Czechoslovakia followed, with its Communist Party abandoning its leading role in society, accepting non-Communist participation in government, and opening the way for reinstallation of a democratic regime.

Equally dramatic were the changes in South-Eastern Europe, where incumbent Communist leaders initially thought they could ride out the changes underway by reforming the regimes in power. In Bulgaria, attempts at reform in November ended up with Zhivkov being ousted from power, followed by mass demonstrations in favour of democracy in December.

Even more dramatic was the upheaval in Romania later that same month. In a matter of hours, following an uprising in Timisoara, what began as a mass demonstration in downtown Bucharest, intended to demonstrate popular support for Ceausescu, turned into a mass protest against him and his wife. Then, when Nicolae and Elena Ceausescu attempted to flee Bucharest by boarding a helicopter on top of the national palace along with their closest supporters, before the helicopter could reach a safe haven it either crashed or was forced to land in the countryside west of the capital. The Ceausescus were seized by their own personal guard, a hand-picked elite group within the Securitate, and transported to the nearby city of Sibiu, where, after a summary trial, they were shot on Christmas Day and their bodies paraded on television. Shortly thereafter, faced with armed rebellion throughout the country and a bitter confrontation with the Securitate (the police force directly accountable to Ceausescu and not to the military), a self-constituted National Salvation Front made up of senior Communist Party members and military officers moved quickly to isolate younger military officers, in what was called the CADA movement favouring more radical change and an end to Communist rule. Having defeated armed insurrection led by the Securitate, they quickly established control of the country in an effort to shore up Romania's variant of state socialism and its command economy – an action which delayed Romania's transition and produced an ambiguous outcome until 1996, when the Democratic Convention Alliance (*Convenţia Democrată Română*, CDR) gained the upper hand and competitive party politics ensued.[1]

Southwest of Romania, change was unavoidable. Even in Albania, the most isolated of the countries in Eastern Europe, rumours began to circulate of internal pressures for change, and it was not long before a successor regime came to power – one that once again was unsuccessful in heading off pressures for more radical change. While Yugoslavia appeared to be in a better position to survive at the outset, in the face of political stalemate and prolonged economic crisis the regime began to disintegrate in 1990. Despite all the emphasis on how the Yugoslav regime differed from the other Eastern European governments, as a function of Tito's break with Stalin dating back to 1948, its decentralized multinational, federal socialist state ceased to be viable – especially as Milosevic in Serbia pushed his hard-line policies, and reformers in Slovenia and Croatia opposed his actions. As 1990 progressed, with Milosevic pressing for more and more control over the federation from Belgrade and the other republics opting for greater autonomy, if not independence, and multiparty solutions to questions of governance, a series of bitter wars broke out – first in Croatia and later in Bosnia. With the military dominated by Serbian officers supporting Milosevic and favouring his hard-line policies, the decentralization of which Tito was so proud, with local militias and arms housed in various regional centres in the Yugoslav republics (in the event of a Soviet invasion), made it possible for those opposed to Milosevic and Serbian dominance of the regime to fight back. Out of this conflict and the disintegration of the old Yugoslavia a new group of successor states emerged, each hostile to and at odds with its previous neighbours in the old federation.

What happened was simply this: once Gorbachev sent the signal that the Soviet Union could no longer guarantee the status quo in the Eastern Europe it had created, and that it would cease to use military force to sustain its control of the region, domestic forces were free for the first time since the late 1940s to pursue their own courses of action. As a consequence, with the Cold War gone, Eastern Europe as a distinct group of states disappeared more rapidly than the outside world was prepared to accept. More unsettling was the fact that Yugoslavia's role in the Balkans as a buffer state between East and West no longer made sense. As a consequence, there was no way its variant of state socialism could survive, or the decentralized federal arrangements elaborated by Tito could sustain a union of the South Slavs.

Eastern Europe in 2004

Today, the old political landscape is gone and in its place are three distinct groups of states: the Baltic states (Estonia, Latvia, and Lithuania), the Visegrad Group in Central Europe (Poland, the former Czechoslovakia – today the Czech Republic and Slovakia – and Hungary), and South-Eastern Europe (the former Yugoslavia – today Slovenia, Croatia, Bosnia-Herzegovina, Serbia and Montenegro, Macedonia – and Albania, Bulgaria, Romania, and Greece). How these countries were incorporated into the Soviet sphere of influence or secured their autonomy from direct Soviet control after 1948, as much as their prior historical experiences before the Second World War, is reflected in their realignment during 1989 and 1990 and how they have handled their external relations since. No longer can these three very different and distinct regional groupings of national communities be hidden behind a façade of uniform political and economic structures.

First, what makes the three Baltic countries different from the rest of Eastern Europe is their strong national identity despite all odds and their orientation towards Europe, regardless of concerted Russian efforts to incorporate them into Czarist Russia earlier and, after 1939, into the Soviet Union. In the effort to suppress their national identity, Sovietization was the most brutal in Moscow's attempt to instigate radical change ethnically by moving large blocs of Russian nationals into these countries. As a consequence, today each of these republics must struggle with ethnic minorities who were previously dominant in their internal politics and were the instruments of a policy designed to obliterate their identity as small national states.

The second realignment is best captured by reference to the Visegrad Group. This is the name given to the four Central European national communities whose representatives first met in Visegrad, Hungary, to cooperate in a strategy to secure their rapid incorporation into the European Economic Community. These are the Central European national communities who gained their independence as a consequence of the collapse of the imperial states of Austro-Hungary, Germany and Russia at the end of the First World War, only to become consigned to the status of satellite states of the Soviet Union after 1945. As realignment in Central Europe expanded and the Visegrad Group evolved into a regional security arrangement whose goal was incorporation into the North Atlantic Treaty Organization (NATO), Slovenia broke loose from its former constraints (imposed by its incorporation into the former Yugoslavia) and affiliated itself with this group of small states. However, this did not take place until 1996, after the most recent round of Balkan wars was brought to a standstill by external intervention in 1994–1995.[2]

Severing its ties with the republics comprising the former Yugoslavia and ending the constraints imposed on the Slovenes (dating back to their inclusion in the wider South-Eastern European settlement of 1919, in which the union of the South Slavs was seen as key to stabilizing the Balkans), Slovenia successfully realigned itself with its Central European neighbours – countries long identified with Western Europe. In returning to the Central European fold, Slovenia has been able to undo its separation from these national communities and rebuild its ties with Austria, originally formed when it was an integral part of Austria in the old Austro-Hungary.[3] Nevertheless, one should always keep in mind that Slovenia's incorporation into the former Yugoslavia and the autonomy granted to it under the reconstitution of Yugoslavia as a Federal Republic in 1946 gave it the opportunity to transform its economy in such a way that, as the leading economy in the old Yugoslavia, it was uniquely situated to re-attach itself to Central Europe and gain access to European markets with minimal disruption. As a consequence, whereas Poland has had a real struggle in rebuilding its economy and the Czech Republic has had to make some painful economic adjustments since the political transition was over, from the moment Slovenia exited from the former Yugoslavia, economic growth and competitive restructuring of its industries and businesses have proceeded apace.

The third realignment, that which has been underway in the Balkans now for more than a decade, involves the European region where the national state idea has been the most conflictive and democratic options the most limited. Each of the major communities in South-Eastern Europe has a long history of seeking to impose its own particular national idea over and above those of other national groups residing in the same physical space. While Greece has had a privileged status among the Balkan states, as a consequence of its long Western alignment since the middle of the nineteenth century and the way it became imbedded in Western economic and security arrangements after the Second World War, its *Megalia Idea* (Great Idea) has never been all that different from any of the other national ideas that the other national communities have used in their attempts to impose their own hegemony over their immediate neighbours in the Balkans.

During the Cold War years it was all too easy for the Greek leadership to convince the West that it was a Southern European state, and to deny the extent to which their struggle to create both state and nation had also entailed the expulsion of its minorities and imposition of an imperfect union of disparate peoples for whom creating state and nation had long remained an illusive ideal. While Greece did successfully define itself as a Southern European state for fifty years, along with Italy, Spain and Portugal, and eventually consolidated a competitive democratic regime, the outcome of the upheavals in the Balkans during the last decade of the twentieth century and the unresolved issues that have spilled over into the twenty-first century have called attention anew to how much it is a part of the politics and economics of South-Eastern Europe. Nothing serves better to illustrate this point than the strong objection made by the Greeks when those leading the move to create an independent Macedonian Republic, as the old Yugoslavia disintegrated, proposed naming their new national state "Macedonia." Greece refused to endorse Macedonia's entrance into the United Nations in April 1993 until they accepted the name of the "Former Yugoslav Republic of Macedonia." Reinforcing this stance more recently has been the refusal of the Greek community in Cyprus to let the Turks on the island participate in the EU now that accession has been achieved.

The impact of European integration and the significance of 1 May 2004

The enlargement of the EU from fifteen to twenty-five members reflects the marked economic and political differences between North and South in the range of countries extending from Estonia, the northernmost Baltic republic, to Albania, in South-Eastern Europe. The Cold War definition of Eastern Europe, as embracing previously independent European states subject to Soviet hegemony after the Second World War, masked this North–South divide. For forty years, political analysts in the West accepted as a given the way in which the Soviet Union had imposed a common set of governmental institutions and political organizations throughout the region, defining what was called the new order of state socialism, based on centralized command economies, and establishing local Communist parties as the vanguard of the new elites in power, over and above popular front political organizations mobilizing urban workers and peasants.

The new Europe of the twenty-five embraces those countries to the East that have had the longest and deepest engagement with Europe historically and culturally, and have made the greatest progress in embracing both market economies and democratic practices since 1989. It excludes, for now, those communities that for one reason or another were perceived by many in Western Europe to be outside Europe prior to the Soviet era, especially in the areas in South-East Europe long subjected to the rule of the Ottoman Turks. In this regard, if one looks at the long trajectory of European history, these new member states drawn from Central Europe and the Baltic region frequently consider the years during which they were incorporated by force into the Soviet sphere of influence to be a historic anomaly. As soon as it became clear that the Soviet Union was collapsing, the realignment of key Baltic and Central European republics and their reconstitution as independent national communities tied to the West was rapid and definitive.[4]

The clearest examples of the close connection between recreating markets and expressing preferences for democratic rule, derived from Western experience, are to be seen in the consensus rapidly established between a new generation of leaders and popular majorities in Estonia, Latvia, Poland, the Czech Republic, Hungary and Slovenia. These six national communities have moved quickly and decisively to install democratic regimes and to integrate themselves as much as possible with the European core – the countries that were the original members of the European Coal and Steel Community (ECSC) that first banded together in 1951 to create a supranational organization (the Benelux countries – Belgium, the Netherlands and Luxembourg – and West Germany, France and Italy). In two cases, those of the Czechs and the Slovenes, this necessitated escaping from prior definitions of statehood assigned to them in 1919, and repositioning themselves as small national states in a new Central Europe. Later, it also became equally clear in negotiating their treaties of accession that this move to European integration could not be accomplished without bringing in Lithuania and Slovakia – areas where the legacies of Communism had proven to be more difficult to eradicate, and the ability to transform the local economy more difficult.

The best way to understand how important achieving this national consensus on integration into the European core has been, in transcending internal political divisions and the enormous differences between those who had collaborated with the Soviets and those who had opposed Soviet rule regardless of the cost, is to look at Poland. There, political brokers such as the Chancellor of the Sejm (who was the government's chief representative or clerk in parliament) worked assiduously to put together support for European integration and market reforms, despite formidable internal obstacles and a constantly changing political landscape. The greatest contrast to this pattern of consensus-building, despite irreconcilable internal differences, is Romania, the largest of the states excluded from this enlargement in 2004. In that country, substantive political and market reforms have become mired down, time and time again, in the inability of leaders and political groupings to transcend internal divisions and the legacies of the Communist era – above all else, how to move beyond the pernicious influence of the Ceausescus.

The legacies of Communism and differential transitions

The legacies of the Communist era are threefold: overcoming the economic gap between Eastern and Western Europe and the different dynamics of market and command economies; dealing simultaneously with economic and political reform; and reconstituting civil society. While there are marked differences between the Baltic and Central European republics, on the one hand, and the Balkans, on the other, it behoves us to keep in mind those legacies which are shared in common.

First, the successful rebuilding of Western Europe after the Second World War, the rekindling of sustained economic growth and the economic integration which has accompanied the movement to a European common market – now reinforced by the development of a common set of governing institutions at the supranational level as symbolized by the Treaty of Maastricht – cannot be automatically transformed into economic convergence that will ensure sustained economic and social progress for all of the newly incorporated economic regions.

The case in point is Eastern Germany. In the Eastern Europe of the Communist era, the DDR was considered to be by far its most advanced economy. But today, after fifteen years of economic and political integration between Western and Eastern Germany, the economic disparity between West and East remains enormous, without an easy solution emerging for reconstituting the economic and social structures which underlay the old Germany to the east, which was as productive in its industrial areas as it was in its rural economy. The mass industries of Eastern Germany more often than not have had to be dismantled, as have the rural cooperatives and collectives; but even when this is done, it has not guaranteed an automatic take-off in terms of new economic growth and integration into existing urban and rural market structures in Western Germany. For all the success that has been touted in the Czech Lands and in Slovenia, there are much wider areas in urban and rural Poland in which the urban and rural landscape is decimated by the empty buildings and structures constructed and sustained under centralized command economies.

Again, the Polish example comes to mind when looking at the difficulty of sustaining simultaneously economic and political reforms over the long term. What can be called the easy reforms are over with: the decrees and the initiatives which put in place new norms favouring markets and new procedures governing elections and the conduct of governmental affairs. The constant turnover in Polish government and lagging economic indices all point to how difficult it is to recreate markets, retool the labour force and revolutionize the incentives which are so essential to encouraging entrepreneurship and sustained group initiatives outside government and political parties.

Yet again, on the civil society side, the enthusiasm unleashed in the Solidarity Movement and the support given to the civic committees which proved to be so very important in triggering the collapse of state socialism in Poland have not been easy to channel into new organizations and associations outside government and the political parties. The enthusiasm for rejoining Europe has not diminished in the least, but the practicalities involved in generating new jobs and economic opportunities, or in breathing new life into local organizations and associations in urban and rural areas identified with the new Poland have proven far more difficult to instigate.

Still, despite these problems and growing awareness that money alone is not the solution to Poland's economic, political and social transformation, and realization that the enormous investment of public and private funds in East Germany has not succeeded in creating a new basis for local economic and social structures, these difficulties pale before the developmental issues which must be confronted and dealt with in South-Eastern Europe.[5]

Successful "reform-mongering" presupposes certain minimal conditions. If the economic and social transformations underway in Poland and East Germany – core European regions – are kept in mind, and one understands the time and hard work entailed in recreating new bases for economic and social activity, in neither case does one have to think about building both state and nation. By extension, throughout the Baltics and Central Europe, the organization and identity which go with state and nation can be assumed to exist already. Likewise, while problems with the Romany (or gypsy) minority present in Hungary present enormous difficulties for the state and non-governmental organizations in terms of protecting minority rights and ensuring equal access to economic opportunities and social services, there is a network of organizations outside government, domestic and international supports from governmental and non-governmental entities which can and are attacking these problems. However, when we move into the Balkans (now minus Slovenia, which is today aligned with Central Europe) there are a whole range of prior questions and issues which must be raised and dealt with.

First, how is society to be organized above the village level in a region where competing claims to physical space by various national communities overlap in such a way as to make the determination of borders difficult, if not impossible, to sustain without engendering conflict? The most painful reminder of the extent to which competing national groups are imbedded in the same physical space is the warfare which followed the break-up of the old Yugoslavia. There is the conflict between Serbs and Croats, in which old issues and bitterness dating back to the 1930s and 1940s resurfaced, and enmities dating back to late medieval outcomes are still nurtured. Enmeshed in this conflict is the subsequent three-way struggle among Serbs, Croats and Bosnians, which generated instances of genocide involving Muslim communities. Coupled with this, as the Bosnian conflict lessened in the face of external intervention, has been the Kosovo conflict, where the Albanian majority seeks to detach that region from Serbia and, failing that, to drive out the Serbian minority. Most recently, the issue of how to define a larger Albania has spilled over into Macedonia, in those areas where there is an Albanian majority that has been hostile to the concept of a small multinational state. Then, there is the long-standing issue of the Hungarian minority present in Transylvania, a region which before 1919 was considered to be an integral part of Hungary and was assigned to Romania on the basis of its Romanian majority.

A second issue concerns acute differences among people speaking the same language separated by circumstance and history in such a way as to undercut programmes designed to stimulate economic development or to increase educational opportunities or to create a more effective safety net for the disadvantaged. The most vivid example of this tension is the long-standing division in Romania between the peoples living east of the Carpathians, where the contact with Europe has been the most difficult to sustain, and those living west of the Carpathians, in Transylvania, where attachment to Europe is long-standing. Yet another latent conflict involves border areas between Bulgaria and Macedonia, and between Moldavia in northeast Romania and the Republic of Moldova, where the language is the same but the cultural identity and the organization of society is markedly different, as a consequence of the way in which Moldavians were incorporated into the Soviet system and how, since the collapse of the Soviet Union, the economic system has begun a rapid decline and a spiral downward which seems unending. In this context, engendering economic and political reforms simultaneously has been virtually impossible to achieve.

The third issue concerns designing and implementing strategies for development in economic terms as well as in terms of social services, in which local communities are involved and where the goal is to move these groups towards sustaining themselves in these endeavours when external assistance ends.[6] When one considers the difficulties encountered in so many parts of the former DDR and the far greater availability of resources in that portion of Central Europe of which Germany is a part, then these issues in development in the Balkans, be it Romania or Albania, are overwhelming. All of these countries fall within the category of those areas most impacted by underdevelopment linked to the failure of their command economies and initiatives in economic and social policy under their variants of state socialism. The variations are enormous, however, given the very different patterns of governance and economic performance in Ceausescu's Romania or Hoxha's Albania and the very difficult transitions which have followed.

Yet, there is one basic difference to be encountered in this group of countries which dates back to the late nineteenth and early twentieth century: this is the residual impact on these areas of the patterns of economic development and organization of society which were identified with the domains of the old Austro-Hungarian empire, and those east of this line, which remained under the Ottomans until the collapse of Ottoman Turkey in the First World War. Hence, today, for all the difficulties and divisions, Croatia (now an independent republic) and Transylvania (which has been Romanian territory east of the Carpathians since 1919) are certainly regions whose development and progress make them more compatible with the European Union than other areas in South-Eastern Europe. Nevertheless, this older division does not present us with a fixed frontier any longer. At this writing, Bulgaria, which is certainly east of this line, has come a much longer way in the direction of restructuring its economy, establishing new patterns of productivity and selecting its political leadership on the basis of open, competitive elections than other Balkan states. In short, however one looks at the Balkans, it remains a complex mosaic of peoples, cultures, regional economies, and small, medium and large states that defy easy categorization. There, consolidating democratic regimes and market economies remain tentative at best.

Implications for Portugal

The challenges for Portugal in the expansion of the EU from fifteen to twenty-five members are, as a small state, continuation of the supports and access to European funding it has enjoyed since 1986, and how to situate itself in an expanded Union where a number of the new member states are more competitive in terms of a skilled labour force, lower industrial labour costs, and proximity to areas of leading economic growth and activity. What is missing from this discussion, however, is a contextualization of what the development of larger, transnational markets and matching integrated institutional structures means in terms of the opportunities and costs for small states or economic regions in larger states in their integration into expanding trading blocs and supranational governance structures.

The link which is most helpful in calculating the opportunities and the risks for regional economies – be they synonymous with existing state boundaries (the case of Ljubljana in Slovenia and its integration into an emerging Central European regional economy), or leading regions in larger national states with the capacity to restructure themselves as the basis of the economy changes and to respond to opportunities for inserting themselves into larger markets (for example, Rhône-Alpes (Lyon), in France, Barcelona (Catalonia) in Spain, and Wielkopolska (Poznan) in Poland) – is the use of city-region constructs as the basic building blocs in restructuring markets, institutions of governance, and civil society. From this base, it is far easier to analyse and develop the various networks that are so essential in moving from the local to the regional and supranational levels, and to assess which are the leading and lagging regions, and why.

How this is to be done, however, depends on whether or not regionally based coalitions can agree on their priorities, maximize those assets needed to leverage change and competitive advantage, and build the necessary linkages by proceeding from the local, to the regional, to the national and supranational levels. In one study of leading and lagging regions, one of the most creative solutions to reversing the pattern of the underutilization of available resources came from investing in human capital available in the region but hitherto not pulled together in terms of a coherent local developmental strategy: Languedoc-Rousillon (Montpellier), an area of France that was a lagging region historically in which substantial economic restructuring has occurred through the use of advanced technology. Outside the EU but imbedded in another emerging transnational regional economy is the case of Austin, Texas, a city-region in the US with an excess of underemployed well-educated human resources in the past, which also used small, medium-size, and large hi-tech firms clustered around a public university in which priority was given to the sciences and engineering to generate jobs and economic growth. There, as opposed to Montpellier, after the first cycle of accelerated growth ended abruptly, economic restructuring is already well advanced in the shifting of available resources into nanotechnology and computational engineering and the sciences, and in creating new more specialized interdisciplinary programmes with appropriate ties with small and medium-size firms.[7]

The other dimension involved here, either in leading regions that have successfully restructured themselves across time as major shifts have occurred in the state and the economy or in lagging regions which have broken the cycle of limited economic performance in the past, lies in identifying variations in institutional performance, linked to the question raised by Robert Putnam: "Why do some democratic governments succeed and others fail?" After an extended examination of the patterns of civil trust in northern Italy, following "norms of reciprocity and networks of civic engagement," and the absence of the incentive to work toward the common good and the prevalence of "the strategy of 'never cooperate'" in the South, he concluded that in all societies these two equilibriums can manifest themselves, and that "dilemmas of collective action hamper attempts to cooperate for mutual benefit, whether in politics or in economics." As Putnam notes, and is appropriate when examining the cases of Montpellier and Austin, the challenge for all of us is that if "history suggests that *both* states *and* markets operate more efficiently in civic settings," how to promote cooperative behaviour, when the logic of "going it alone" is the easier to pursue in a complex world.[8]

While these are difficult questions and challenges to sort out, the answer lies somehow in making the complex regional market now in place in Europe and the other emerging regional markets work in terms of promoting strategies of accelerating economic and institutional change in leading regions while minimizing the drag of lagging regions and the logic of going it alone. As is true of all systems of governance, instances of democratization and endeavours to stimulate markets, it is important to remember that these undertakings are essentially cyclical in nature. There is nothing inevitable about continued growth and expansion of the economy and new endeavours designed to improve governance and institutional performance, any more than is democratic consolidation a permanent state – for all such undertakings are, after all, subject to reversible change.[9]

Notes

1 This section draws upon a more extended article published by the author in early 1990 under the title "The Economic and Political Outlook for Eastern Europe," *Alcalde: UT Austin Alumni Magazine*, 78 (4), 1990: 7–9.

2 Misha Glenny, *The Fall of Yugoslavia: The Third Balkan War*. New York, NY: Penguin Books, 1996. For him, the first Balkan War was the long-term struggle between Austro-Hungary and Ottoman Turkey for the control of the Balkans up to the First World War; the second was among the Partisans, Ustashe and Chetniks at the end of the Second World War.

3 Margaret McMillan, *Paris 1919: Six Months That Changed the World*. New York, NY: Random House, 2002. This is by far the most succinct and lucid discussion available of the post-First World War settlements which have continued to have ramifications for the present.

4 In understanding these ties between past and present and the different tracks the Eastern European countries have been following since 1989, as well as their passion for reintegration into Europe, the most helpful history, in my opinion, is: Norman Davies, *Europe: A History*. London: Pimlico/Random House, 1997. The paperback copy I currently have on my shelf is one that I received some seven years ago from a Polish colleague, who in the Polish transition had abandoned his academic career, as was true of so many of his associates in Solidarity, had become the Chancellor of the Sejm, and was at the time the Polish ambassador to the Court of St James. Whether Pole or Lithuanian, these are people who never forgot for a moment during the Cold War years their cultural and historical ties with Europe.

5 The recent article in the *Financial Times* "The Best and Worst of Times in a Tale of Two Economies," (4 June 2004: 14) provides an excellent case study of two German communities, the Freising administrative district, north of Munich, one of Germany's most successful regions economically, and Weisswasser, "a similar-sized town in Saxony near the Polish border." As Bertand Benoit, the journalist writing this article, notes,

> The tale of affluent Freising and dying Weisswasser reflects Germany's failed economic reunification. It could also be the shape of things to come in two regions that, 15 years after the fall of the Berlin wall, remain two different countries. Although Berlin has pumped more than €1,200 (US$1,470bn) in infrastructure development, subsidies and welfare benefits into East Germany since reunification, the region remains mired in economic difficulty.

6 The two most effective books regarding these difficulties in a specific country context and more generally are: Thomas Carothers, *Assessing Democracy Assistance: The Case of Romania*, Washington, DC: Carnegie Endowment Book, 1996; and his *Aiding Democracy Abroad: The Learning Curve*, Washington, DC: Carnegie Endowment for International Peace, 1999.

7 See: Lawrence S. Graham, "The Political Economy of Regional Accommodation: A New Dynamic in Restructuring," unpublished paper prepared for the 1999 Annual Meeting of the American Society for Public Administration in Orlando, Florida. It summarizes the results of an initial meeting of six members of a cross-national research team at the Rockefeller Foundation Bellagio Study and Conference Centre in Italy in November 1996, to develop a project on new patterns and developments in regional economies. Thereafter, seven two-person country teams were selected to prepare theoretically relevant case studies in Europe and the western hemisphere from the EU, the North American Free Trade Association (NAFTA) and the Southern Common Market (MERCOSUR). In Europe, these were: Rhône-Alpes (Lyon) and Languedoc-Rousillon (Montpellier), Catalonia (Barcelona) and Andalucía (Sevilla) in Spain, Wielkopolska (Poznan) and Upper Silesia (Katowice) in Poland, Slovenia (Ljubljana) and the Federal Republic of Yugoslavia (Belgrade). In the western hemisphere, they were Quebec (Montreal) and the Maritime Provinces (Moncton) in Canada, Nuevo León (Monterrey) and Chiapas in Mexico, and Paraná (Curitiba) and Ceará (Fortaleza) in Brazil. The pairing of leading and lagging regions laid the foundation for a collaborative project focused on the new regionalism.

8 Robert D. Putnam, *Making Democracy Work: Civic Traditions in Modern Italy.* Princeton, NJ: Princeton University Press, 1993, pp. 176–7 and 181.
9 After this chapter was completed and revised, according to the schedule set by the editors, negotiations with Romania and Bulgaria regarding necessary market and political reforms were successfully completed and they were admitted into the EU in 2007, thus bringing the Union's membership up to twenty-seven states.

9 External dimensions of democratization

The case of the Middle East

Richard Youngs

Introduction

Issues relating to political reform in the Middle East have attained unparalleled significance across a range of international policy concerns. The Middle East is a case study that is uniquely compelling in the way it reveals the international domain's profound and complex impact on political processes. In the context of this volume, this chapter on the Middle East proceeds from a striking peculiarity: while other contributions have analysed international factors in cases where democratic transitions *did* take place in the Middle East, we must assess their relevance in a context where democratization has *not* (yet) occurred. The chapter offers assessment of the role played in the Middle East by a number of international dimensions: Western relations with authoritarian regimes across the region; transnational networks; and the relationship between the global economy and the prevalence of rentier economic structures in the Middle East.

It is argued here that in each of these spheres there are factors that have been influential in rendering democratization more difficult in the Middle East. Some of the standard categories of positive, pro-democracy international influence posited in the academic literature either have been weak or have acted in reverse form in the Middle East. At the same time, the chapter suggests that these international dimensions contain the seeds of a potentially more positive impact. Increasing variety and diversity within the Middle East, along with apparent changes in outside perspectives on the region, combine to require a more balanced assessment of the international dimension's impact on the prospects for political change.

Contrasting trends in the Middle East

A detailed overview of the state of democratic reform in the Middle East is well beyond the scope of this chapter. However, to help understand the backdrop against which the role of international dimensions must be assessed, a mixed picture can be outlined of limited reform, atrophy and de-liberalization witnessed in the Middle East in recent years.

While the Middle East remains the region least touched by the "third wave" of democratization, some political liberalization is clearly afoot in many Middle Eastern states. By early 2006, democratic elections had taken place at both the presidential and legislative levels in the Palestinian Territories, with the parliamentary poll significant in breaking the ruling faction Fatah's stranglehold on political power and handing a majority to Hamas. By the same stage, Iraq had organized three national elections – made all the more remarkable, if also somewhat compromised, by deepening violence in the country. In 2005, multi-candidate presidential elections were held in Egypt. A lively, critical opposition movement, Kifiya (Enough), gained prominence, and Egypt's judges pressed the Mubarak government through a process of electoral scrutiny. While Mubarak won the September 2005 presidential elections, the ruling National Democratic Party lost some ground to the Muslim Brotherhood in subsequent parliamentary elections. By this stage, pluralistic and outspoken debate had firmly taken root on issues of political reform in Egypt.

Pro-democracy protests erupted in Lebanon after the assassination of former premier Rafik Hariri, and helped eject Syrian troops from the country in May 2005. In Saudi Arabia, Crown Prince Abdullah launched a national dialogue on political reform in 2003, and in early 2005 competitive municipal elections were held. In Algeria, the army's direct control over the political sphere subsided to a modest degree, while president Bouteflika implemented a number of governance and human rights reforms. In Morocco, a new civil rights code was implemented, which strengthened women's rights, while an Equity and Reconciliation Commission delved into previous human rights abuses. In Jordan, a National Agenda for reform was introduced, piloted later by a reformist government appointed in mid-2005.

Since taking office in 2002 Turkey's Islamist-oriented government has surprised many observers by pushing hard to deepen democratic reforms, appearing to combine successfully religious identity with the development of a competitive, secular political system. The government of Recep Tayyip Erdogan has introduced a raft of reforms improving human rights provisions, expanding Kurdish cultural rights, and targeting corruption in the public administration and judiciary. Crucially, the government has also moved to undercut the army's political pre-eminence, through reducing the powers of the National Security Council (NSC), giving parliament greater control over the military budget, and giving civilians majority representation on the NSC.

Like looking into a reverse mirror, however, each advance almost seems to contain its opposite; like the laws of Newtonian physics, each move forward has generated its own counter-reaction. Some polities in the Middle East have remained resolutely closed. Syria's "Damascus Spring" of apparent opening under Bashar Assad was almost immediately reversed, as the "discussion circles" that had appeared were closed down almost overnight. As hardliners have regained ascendancy in Syria, any contemplation of political reform has been dropped and there have been new clampdowns against democracy activists. Iran's reformist movement propelled by President Mohammed Khatami lost ground to conservatives after 2001. Anti-reform sectors regained primacy within Iran's complexly bifurcated political system, prior to the election of conservative President Ahmadinejad in June 2005. Tunisia has been perhaps the most spectacular "backslider," as the Bin Ali regime has extended its repression of Islamists to stifle any criticism or genuinely autonomous civil society activity.

In Egypt, early 2006 saw an extension of emergency law provisions, harsh security force interventions against opposition demonstrations, the closure of a number of liberal newspapers, and the imprisonment of opposition leader Ayman Nour. The Muslim Brotherhood was still denied official recognition, and had a large number of its supporters detained.

Critics argue that Saudi Arabia's incipient system of consultation – based on the personal petitioning of princes – has in practice simply increased the Al Saud's patronage-based influence. Across the Gulf, limited reforms have been carefully orchestrated by ruling families and parliaments still possess relatively limited powers; reforms have been pursued in a highly top-down fashion, as a means of shoring up the declining legitimacy of the ruling emirs. While still functioning within a nominally reformist mandate, Yemen has suffered a gradual tightening of political space over recent years under the Saleh government and what is increasingly the dominant party system of the General Popular Congress (GPC).

Even in the most reformist states, political liberalization appears to have been tightly controlled. Lebanese elections in the spring of 2005 resulted in a familiar distribution of posts between pro- and anti-Syrian factions, and hopes that the withdrawal of Syrian troops would open the way for a full democratization of Lebanon remained unfulfilled. In Morocco, the Palace retains control over key areas of policy, has clamped down on journalistic freedoms and continues to bar the biggest Islamist organization, Sheikh Yassine's Justice and Solidarity movement. Political *alternance* allows for limited contestation, while serving to broaden the consensus behind the monarchy's continuing dominance. After the 16 May 2003 bombings in Casablanca, the government tightened restrictions on Islamists and removed many critical clerics. A government imposed by the King following elections in 2002 led to an uneasy multi-party coalition, united only by a common support for the monarchy.

In Jordan, soon after taking power King Abdullah moved to suspend parliament and postpone new elections. While elections were eventually held in 2003, limited political reform has been accompanied by deliberate gerrymandering to prejudice both the Islamist opposition and Jordan's Palestinian majority. Reform has been conceived as a vehicle for legitimizing the Jordanian regime through direct plebiscitary links between the government and tribal independents. It has, in contrast, precluded support for countervailing institutions and parties. Change has been directed in a heavily top-down fashion by the King, and even most of the cabinet remains politically illiberal. Both Jordan and Morocco suggest that, rather than relatively free elections being a basis for more critical scrutiny of governments, parliaments have more often become increasingly co-opted into reform processes tightly controlled by regimes.

In similar vein, some observers fear that the continuing prevalence of a nationalist security culture in Turkey constitutes a barrier to full democratization. Frequent skirmishing over second-order issues has been witnessed between the Erdogan government and the Turkish army, and some caution that it remains unclear how broad is the support for the Justice and Development administration to continue re-moulding the country's military-guaranteed constitutional order.

In sum, significant diversity in political trends has emerged across the Middle East, while the limited advance of fully democratic reform is a striking feature throughout the region. Even if the glass of reform is not entirely empty, it would be premature to start posing the standard question of whether it is half full or half empty: a few scarce drops of reform have generated new debate and expectation, but any fundamental reordering of underlying power structures remains generally absent. It may, of course, be seen as entirely unsurprising that Middle Eastern regimes have entertained only cosmetic reform; as in other regions, the issue to be monitored is how far such "managed" change has the unintended consequence of spilling over into more meaningful political liberalization that escapes the containment of autocratic governments.

The focus of analysis of this volume is set by this context. The question here is, what role have international dimensions played in this lack of Middle East democratization? And what significance do they have in relation to the more recent limited and "managed" form of political liberalization entertained by some Middle Eastern governments?

Western foreign policies: a persistent external impediment?

While the primacy of domestic factors must be acknowledged in the Middle East as in other regions (and our study of the international dimensions should not be taken to imply the contrary), the argument can convincingly be sustained that the paucity of political pluralism owes much to external influences. It is widely agreed that international factors have for a long time worked against the prospects for democratic change in the Middle East. A reordering of the international environment since the terrorist attacks of September 11, 2001 has engendered much debate over whether this is in the process of changing. A pertinent question is whether we stand at a watershed moment where external factors can move from being obstacles to being facilitators of Middle Eastern democracy.

The external impediments to democratization in the Middle East originate in the region's process of decolonization. The new Arab elites sanctioned by departing European powers often lacked local credibility, and were rarely noted for their democratic credentials. The uncertain circumstances in which independence was born gave Arab security forces a strong and legitimized hold on power. The nationalist iconic leader soon became central to imbuing the post-colonial state with its legitimacy against a hostile world. National identities had to be imposed and carved out from the top, as colonial powers left legacies of arbitrarily drawn boundaries, with states incorporating a complex mix of ethnic, religious and tribal groupings. Sometimes European powers left minority groups to take over the reins of power, and these quickly assembled the instruments of firm state control in protection against majority ethnic and religious constituencies.

The Middle East's struggle for effective autonomy has been seen by many as the primary factor explaining relations with the West. There was incongruence between the artificial territorial boundaries imposed by colonial powers and Arab identity, which many argue militated against democratization. System-level competition fostered by the international order further undermined Arab solidarity, with destabilizing consequences. Then the 1967 defeat by Israel broke the back of Arab nationalism and led to a re-revival of political Islam as an alternative counter-hegemonic project.[1] This historical legacy continued to inform perspectives on democracy in the region for many years, and often still compromises the potential role of Western powers. Charges are routinely heard that democracy is a specifically "Western" concept, but we should be reminded that many of the state-building concepts that underpinned *non*-democracy in Arab states were equally Western inspired.

As elsewhere in the world, during the Cold War Western powers supported friendly authoritarian states in the Middle East. The logic of containment was compounded as religious extremism intensified and authoritarian regimes came to be seen additionally as a bulwark against political Islam. Political Islam was during this period invariably seen in an unremittingly negative light, as fundamentally hostile to the West and to democratic norms. Islamic doctrine and democracy were commonly assumed to be incompatible. Many saw the rise of "Islamic identities" as irreconcilable with democracy and a pluralist civil society. Critics asserted that Muslims needed to make an enemy of the West as an integral part of their fundamentalism. Deep problems were held to afflict emergent Islamist movements, related with feelings of subjugation, limited con-cepts of individual human rights and historically-rooted pride – not factors that could be easily transcended by a few moderating tweaks to Western policies.[2] For a long time, the standard claim was that Islamists were at best likely to favour democracy merely as an expedient means of obtaining power; power that would be used to disenfranchise the electorate. "One man, one vote, one time" was presumed to be the extent of the Islamist agenda. Moreover, intellectual "Orientalism" remained sceptical that "Western" measures of social and political freedom could be appropriately applied to the Middle East. From various analyt-ical perspectives, indeed, it was cautioned that democratic values were alien to the Middle East, were not what people wanted, and were likely to be poorly understood and destabilizing if shoe-horned into the region. While such assump-tions have mercifully been increasingly rebutted, their sway over many policy-makers in the international community was for a long time difficult to deny.

There was in this sense a profoundly symbiotic and mutually entwined rela-tionship between external dimensions and developments within the region. While external powers sought to shore-up pro-Western autocrats as a defence against radical Islam, political Islam's very radicalism was, at least in part, a product of those same Western policies. This was, of course, seen most dramatically in Iran, where external support for a pro-Western autocrat added to the resentment and frustration that helped to deliver the country into the hands of a theological dictatorship. Similar dynamics were fed by Western involvement in Afghanistan and by the Gulf War in 1990–1. Many feared that such trends were becoming pervasive across the Middle East, the external environment coming to represent a pre-eminent obstacle to democracy and a primary source of illiberal, counter-hegemonic identities in the region.

Against this background, the terrorist attacks of September 11, 2001 appeared to herald a potential change. Western governments seemed to have taken on board the critique of their containment-based strategic policies in the Middle East. It has increasingly been recognized that Middle Eastern resentment against the West can be traced to Western support for the region's repressive authoritarian regimes. One comprehensive study suggested that violence represented a response to political repression more even than to economic deprivation: on economic criteria, Jordan and Morocco should, for instance, have experienced more, not less, violence than Egypt and Algeria.[3] Many analysts suggest that if democracy enabled Islamists to assume power, the mystic appeal of the latter would soon dissolve and (what some saw as) the insularity of their approaches to economic and social imperatives become apparent. The seminal 2002 *Arab Human Development Report* enshrined the first explicit link on the part of the UN between the region's lack of democracy and its economic and social travails; the second report located the region's low knowledge and skills base in the lack of political openness; the third was even more explicit in its focus on the need for democratic reform.[4] Arab regimes have come to spend more than any other region on military expenditure, have created the biggest public sector in the world, and are more reliant on migrants' remittances than any other developing region.

If authoritarianism was initially welcomed as a bulwark against resurgent Islam, its limited success in fulfilling this function was increasingly acknowledged by Western governments. Across the region, nominally pro-Western autocrats had stoked up anti-Western feeling and played to Islamist opinion in order to shore up the precarious legitimacy of their own rule. A vicious circle had taken hold: regimes had often played up the dangers of radical Islamism to justify to the West their own repressive powers, which merely served to foment that radicalism further. This was a particularly notable trend during the late 1990s in Egypt and Jordan, and has, *inter alia*, compromised regimes' containment of opposition to the Oslo peace process. Regimes have neither in practice been cocooned from domestic pressures nor provided the material basis and incentive for moderation within their populations. In a shift away from the "big power" weapons of mass destruction (WMD) security logic of the Cold War, Western analysts and diplomats have come to argue that counter-proliferation strategies are hindered mainly by the lack of transparency of regimes and their fomenting of sub-state actors

These concerns appear to have been reflected in the policies of Western governments. As is now well-known, there have been frequent assertions from Western powers that new strategies are to be implemented to encourage political liberalization in the Middle East. Through both its Middle East Partnership Initiative (MEPI) and the new National Security Strategy (NSS), the rhetorical US commitment to supporting democracy in the region has increased. Both the US and European governments have increased resources going to democracy projects in the Middle East, and have established a range of dialogue forums focusing on political change. These developments led to agreement at the June 2004 G8 meeting on a Broader Middle East and North Africa Initiative, designed to enshrine transatlantic cooperation on democracy promotion in the region.

However, the substance of Western democracy policies in the Middle East has so far remained limited. Western criticism of a number of Arab regimes intensified in the aftermath of September 11 only then gradually to subside, this being the case in particular with Saudi Arabia and Syria. Both the US and the EU have criticized the Egyptian government slightly more than in previous years, but within the scope of policies still based on strategic partnership and generous aid donations. In Morocco, Jordan and Yemen, the partial liberalization described above has been supported and encouraged by Western powers, but the latter have shown little desire or concrete policy intent to push these limited processes of political reform towards democratization. Hamas's victory in the January 2006 Palestinian parliamentary elections met with an international response whose ambivalence suggested that the stated desire to encourage democratization would still be counterbalanced by more direct security concerns.[5]

Geoffrey Pridham argues in this book that the most significant change in the international dimension of democratization has been the increasing imposition of political conditionality.[6] If this is indeed the case, then the Middle East remains an "outlier." Formal democracy-related conditions have been included in a range of both European and US trade and cooperation agreements, but have had a relatively limited impact on the actual substance of engagement-oriented international policies. In early 2006, Yemen was excluded from one US aid programme, and a US–Egyptian free trade agreement was delayed. But, in general, even the more "forward-leaning" US approach to democracy promotion did not bring with it systematic exertion of critical pressure.

Also in this volume, Philippe Schmitter reports a modest, positive correlation between international democracy assistance and political liberalization in four Middle Eastern states between 1980 and 1999.[7] This might be extrapolated to the subsequent period and the argument is made that increases in democracy assistance to the Middle East since 2002 have played a role in generating more intensive debates over reform in the region. In general, however, across these two periods amounts of democracy aid in the Middle East were limited; funding went to relatively "safe" civil society groups, not necessarily the most effective in or desirous of democratic reform; democracy projects were not significantly backed up by focused diplomatic sticks and carrots; and doubts remained over what the West's real intentions were in terms of the extent of reform sought. International democracy support did as much to sanction the cosmetic nature of reform as it did to assist the process of change.

Notwithstanding these limitations, the new international discourse on Middle Eastern democracy does appear to have galvanized debate in the region. The new positions of Western governments have emboldened liberal activists. A series of pro-democracy gatherings have been held and reform declarations issued. Even the Arab League adopted a thirteen-point reform action plan at its meeting in May 2004. This plan was first presented to the Arab League by Saudi Crown Prince Abdullah at the beginning of 2003, but rejected; by 2004, talk of reform had become sufficiently widespread for Arab ministers to feel obliged to adopt a statement based on this plan. Some very specific moves have been made, clearly in response to the apparent shift in Western rhetoric. Examples include the licensing of a slightly wider range of opposition activity in Egypt, the introduction of more liberal women's rights protection in states such as Kuwait, Morocco and Algeria, and the inclusion of "liberals" in government in Yemen and Jordan. Some feel that such debate has fed into gradual genera- tional change, helping younger reformers gain a foothold among Arab political elites. As pointed out, it is clear that governments' changes represent a tactical means of heading off external pressure. The optimist might point out, however, that this was also the case with initial moves in other regions, where cosmetic reforms did unwittingly unleash an ultimately unstoppable momentum of change.

Many analysts, Western diplomats, donors, funding organizations and inter- national institutions claim to have bought into the argument that Islam can be a positive mobilizing force for democracy, social justice and stability in the Middle East.[8] However, despite frequent assertion of a commitment to engage with moderate Islamists, in practice Western governments have remained reluct- ant to offer such groups support. Many talking shops have been convened on "Islam and democracy" and "cultural understanding" between Islam and the West. But Western governments have declined to provide concrete backing for moderate Islamists engaged in pro-democracy campaigning. Dialogue with Islamists has been low key and invariably secret, carried out at the discretion of individual Western ambassadors. While many analysts have suggested that Islamists' control of many professional syndicates offers the possibility for engagement on relatively apolitical issues, donors have distanced themselves from this area of civil society as it has become "Islamatized."

The external factor has been nowhere greater than in the way that European Union policy has enticed Turkey along its protracted path of political reform. At the time of this writing, however, even this apparent successful case of interna- tionally assisted democratization in the Middle East looks open to question. Since the EU accepted Turkey's application to join the EU in 1999, prospective accession has been used by reformists to help propel change. The fluctuating positions of the EU have been used by both sides of the debate in Turkey, and have inextricably entwined themselves into domestic Turkish politics. Definitive judgement on the role of external factors in the long-term success or failure of Turkish democratization must wait until the final decision of the EU on accession is known. While the EU agreed to open formal accession negotiations with Turkey in October 2005, it did so at a time when apparent domestic opposition to Turkey's entry from within Europe rendered it increasingly possible that the EU would renege on its commitments to Ankara. Some fear that the EU has undermined reformers by setting the hurdles higher for Turkey than for other candidates.

The question is whether the carrot of EU accession has sufficed to cajole Turkey sufficiently far towards full democratic consolidation to make any "backsliding" unlikely, even if some in the EU do block Turkey's final steps towards full membership. Current debates within the army and the Justice and Development Party (*Adalet ve Kalkynma Partisi*, AKP) suggest that, while this may indeed generally be the case, the prospect of minor democratic reversals is present. What might safely be concluded is that they way in which the EU–Turkey relationship unfolds will in turn condition Turkey's influence over reform prospects in the wider Middle East. If at least the possibility of EU accession has ignited profound reform in Turkey, the next phase of decisions on the eventuality and timing of Turkey's entry could be one of the most important external determinants of reform potential elsewhere in the Middle East.

Transnational dissemination: the Middle East's weak link?

If this first level of focus on Western foreign policies remains bereft of clearly positive influences on Middle Eastern democratization, so also does a second level of concern with international demonstration effects. Analysis of transnational linkages and the dissemination of norms has become a staple part of intellectual work on the international dimensions of political change. This domain has exhibited a number of significant features in relation to the Middle East.

The dynamics of norms socialization, articulated through transnational civil society linkages, have remained of comparatively limited import in the Middle East. Nothing approaching the same density or "thickness" of transnational liberal civil society links has taken shape as in (most) other regions. The kinds of linkages between political parties and party foundations that were so crucial in Latin America and Eastern Europe are only weakly present in the case of the Middle East. Many such party foundations have struggled with the fact that obvious fraternal counterparts, free of state colonization, can be difficult to identify in Arab countries. In 2005 and 2006, countries such as Bahrain, Syria and Egypt began to restrict even further the scope for such international organizations to operate freely. Western political and civil society organizations have invariably been reluctant to include Islamist organizations within their transnational networks, with a few exceptions, such as the Moroccan Party of Justice and Development (*Parti de la Justice et du Développement*), whose inclusion merely serves to demonstrate the broader trend to the contrary.

The supposed normative appeal of Western democracy has been the subject of fierce debate inside the Middle East. The Kifaya movement in Egypt did take its orange-coloured symbols from the Ukraine. In general, however, most Middle Eastern reformers have placed greater stress on what they insist are persistent differences and specificities. Few Arab reformers appear to have the US or even Europe as normative models present in their political strategizing. Increasingly, they argue, the main demonstration effect is that of democracy failing to protect Muslim rights in the West. This judgement may or may not be proportionate, but the perception must be counted as a negative factor influencing the relative weakness of pro-democracy activism in the Middle East.

Interestingly, democratic socialization dynamics appear not to have fully filtered into concrete democratic reform even with Kings Mohammed VI and Abdullah, whose personal histories could hardly have been *more* exposed to Western-influenced socialization dynamics. At the same time, the regional dimension might be raised as one of the areas of notable change in recent years, with a whole range of pro-democracy forums and gatherings established since 2003.

The nature of political Islam is of particular importance to this transnational dimension. This chapter is not concerned directly with the nature of internal debates within Islam (a subject covered in this volume by George Joffé). What *is* of relevance here is the nature of transnational Islamist dynamics. Political Islam can be seen as having a bearing on international dimensions in the way in which it conditions the kind of transnational civil society networks that have been instrumental to democratic change in other regions. If it is the case that avowedly liberal transnational linkages remain "thin" (both within the Middle East, and between the latter and Western societies), it might be suggested that the potential for norm dissemination has been located far more within cross-border linkages between religious organizations.

It might be argued that such linkages have played their part in the evolution of the "Islam and democracy" debate. The fact that few serious analysts would today question that Islam and democracy are in any way intrinsically and unavoidably incompatible could be seen as itself reflecting social learning and normative entrapment in a changing international system. The continuing focus on this question in some policy quarters is dismissed by those cognizant of Islamist political strategies as a tiresome, long-resolved diversion (even if some at the time argue that genuine concern remains over Islamists' conceptions of individual liberal rights).[9]

However, it might also be asked whether international linkages have not had a negative rather than a positive impact. The prominence of radical Islamist groups has led to concern that, far from democratic norms being internationally disseminated, the trend is more one of *reverse* dissemination. The growing *de*-linkage of "European Islam" and "home country" political pathologies has been the centrepiece of some of the most notable work on changing Muslim identities.[10] Many fear that anti-democratic Islamist clerics have enjoyed increasing influence in Europe. Even though such phenomena are clearly often overstated for domestic political agendas in the West, they do at least add complexity to the standard investigation into democratization's international dimension. An apparent spread of Islamist ideas to the West – even if not presenting the same kind of all-embracing ideological competition as Communism's erstwhile challenge – is seen by critics as sometimes sitting uneasily with Western concepts of individual liberal rights. If international influences work both ways, not only *from* but also *into* the West, this can pose a real predicament for democracy's advance. One prominent analyst opines that if at one extreme lies the danger of a self-fulfilling prophecy of civilizational clash, at the other extreme there is the danger of over-indulging a supposedly homogenous "other" in a fashion that militates against a necessary applicability of universal political values.[11] In short, transnational Muslim networks imbue the politics of democratic dissemination with contrasting dynamics. On the one hand, Muslim communities in the West are regularly posited as potential conveyors of democratic norms to the Middle East; on the other hand, many fear that they also facilitate the spread of Islam's more illiberal strands.

A still different perspective questions just how strong the transnational dimensions of political Islam actually are. Islamists have often cited as a reason for their withdrawal from politics into religious textual doctrine and social activity the judgement that international factors have been prejudicial to Islam – a perception that has sullied the ethical appeal of the democracy promoted through that same international dimension. While political Islam appears to have developed such potency as an international network, some analysts highlight the extent to which Islamists have in practice invariably organized around national agendas, not a pan-Arab political reform programme. Tensions between Arabs, Afghans and Persians; the different political perspectives of Sunni and Shi'a; the distinctive voice of other minorities, such as the Berber; the Arab treatment of Palestinian refugees – all these factors serve to dilute the notion of a common Muslim international political agenda or vision. Conversely, those recognizing the elements of unity in political Islam as an international movement argue that the main focus of these elements has rarely been on a precisely defined political system. Indeed, one view is that Islam has increasingly manifested itself as the "reincarnation of an older Arab nationalism," dressed in what is seen as a more indigenous language and belief system.[12] In sum, despite shifts in the identities of international Islamist networks and in the way these are perceived by Western powers, the international dimension remains an equivocal factor in the prospects for realizing Islam's democratic potential.

The nature of Western policies towards the Israeli–Palestinian conflict also weaves its influence into democracy-related transnational dynamics. The failure to secure a final settlement between Israel and the Palestinians makes it harder to sell democracy, and diverts the energies and focus of linkages between Middle Eastern civil society and international organizations. It is often pointed out that democracy has not become a rallying cry and motivation for action in the Middle East, and that all such protest has rather focused on reacting against Israeli heavy-handedness and perceived Western support for Israel. Ensuring greater civilian democratic control over militaries is complicated by the legitimacy that the non-resolution of the Israeli–Palestinian conflict bestows upon the significant powers retained by militaries. This has fed into radicalism across the region. One view equates Islamic fundamentalism to a "balloon" that will deflate once a Palestinian state is created.[13]

The long-cited Arab–Israeli dispute has now been joined by another international conflict that is regularly judged to have entwined itself deeply into Middle Eastern domestic politics. The Iraqi conflict has been marshalled by both sides of the democracy debate. Even if one discounts the more hyperbolic US claims that Iraqi regime change would provoke a tsunami of democracy across the Middle East, some in the region have noted how Iraq's lack of democracy made it such a weak and polarized society. However, the balance of opinion has seen events since April 2003 as undermining democracy's cause. US policy has led to "democracy promotion" being seen as synonymous with heavy-handed, sovereignty-compromising Western intervention. Shi'a-inspired instability in Iraq has already been used by incumbent Sunni regimes as further justification for a lack of reform. Arguably, the most notable significance of Iraqi events lies in their re-igniting of the Sunni–Shi'a split as a major factor in Middle East politics. The United Nations Development Programme (UNDP) 2003 *Arab Human Development Report* opined that: "The issue of freedom in Arab countries has become a casualty of the overspill from the Anglo-American invasion of Iraq" and that because of Iraqi democracy's predicament was "even graver than before."[14] Of course, the full story of regime change in Iraq remains untold, but as of early 2006 it looked set to do as much to hinder as to spur democratic reform in southern Mediterranean states.

In sum, it would be difficult to deny that Western policies in Palestine and Iraq have had the spill-over effect of weakening the "normative appeal" of Western democracy. This ties in closely with the suggestion made by Laurence Whitehead in this volume that key to the international dimension is an appreciation of the extent to which democratization has increasingly lost its "counter-hegemonic" appeal.

On the other hand, much polling evidence suggests that Arab citizens are perfectly able to distinguish between a dislike for Western foreign policies and their views on the kind of democracy that prevails in the West. Tensions are striking in evolving Arab identities. On the one hand, it is possible to detect more openly stated desires for political modernization of the type that has now spread, to some greater or lesser degree, to every other continent. On the other hand, there appears to be ambivalence amongst Middle Eastern citizens over the prospects of full immersion into a transnational liberal normative community. Whether one views this tension with concern or in positive light, it has important and distinctive implications for our concern here with the impact of international dimensions.

A final factor relating to dissemination dynamics relates to the means through which the Arab nationalism often inspired by these aspects of the international context has spread on a regional basis. The role of dissemination effects conveyed by a newly influential international Arab media has become the subject of fierce debate. The emergence of critical media outlets, linked by new technology across national borders, has played a crucial role in democratization processes across the world. Yet in the Middle East, increasingly popular satellite channels are widely seen in the West as more cause for concern than for hope. Concern over the Al-Jazeera phenomenon has become rife in the West. Positions advanced by the host of London-based media, such as Al-Hayat and Al-Quds, with an increasingly broad reach across the Middle East, are also often uncomfortable for some in the West. But Al-Jazeera and other stations have pioneered coverage of many topical issues that have previously been marked forbidden territory by regimes. Lively and open debates have ensued, incorporating a range of voices. Contrary to Western perceptions, some observers note that many of these discussions do not centre on the evils of the West but instead on a wide range of social issues. The output of publicly-owned media is sometimes more inflammatory and more unhelpful to Western policies than that of the new satellite channels. Al-Jazeera and other international Arab media might be pointed to as democracy's allies and potential carriers of open debate and the dissemination effects seen as so important in other democratic transitions. Optimists argue that state propaganda is no longer the sole source of information in the Middle East, and the state is no longer able to control the international flow of information and debate. If this is the case, US eagerness to suppress these Arab outlets represents an international obstacle to what might serve as a genuine fillip to democratic culture in the Middle East. Some experts remain sceptical, however, that the satellite channels are as yet harbingers of democracy, to the extent that they in practice remain under regimes' control.[15]

International economy and the rentier state

The importance of rentier-based economic activity in the Middle East is routinely cited as a factor militating against democratization – in accordance with the maxim that where states are concerned mainly with the distribution of largesse from natural resource production, a lack of taxation implies less need for representation. Crucial to our analysis here, the relationship of the Middle East's economic structures and the international economy has profoundly conditioned the potential for democratic change. The constraints of globalization promised to unleash political change, but did so in such a destabilizing manner that it ultimately reinforced repressive rule. External factors have done little to temper the prevalence of rentier economics. International investment has been largely limited to the oil and other natural resource industries, and these have remained isolated enclaves within Middle Eastern economies. The Middle East has suffered the highest rate of capital flight of all developing regions, and economic diversification has failed to materialize.[16]

The tender shoots of political liberalization that appeared throughout the region in the late 1980s and early 1990s were driven by international economic factors. Economic crisis provoked by the constraints of globalization and international financial organizations' neo-liberal strictures unleashed waves of protest on the Arab street. Middle Eastern governments became eager to change: giving citizens a political voice was seen partly as a necessary quid pro quo for economic reform and partly as a way of distributing blame for painful reforms. Social mobilization ultimately rested on thin foundations, however. No solidly pro-democratic constituency had assembled itself, middle classes remained nervous about breaking their privileged links with regime elites and, as Algeria showed most starkly, it was radical Islamists who promised to fill the void opened by precipitate signs of political reform. If economic internationalization appeared to open the door for reform, it was subsequently the pretext used by regimes for slamming closed this opportunity and arguing that economic reform required an even firmer governmental hand on the tiller. As general critiques of globalization have so often noted, the lack of effective popular say over altern- ative economic models can undermine the whole notion of democratic choice – in the Middle East, this fed into a disillusion that provoked a repressive backlash from the political elites that had begun to cede some control.

The question here is whether internationally driven globalization and eco- nomic liberalization might ultimately prove a key to change in the Middle East. In some respects this international economic dimension would seem to be particularly apposite in this region, as its problems have so much to do with pat- terns of state control over economies dependent on natural resource exploitation. In comparative terms, what is still striking is the absence from southern Mediter- ranean states of any overwhelming and unambiguous middle-class agitation for democratic reform. Economic reform does not appear to have entailed a diminu- tion of rentier-type dynamics sufficient to foster pressure for democratic control over the exercise of public administration. No other region has reached similar levels of economic development with such a paucity of organized and effective private-sector support for democratization. Secular actors have notoriously either backed or at least tolerated regimes as a bulwark against Islamists. At the same time, regimes have skilfully built up cross-cutting alliances amongst eco- nomic actors, bureaucracies and unions, playing these off against each other and retaining relations of dependency.[17]

The economic liberalization subsequently pushed by international institutions since the 1990s has not yet had unequivocally positive implications for demo- cratic potential. In the region's star economic reformer, Tunisia, market reform has been accompanied by – and indeed facilitated by – tighter political control. Across the region, regimes have succeeded in tightly managing economic reform, and patrimonial style rule has actually intensified as regimes have taken it upon themselves to allocate the benefits of new market and regulatory activity. In many states, as economic reform has forced the retreat of the welfare state, it has been Islamist organizations that have filled the vacuum, providing local welfare services. Economic change forced by globalization has in this way been associated more with the rise in Islamic than in democratic identities. Economic liberalization has failed to convert into sustainable political change as it rests upon such fragile foundations, and not upon economic structures that are sufficiently modernizing and diversifying. One contrasting case may be Turkey, in many ways already the region's most diversified and modern economy; here, a process of gradual economic change followed by a severe crisis, in 2002, did feed into democratic reform. Fluctuations in international oil prices have also unleashed contrasting dynamics: the gradual decline in oil prices had done more than anything to occasion talk of Saudi Arabia needing to broaden its representative legitimacy; the rapid rise in oil prices since 2004 has refilled the Al Saud's coffers and potentially reversed the main factor driving change, but has also lain behind the increasing instability of the kingdom, that might yet tip over into dramatic political change.

Conclusions

Two extremes must be avoided in the Middle East; on the one hand, the view that features of modernity have all come to the region from outside; on the other hand, the perceived need to justify everything in terms of purely domestic tradition. International influences could readily play a more positive role in the Middle East's political modernization, within a clearer understanding of this balance between national specificities and desired external linkages. There is some evidence that international factors might at least be moving to constitute less of an unmitigated barrier to political liberalization. It must, of course, be recognized that the models of internationally-influenced change witnessed elsewhere cannot be replicated in the Middle East. This would fail to conceive Islam as something of positive value, and risk assuming it to be simply an aberration caused by social and economic problems. But it might also understate some of the undeniable challenges relating to Islam that cannot easily be dismissed. Even if Islamists have shifted back towards modernism, their influence still provokes profound polarization, which renders the prospect of change more destabilizing for many, and prohibits unity in civil society as a force for change. This is a key to understanding the difficulty in building broad-based consensus for reform across the region, and to explaining why international linkages have been hard to establish in the Middle East around the kinds of negotiated or "pacted" transition often supported through external agency in parts of southern Europe and Latin America. Yet, the danger also exists of seeing the region entirely through the lens of political Islam, and of thus neglecting the way that economic and communications internationalization might indeed be better managed to assist democratic potential. The nexus of factors considered in this chapter – regional conflict, religious identity, economic change, and security alliances – presents increasing diversity in the way that linkages to the international sphere impact upon domestic political trends. The international dimensions of potential democratization are both more prominent and more varied than they have ever been in the Middle East.

Notes

1 Raymond Hinnebusch, *The International Politics of the Middle East*. Manchester: Manchester University Press, 2003.
2 Bernard Lewis, *The Crisis of Islam: Holy War and Unholy Terror*. London: Weidenfeld & Nicolson, 2003, 21.
3 Mohammed M. Hafez, *Why Muslims Rebel: Repression and Resistance in the Islamic World*. Boulder, CO: Lynne Reinner, 2002.
4 United Nations, *Arab Human Development Report 2002*. Geneva: UNDP, 2002, Chapter 10; United Nations, *Arab Human Development Report 2003*. Geneva: UNDP, 2003, Chapter 8; United Nations, *Arab Human Development Report 2004*. Geneva: UNDP, 2004.
5 For a detailed account of European strategies, see Richard Youngs, *Europe and the Middle East: In the Shadow of September 11*. Boulder, CO: Lynne Reinner (2006).
6 Geoffery Pridham, Chapter 3 in this volume.
7 Philippe Schmitter, Chapter 2 in this volume.
8 One example is François Burgat, *Face to Face with Political Islam*. London: IB Tauris, 2003.
9 Carnegie Endowment for International Peace and Herbert-Quandt Stiftung, "Islamist Movements and the Democratic Process in the Arab World: Exploring the Gray Zones," Carnegie Working Paper 67, March 2006.
10 Olivier Roy, *Vers un islam européen*. Paris: Éditions Esprit, 1999.
11 Fred Halliday, op. cit., pp. 122 and 131.
12 François Burgat, op. cit., p. xiv.
13 Etel Solingen, "Toward a Democratic Peace in the Middle East," in: Amin Saikal and Albrecht Schnabel (eds.), *Democratization in the Middle East*. Geneva: United Nations University Press, 2003, pp. 52 and 56.
14 United Nations, *Arab Human Development Report 2003*. Geneva: UNDP, 2003, pp. 31–2.
15 Fred Halliday, *100 Myths about the Middle East*. London: Saqi Books, 2006, p. 41.
16 Raymond Hinnebusch, op. cit.
17 Daniel Brumberg, "Liberalization versus Democratization: Understanding Arab Political Reforms," Carnegie Endowment for International Peace Working Paper 37, 2003.

10 Democracy and the Muslim world

George Joffé

Introduction

There is an increasingly widespread view that the root causes of social and political tensions in the Muslim world, together with economic failure, arise from poor governance. In the Middle East and North Africa in particular, the persistence of despotic regimes is adduced as the source of regional failure, quite apart from the specific political issues in the region or the economic problems associated with the rentier states resulting from dependence on hydrocarbon production as the source of economic wealth. There is thus growing pressure on Arab states to engage in the process of democratization, in the belief that this will, alone, provide the basis for a resolution of the region's problems. This, certainly, is the view of the neo-conservatives who have recently dominated the foreign policy and intellectual establishment in Washington.[1] It has, as a result, also become the normative theme in much international relations discourse throughout the West and in the Middle Eastern and North African region itself.

The nature of democracy

The assumption that the advent of democracy, alone, will resolve the manifold problems of the Middle East and North Africa is questionable, to say the least. It is, nevertheless, true that few regimes in the region are "participatory" in that they actively encourage meaningful popular political participation in the process of governance. Nor are they "democratic" within the dictionary definition of the term.[2] In addition, it also seems to be the case that there are ideological and cultural objections to the usual interpretation of the term "democracy," at least as it is portrayed in the United States and Europe.[3] Thus Ali Bel Hadj, one of the Algerian Islamist leaders of the early 1990s, was widely reported as saying in February 1989 that: "there is no democracy because the only source of power is Allah through the Koran, and not the people. If the people vote against the law of God, this is nothing other than blasphemy." In December 1989, his colleague, Abbasi Madani, then president of the Islamic Salvation Front (*Front Islamique du Salut*, FIS) remarked: "We do not accept this democracy which permits an elected official to be in contradiction with Islam, the *Shari'a*, its doctrines and values."[4]

This apparent rejection of democracy within the Islamic world leads one to speculate whether "democracy," as understood in secular Western states, is really incompatible with Islamic values and principles.[5] This, in turn, raises other considerations, not least about what the nature of "democracy" really is, and what it actually represents within the process of governance. Governance within a state is essentially a process of manipulating power for the purposes of administration and control – hence Max Weber's famous dictum that the state is the entity with the monopoly of the legitimate use of violence.[6] Democracy, then, is a means for controlling and legitimizing that power. It is, in other words, a technique of governance legitimized by the fact that it provides a mechanism – the electoral process – by which all members of society may, directly or indirectly, participate in the process of decision-making and the subsequent articulation of power.

It is also, however, a mechanism for limiting the application of power. Friedrich Hayek, who seems to have had a poor opinion of democracy, for he saw within it the potential for dictatorship by the majority, nevertheless admired its potential to ensure the replacement of government without violence on a regular basis.[7] Democracy is limited in another sense, for it also defines the arena for permissible political action by excluding the possibility of political change through violence, in addition to its function of enabling popular participation in governance. This implies that there must be an agreed and independent system for determining where the barriers to such action may lie, and which can also sanction action that extends beyond it.

There must be, in other words, an independent system of the rule of law, which can sanction government, should it exceed the limits placed upon its freedom of action,[8] which itself also enjoys legitimacy through popular support because of the way in which it has been instituted – by popular consent and by reference to generally accepted and sanctioned standards of social and political behaviour. It is based, in essence, on the codification of a consensus of what inalienable individual rights should be, and is a mechanism to protect the individual, whether as an individual or as a member of a collective – society, in short – against the depredations of unfettered governance.

Associated with it is the idea that counters, in part at least, Hayek's objection of the paramount nature of democratic political power in the interstices of the electoral process, at least in liberal democracies based on indirect participation. This is the role of civil society, which mediates between the state and society, acting as a brake on the potential excesses of the former and a medium of communication with the state for the latter, which it also democratizes. This concept of civil society, of course, is a modern variant of the original term, which goes back to Locke and reflects the individual's social actions to protect property rights. It thus, according to Hegel[9] and, after him, Marx and Gramsci, evolved into a mechanism designed to evade the coercive power of the state, particularly in social and economic spheres. In its modern form, however, it is not just the prerogative of the bourgeoisie but applies to society at large, filling the political space between family and state as mediator between the two.[10]

The ideal Islamic vision

Behind all of these attributes, however, lies a fundamental assumption, in which lies the apparent rejection of the democratic process by Islamists. It is that the sovereign use of power in Western societies is a popular attribute.[11] In other words, the ultimate operation of political power lies in the hands of the society embodied in the state, for which the state acts as organizing principle. Further-more, because society itself is composed of individuals, the ultimate repository of sovereignty lies within the individuals who themselves make up society. In Islamic political and constitutional theory, however, sovereignty is a divine attribute which may be delegated to those qualified to use it but is still the prop-erty of divinity, a consequence of the overriding Islamic principle of *tawhid* (unity).[12]

This very significant and fundamental difference in the mode of legitimiza-tion of power – popular versus divine sanction – has a profound consequence for the devout Muslim in that it means that democratic sanction is, at least in prin-ciple, impossible in the Western sense. Instead, the legitimacy of political action is decided not by popular approval – even if limited by the autonomous exist-ence of a code of law or by the actions of civil society – but by its concordance with divine revelation or sanction. In other words, it is not open to society to provide majoritarian approval of the exercise of power to make it legitimate and viable. Instead, there is a hierarchical pattern of authority, by a process of dele-gation, in accordance with divine precept, from the divine principle to the ruling body for the exercise of state power.

Although this would appear to exclude any question of popular participation in the political process, this was not entirely the case because of the way in which those to whom divine sovereignty was delegated were chosen. In essence, the community had to authenticate the choice that was made, for only in Shi'a political theory were rights of authority subject to agnatic inheritance. There were, it is true, a series of criteria available to establish the choice of *khalīfa* (caliph-delegate), largely derived from the experience of the first four *rashīdun* ("rightly-guided") caliphs after the Prophet Muhammad, who were held to exemplify the caliphate ideal type.[13] However, there was a general consensus that the caliph should be elected from suitable candidates by leading members of society, the *ahl al-h?all wa'l-'aqd* ("those who unbind and bind," usually doctors of religious law, the *ulamā*) and that the election should be subsequently authenticated by groups and individuals within the community – in this case, of course, the *umma*, the unitary community of Muslims – by the delivery of a *bay'a*, a formal, written ratification of the contract implied by the electoral process. The contractual implication was that the community offered the caliph obedience in return for him discharging the function of governance in accord-ance with Islamic precept.[14]

In addition, although one of the major concerns of the ideal Islamic system was to avoid *fitna* (disorder) at almost any cost, which implied that rebellion against established authority was innately and absolutely illegal and unacceptable,[15] there were also legitimate mechanisms to unseat a caliph who breached his religious and legal obligations, given that "there is no obedience in sin."[16] Thus, a breach by the caliph of the terms of his *bay'a* could legitimize rebellion. This particular principle has been revived in modern Islamist movements and, as Sayid Qutb said, "This is an emphasis on one of the main principles of authority in Islam; the unjust ruler has no claim to obedience."[17]

There was also a code in the *Shari'a* telling the caliph what should guide his actions. This was the corpus of Islamic religious law, derived from the *Qur'an*, and the traditions of the Prophet Muhammad[18] – the *sunna* – and the Prophet's sayings, the *hadīth*. This could be supplemented by *qiyas* (argument by analogy) and, up to the fourteenth century at least, by *ijtihād* (innovative reasoning in accordance with established Islamic principles). Such innovation, otherwise normally excluded as *bid'a* (innovation) and thus leading to *fitna*, was legitimized by the principle of *ijmā'* (consensus), initially amongst the learned in law (the *fuqahā'*), but subsequently amongst Muslims as a whole, in accordance with one of the traditions, which claims that "my people will never agree upon an error."

In fact, there were implicitly two contradictory concepts of the caliphate within this ideal structure, namely the view that the caliph's power was absolute and immutable, for he was the "Shadow of God upon earth," and the vision of the caliphate as a contractual institution, limited by law and popular consensus. Such consensus was reflected in the much later institution of *shura*, the consultation by the ruler of senior figures within Muslim society over the process of governance on the basis of the tradition cited above. Indeed, such an institution never existed under the caliphate as a formal council within government, certainly not before the Abbasid caliphate in Baghdad was destroyed by the Mongol invasion in the mid-thirteenth century. It is, in effect, a very recent institution that emerged out of the nineteenth-century confrontation with European colonialism in the Middle East.

Yet, although the caliphate fragmented into autonomous states after the collapse of the Abbasids in 1258 CE, each of the subsequent states that emerged operated along similar lines, using the principles of delegation of sovereign authority described by al-Mawardi.[19] The same principles generally applied during the Ottoman Empire where, as states broke away, they still recognized the suzerainty of the Ottoman ruler in Istanbul, even accepting his dubious claims to the status of caliph, until the caliphate was formally abolished by Kemel Ataturk in 1924.[20] But the concept is still not dead, for its abolition gave rise to the *Khalafiyya* movement in the Indian sub-continent in the immediate aftermath of its abolition, and to the revival of the concept of the caliphate inside political Islamic discourse since the 1970s.

Democracy and Islam

At first sight, therefore, there appears to be no real basis for accommodation between the democratic and Islamic ideal-type traditions of governance. One is essentially temporal and secular in its concept of sovereign legitimization, while the other locates sovereignty within the sphere of divinity. One involves direct popular participation in governance, and the other sees authority as hierarchical and divinely inspired. One establishes political choice as ultimately being a popular majoritarian prerogative, and the other only allows for consultation and consensus within society as a contribution to the individual decisions of a ruler and the principles of doctrine. Yet there are similarities, too, for both require authority to be exercised in accordance with autonomous concepts of law over which neither has control. Both do involve popular consultation over the exercise of power, and both involve, at some level, electoral choice.

The essential problem resides, of course, in the definition of sovereignty, for as long as this remains a divine attribute, it is extremely difficult to see how (in principle at least) a political system of the kind we consider to be democratic can be based on Islamic precepts. Of course, this does not preclude the creation of democratic systems in the Middle East and North Africa, or even in the wider Muslim world, but it does engender philosophical tensions which filter through into demotic political cultures in the region, undermining not the formal institutions of democratic governance but threatening much of its philosophical and moral import. It is this phenomenon, alongside the cynical behaviour of authoritarian governance seeking to adapt to external pressure, that produces the self-destructive concept of "façade democracy," in which democratic institutions are denuded of all meaningful democratic content.

There is no doubt that, in its Western sense, "democracy" is an aggressively secular concept, as its assumptions about sovereignty make clear. Its focus revolves around the concept of "the people," and its concerns are exclusively related to the temporal world, as Abraham Lincoln revealed when he defined it as "government by the people, for the people and of the people."[21] This is, in large measure, a consequence of the tripartite secularization process introduced by the Reformation in Europe – of intellectual activity, of the political process and of economic activity, all of which had previously been subject to religious sanction as a consequence of revealed truth.[22]

The immediate consequence of this was to exclude religious sanction from public life, for it was no longer necessary for the purpose of authenticating political action or intellectual activity. Rationalism alone was all that was necessary to determine the nature of the public, temporal sphere of action, and thus reflected the secular environment in which it operated. Religion, of course, remained and remains a vital personal activity – as the religious right in America has demonstrated. But attempts to re-establish it as the moral principle of public political life provoke massive resistance because the principle of secular politics is so central to the democratic political process.

This is certainly in direct contradiction with the idealist version of political governance in Islam, which is explicitly based on the concept of revealed truth. It is this fact that has led many to argue that Islam must undergo its own "reformation" and thus domesticate religious belief to the private sphere of individual activity, rather than allowing it to dominate the public sphere. Only then, it is proposed, can the Islamic world adapt to the practicalities of democratic governance. In fact, such an approach is to ignore the richness of the Islamic tradition, for there are other traditions that might have achieved the same purpose as the Reformation.

One of these, which dates back to the very early days of Islam, and runs hand-in-hand with the astonishing outburst of intellectual activity that attended the discovery of the philosophical and scientific heritage from classical Greece, was the *mu'tazila*. The ideas of this group arose from an attempt to circumvent the extremism of other currents which challenged Islamic orthodoxy. Its members argued that God was in essence infinite justice, and as such could not be responsible for human evil, so that man had free will.[23] Over time, their concept of God was increasingly determined by their appreciation of Platonic thought and argument, in which He was increasingly removed from the realm of human action. Indeed, "in one sense, Mu'tazilism ended up as a philosophical religion where reason was for a little raised to a position superior to that of the Divinity Himself."[24]

One interesting by-product of their philosophy was that the religious role of the caliph – as *imām* setting the normative parameters of collective behaviour – was not essential if the *umma* were unified, particularly if they were unified around *mu'tazili* doctrine[25] – an idea that seems suspiciously close to the idea of a self-justifying political entity inherent in the democratic ideal, although the *mu'tazila* would never have drawn such conclusions themselves. Perhaps the most important historical consequence for our purposes was that the *mu'tazila*, after they had been crushed by orthodox Islamic thought, had paved the way for the *falsafa* tradition, epitomized by Ibn Sina and Ibn Rushd. Both argued that an awareness of God was accessible through reason as well as through belief, and Ibn Rushd in particular argued that the natural world was accessible to rational explanation – although he would not have admitted that there was any inherent distinction between rational and revealed truth.[26]

As has been pointed out, such views produce the result that:

> In fact, it was religion which was to pay the price of this "agreement" [between rational and revealed truth]. It was philosophy which was to discount the apodictic truth; religion did no more than "clothe" the images to bring them to the level of the mass of the people. This accounts for the attempt of some Christian thinkers to interpret this attitude as the acceptance of a "double truth," which the Commentator [Averroes; Ibn Rushd] would have professed and which they would have willingly accepted as their position. But in fact it meant destroying religion and theology, since it was estimated that on the essential points they would be in contradiction with reason.[27]

In other words, such views would inevitably lead to the secularization of the public arena within the Islamic world, thus creating precisely the conditions in which democracy can flourish. Indeed, the Young Ottoman movement, in the late nineteenth century, revived the ideas of the *falsafa* movement in order to justify calls for a democratic constitution for the Ottoman Empire, which was granted in 1876. They called for constitutional and parliamentary government on the basis of a return to the spirit of early Islam, "which recognised the sovereignty of the people and the principle of government by consultation."[28] Lying behind this was what Sadyk Rifat Paşa regarded as the essential principle of justice, rather than liberty, and of the essential right of the individual to benefit from just rule.[29]

Interestingly enough, the same principles apply today within the moderate Turkish Islamist movement. It is typified by the arguments contained inside the influential intellectual review *Girişim*, which has argued that "pluralism" is innate to Islam, limited only by adherence to the basic principles of the *Qur'an*, the *sunna* and "belief," and by the requirement that no attempt be made to align the West and the Muslim world in terms of political institutions, for Islam and democracy are incompatible. Pluralism itself, however, is a consequence of the faculty of reason (*aql*), which is itself of divine origin.[30] Although the argument was developed in the 1980s to counter tendencies towards authoritarianism, not to promote democracy (which it specifically excludes), it does demonstrate that there are traditions of multiple interpretation based on reason within the Islamic context that provide opportunities for the construction of political plurality. This, in turn, raises the speculation as to whether secularism is essential for forms of governance based on political participation.

It seems that many contemporary moderate and innovative Islamic political theorists do not see this requirement as a bar to democracy inside the Islamic context. Rachid Ghannouchi, for instance, makes the point that:

> Islam is unique in that it alone recognizes pluralism within and outside its own frontiers. Within, no religious wars are known to have ever taken place. While on the one hand Islam guarantees the right of its adherents to *ijtihad* in interpreting Quranic text, it does not recognize a church or an institution or a person as a sole authority speaking in its name or claiming to represent it. Decision-making, through the process of *Shari'a*, belongs to the community as a whole. Thus, the democratic values of political pluralism and tolerance are perfectly compatible with Islam.[31]

Ghannouchi's argument, however, does not address the problem of freedom of expression, which implies that the public sphere must be secular, although he implies that this is a false issue.

It is unlikely that most observers would agree with him, and the problem has been addressed by the Iranian philosopher, Abdolkarim Soroush, who bases his arguments on Shi'a tradition – which some have argued was originally paralleled by the *mu'tazila*.[32] He has argued that, in general, the political application of Islamic theology deforms religion and prevents genuine popular participation in the process of governance. The only form of religious government that does not do this, he argues, is one that is democratic, for democracy is a form of government which is compatible with a multitude of political cultures, including

Islam. Furthermore, "Any religious government that rules without societal consent, or restricts this right, abrogates the public's conception of justice and sacrifices its legitimacy." A commentator on his views suggests that:

Democracy is both a value system and a method of governance. As a value system, it respects human rights, the public's right to elect its leaders and hold them accountable, and the defence of the public's notion of justice. As a method of governance, democracy includes the traditional notions of the separation of powers, free elections, free and independent press, of freedom of expression, freedom of political assembly, multiple political parties and restrictions on executive power.

Soroush argues that no government official should stand above criticism, and that all must be accountable to the public. Accountability reduces the potential for corruption, and allows the public to remove or restrict the power of incompetent officials. Democracy is, in effect, a method for "rationalizing" politics.[33]

Soroush, however, does not offer a *carte blanche* to Western liberal concepts of democracy, for he distinguishes between "political democracy" and "liberal democracy," in which liberal democracy was castigated for its moral licence,[34] the ultimate consequence of its libertarian values. This was a point that he repeated in his address during the award of the Erasmus Prize to him in November 2004:

I am of the firm conviction that mankind today is in dire need of a spiritual interpretation of the universe as well as a spiritual emancipation (as Mohammad Iqbal once said). In my humble endeavours, therefore, I try to emancipate spirituality from the cage of officially-organized religions. As for the masses who seek spirituality within an organized religion I offer a more tolerant interpretation thereof. In the field of political ethics I always remind myself and my friends of the horrible gap between rights and duties in modern society. Too much emphasis on the rights in the liberal West has led to the virtual neglect of human duties and responsibilities. On the other hand, too much concentration on obligations has made rights practically invisible in the East. A balance therefore has to be struck between the two in order to readjust the human condition to ideal human values.[35]

One interesting speculation regarding the reasons justifying the rejection of secularism and the retention of the concept of divine sovereignty in Islamic governance is provided by Fatema Mernissi.[36] She argues that the classical Islamic social and political environment is one of order and boundaries, based on the collective, not the individual. In some respects, the aggressive secularism of Western-style democracy evokes the chaos of *jāhiliyya*, the pre-Islamic world that lacked order and divine sanction. Thus resistance to democratic modernity is also a reflection of a conservative political culture which fears the damage wrought to its institutions and traditions by democratic change, for the two cannot be melded together. Indeed, as Dr Soroush pointed out, there is a cultural clash as well as a definitional contradiction which bedevils the process of adapting democracy to the Muslim environment.[37] Interestingly enough, similar ideas of fear of the democratic alternative have been used to explain European reluctance in the past to wholeheartedly adopt such institutions and processes. De Tocqueville, for example, identified conformity and anxiety as the cultural and psychological consequences of such fear – a situation not unlike that described by Fatema Mernissi.[38]

An alternative approach

Indeed, it seems impossible to find a complete coincidence between Western democratic paradigms and the principles which inform legitimate political structures within an Islamic context, largely because of the difficulty of excluding Islam from the public sphere. Yet it is also clear that Muslims, as much as anybody else, seek the alleged benefits that emerge from the democratic process, and Islamic intellectual tradition seems, in many respects, to seek the same outcome as democracy in the West. Indeed, some Muslim countries, such as Turkey and Indonesia, apparently operate democratic systems without too many problems, while others, such as Iran or Morocco, operate political systems that are plural in nature.

Perhaps the attempt to establish a coincidence between two systems that are, at base, techniques of governance is in itself misguided, and a more productive approach would be to consider outcomes. In the West, good and bad governance is usually equated with liberty and tyranny; in the Muslim world, the parallel to liberty was traditionally justice, for, as Bernard Lewis points out, liberty had a legal, not a political significance.[39] "Liberty," however, has increasingly been defined in terms of individual human rights, in which the state guarantees the individual essential rights of freedom of expression, assembly and association – a view which approximates to the traditional Islamic vision of social justice. Many Muslim states, moreover, subscribe to the Universal Declaration of Human Rights, although some enter derogations or have not signed for specifically religious reasons – eight of the original forty-eight signatories were Muslim states.[40] Thus, in many respects, it might be a more useful question to ask whether or not the appropriate political conditions exist within the Islamic world and within the political corpus of Islam to guarantee such rights.

In this context, it seems that the institutions that are available to guarantee and protect such rights are very similar in each political system. Both provide mechanisms for popular political participation, and provide for accountability. Both maintain autonomous legal systems as part of this process, to protect the individual and to restrain the process of governance. And both offer informal mechanisms to mediate between family and state in the form of civil society. Indeed, in the Arab World, such traditions are of considerable antiquity, even though they may not yet form the dense network of organizations that characterize the Western model and render it so effective.[41] The elements necessary to achieve such social justice thus seem to exist in both political systems, separated only by the demand for one to acquire divine sanction and for the other to justify itself by an egalitarian secularism.[42] But, as de Tocqueville pointed out, a shared Christian morality was essential to the survival of American democratic republicanism in the nineteenth century, since it was the only way in which unrestrained liberty could be checked and the danger of a descent into anarchy avoided!

Indeed, there are grounds to consider whether or not this is a distinction without also being a difference, for de Tocqueville's views mirror those of Abdolkarim Soroush. In the end, it is the way in which either system is operated that provides it with the ability to guarantee the individual rights to which both – at least as far as the Arab world is concerned – subscribe. And for that to succeed, the real issue is the one highlighted in the middle of the nineteenth century by Alexis de Tocqueville, when he claimed that:

> I am thoroughly convinced that political societies are not what their laws make them but what they are prepared in advance to be by the feelings, the beliefs, the ideas, the habits of heart and mind of the men who compose them.[43]

In short, it is not so much the question of the construction of political institutions but the fostering of political culture that will eventually achieve the objective of good governance in the Middle East and North Africa.

Notes

1 See: Stefan Halper and Jonathan Clarke, *America Alone: The Neo-Conservatives and the Global Order*. Cambridge: Cambridge University Press, 2004, p. 218.

2

> Government by the people; a form of government in which power resides in the people and is exercised by them either directly or by means of elected representatives; a form of society which favours equal rights, the ignoring of hereditary class distinctions, and tolerance of minority views.
> Lesley Brown (ed.), *The New Shorter Oxford English Dictionary*.
> Oxford: Clarendon Press, 1993, Vol. I, p. 629.

3 See: Fatema Mernissi, *Islam and Democracy: Fear of the Modern World*. London: Virago, 1993, p. 3.

4 This is quoted in the shadow report for the United Nations Human Rights Commission (UNHRC) in 2001, prepared by the International League for Human Rights.

5 Bernard Lewis certainly considers that proponents of political Islam as a specific holistic ideology – Islamists – are not prepared to consider democracy as anything other than a means to attain power. As he says,

> For Islamists, democracy, expressing the will of the people, is the road to power, but it is a one-way road, on which there is no return, no rejection of the sovereignty of God, as exercised through His chosen representatives. The electoral policy has been classically summarized as "One man (men only), one vote, once."
> Bernard Lewis, *The Crisis of Islam: Holy War and Unholy Terror*.
> London: Phoenix, 2003, p. 88.

6 Max Weber, "Politik als Beruf," in: Max Weber, *Gesammelte Politische Schriften*. Munich: Duncker and Humblot, 1921, p. 397.

7 Friedrich Hayek, *New Studies in Philosophy, Politics, Economics and the History of Ideas*. London: Routledge & Kegan-Paul, 1978, p. 152.

8 There is, of course, an inherent contradiction in this, in that the usual mechanism for establishing law is the prerogative of a legislature – which itself is to be restricted by it! This is at its most evident in the sovereignty of the House of Commons within the British democratic system, and clashes between government and the judiciary are often, at base, clashes between a sovereign legislature and the judiciary. In most cases – and this does not apply in Britain – this potential contradiction is overcome by the definition of basic legal principle upon which the state should operate in a constitution. Interestingly enough, in Britain, this function is increasingly provided by the effect of external, supra-national institutions and provisions, such as the United Nations Charter of Human Rights (UNCHR) and the European Charter of Human Rights (ECHR) which have been incorporated into British law by parliamentary decision. The term "rule of law" is nevertheless inherent to British constitutional practice, even though no formal constitution exists. See Albert Venn Dicey (1885, 1985), *Introduction to the Study of the Law of the Constitution*. London and New York: Macmillan, 1985.

9 Georg Wilhelm Friedrich Hegel, *Grundlinien der Philosophie des Rechts*, 1821 (translated by Hugh Barr Nisbet, in Allen W. Wood, Raymond Geuss and Quentin Skinner (eds.), *Hegel: Elements of the Philosophy of Right*. Cambridge: Cambridge University Press, 1991, pp. xvii and 220–39.

10 Jillian Schwedler (ed.), *Toward Civil Society in the Middle East? A Primer*. Boulder, CO: Lynne Rienner, 1995, pp. 6–7.

11 Anthony Arblaster, *Democracy*. Milton Keynes: Open University Press, 1987, p. 8.

12 Amin Saikal, *Islam and the West: Conflict or Cooperation?* London: Macmillan/Palgrave, 2003, p. 124.

13 Abu al-Hasan Ali al-Mawardi, *Al-Ah?kām al-Sultāniyya*, 1058 (translated as Edmond Fagnan, *Mawerdi: les statuts gouvernementaux*. Paris: Editions Sycamore, 1982), describes seven such criteria, for example.

14 Anne K. S. Lambton, *State and Government in Medieval Islam*. Oxford: Oxford University Press, 1981, pp. 13–18.

15 Moroccan jurists coined the adage that, "To him who holds power, obedience is due." See: Elie Kedourie, *Politics in the Middle East*. Oxford: Oxford University Press, 1992, p. 9.

16 Anne K. S. Lambton, op. cit., p. 19.

17 Sayed Kotb, *Social Justice in Islam*. Washington, DC: American Council of Learned Societies, 1953, p. 187. This is a translation of S. Qutb, *Al-'Adālah al-Ijtimā'yah fi al-Islām*. Cairo: Maktabat Misr, 1945.

18 In fact, this was the traditions of the behaviour of his Companions, the *Ansar*.

19 Edmond Fagnan, op. cit., pp. 43–57.

20 Bernard Lewis, *The Crisis of Islam*, op. cit., p. xvi.

21 President Lincoln's address, delivered at Gettysburg on November 19, 1863.

22 George Joffé, "Democracy, Islam and the Culture of Modernisation," *Democratization* 4 (3), 1997: 136–8.

23 Anne K. S. Lambton, op. cit., pp. 36–42.

24 Dominique Sourdel, *Medieval Islam*. London: Routledge & Kegan-Paul, 1983, p. 76.

25 Ian R. Netton, *Muslim Neo-Platonists: An Introduction to the Thought of the Brethren of Purity*. London: George Allen & Unwin, 1982, p. 103.

26 William Montgomery-Watt, *Islamic Philosophy and Theology*. Edinburgh: University of Edinburgh Press, 1962, p. 97. See also: Majid Fakhry, *A History of Islamic Philosophy*. London: Longman, 1983, p. 276.

27 J. Schacht and C. E. Bosworth (eds.), *The Legacy of Islam*. Oxford: Oxford University Press, 1974, p. 384.

28 Bernard Lewis, *The Emergence of Modern Turkey*. London and Oxford: RIIA-Oxford University Press, 1961, p. 169.
29 Bernard Lewis, ibid., p. 130. He was one of the precursors of the Young Ottomans in the late 1830s, as was Ziya Paşa who, some years later used a Prophetic tradition to justify an assembly expressing different opinions and entitled to examine and criticize ministers (p. 137) and Namyk Kemal who, in the 1860s and 1870s, linked parliamentary governance with human rights on the basis of Islamic exegesis (p. 140).
30 Ayse Güneş-Ayata, "Pluralism versus Authoritarianism: Political Ideas in Two Islamic publications," in: Richard Tapper (ed.), *Islam in Modern Turkey: Religion, Politics and Literature in a Secular State*. London: IB Tauris, 1994, p. 263.
31 Lecture to the Royal Institute of International Affairs (London) on 9 May 1995, published in *Maghreb Quarterly Report* 18, 1995: 58.
32 Ian R. Netton, op. cit., p. 100.
33 Vala Vakili, *Debating Religion and Politics in Iran: The Political Thought of Adbolkarim Soroush*. New York, NY: Council of Foreign Relations, 1996, pp. 21–3.
34 "Islam and Democracy," excerpts from a speech by Dr Soroush to a conference in Mashhad on 6 November 2004.
35 See: www.drsoroush.com
36 Fatema Mernissi, op. cit.
37 Interestingly enough, the importance of political culture in the achieving of a democratic political system was highlighted by Alexis de Tocqueville, in his analyses of French, British and American political systems. In 1853, in what has been called his "political credo", he wrote:

> You know my ideas well enough to know that I accord institutions only a secondary influence on the destiny of men. Would to God I believed more in the omnipotence of institutions!... political societies are not what their laws make them, but what sentiments, beliefs, ideas, habits of the heart, and the spirit of men who form them, prepare them in advance to be, as well as what nature and education have made them.
>
> Alexıs de Tocqueville, *Selected Letters on Politics and Society*. California, CA: University of California Press, 1985, p. 294.

38 Corey Robin, "Fear: A Genealogy of Morals," *Social Research* 67 (4), 2000: 10.
39 Bernard Lewis, *What Went Wrong? Western Impact and Middle Eastern Response*. London: Phoenix, 2002, pp. 60–61.
40 All Muslim states subscribe to the Islamic Declaration of Human Rights, drawn up on 19 September 1981, although this does not correspond with the Universal Declaration of Human Rights, specifically in not mentioning democracy and in emphasizing the role of religious sanction and divine sovereignty. Interestingly enough, Arab League states subscribed to the Arab Charter of Human Rights (ACHR) on 15 December 1994. This document, which is a binding international instrument, fully endorses the Universal Declaration of Human Rights, implying that the states concerned are prepared to endorse democratic political systems. Mustapha Benchenane, "Les droits de l'homme en Islam et en Occident," *EuroMeSCo Brief* 9, March 2004 (at: www.euromesco.net).
41 Jillian Schwedler, op. cit., pp. 9–11. Indeed, there are two separate concepts that are used: *al mujtama' al-madani* (which really means "civic society" and would include secular organizations) and *al-mujtama' al-ahli* (civil society, including Islamic associations and organizations). Ibid., footnote 22, p. 26.
42 Jon Roper, *Democracy and its Critics: Anglo-American Democratic Thought in the Nineteenth Century*. London: Unwin & Hyman, 1989, p. 11.
43 Jon Roper, op. cit., p. 22.

Conclusions

Laurence Whitehead

The conference at which the chapters that make up this book were originally presented in Óbidos, Portugal, took place on the thirteenth anniversary of the Portuguese revolution of April 1974 that inaugurated what Huntington dubbed the "third wave" of democratization – the most powerful of its kind in the history of constitutional government and of the diffusion of basic political freedoms. In practice, this thirty-year period can be neatly divided into two quite contrasting segments – before and after the disintegration of the Soviet bloc. Other sub-periods can also be considered (for example, since September 11, 2001), and different large regions of the world have undergone concerted shifts in regime type in a succession of much more specific short periods (southern Europe in the 1970s, Latin American in the 1980s, sub-Saharan Africa and much of eastern Europe in the early 1990s, the Balkans at the end of that decade, and so on). Any overview of this rich and varied interweaving of national experiences would produce a proliferation of sub-types and alternative dynamics. No one "unified theory" of democratization seems likely to encompass all the variations. Indeed, each time a dominant paradigm has seemed about to establish its ascendancy in the academic literature, some new set of democratic developments have come to the fore and destabilized any emerging interpretative framework. Nevertheless, some rather clear lessons from experience can be extracted from this complex and diverse tapestry.

One such lesson is that it is always appropriate to examine the international dimensions shaping and constraining each national trajectory. During the 1980s the "transitions" literature was sometimes tempted to screen out these considerations, and to focus attention on the strategic interactions between dominant coalitions of political actors, together with their various domestic constituencies. That was not an entirely inappropriate simplifying strategy at a time when almost everything about these processes of regime change was uncertain, but it came at a price. Perhaps it was particularly driven by the Spanish case (which exercised a tremendous influence over that generation of theorists of democratization, especially in Latin America). But, as underscored by the chapter by Juan Carlos Pereira on Spain in this volume, even there the international elements were more significant than was recognized in this literature. It was therefore highly appropriate for the organizer of the conference and editor of this book to call us together to reappraise the international dimensions of all these democratizations.

In this concluding chapter I will not try to cover all the important insights offered by the various authors. For the sake of clarity, I propose to organize my observations around two axes, one temporal and the other geopolitical. In terms of periodization, it may be instructive to contrast the first half of the 1990s (the highpoint of international consensus and optimism concerning the pace and coverage of democratization around the world) with the first half of the following decade (a much changed international context, full of security fears and characterized by "overstretch" of the rhetoric of democratization). In terms of geopolitical coverage, this conclusion will contrast the western hemisphere (strongly under influence of the US and its closest allies) with enlarging Europe (also influenced by developments in Washington and the expansion of the North Atlantic Treaty Organization (NATO) but, above all, structured by the enlargement of the European Union, EU). This choice of coverage was governed by the extent of this book, in which the western hemisphere is discussed (Brazil by Alexandra Barahona de Brito, and Argentina by Andrés Malamud), and European cases analysed by Geoffrey Pridham (EU conditionality regimes), Lawrence Graham (Eastern Europe), Juan Carlos Pereira (Spain) and Nuno Severiano Teixeira (Portugal). Further, the focus on the transatlantic dimension serves to shed more light on the current difficulties that European countries and the US face when dealing with democratization in the Middle East (discussed in the chapters by George Joffé and Richard Youngs).

Clearly, this selective coverage does not exhaust the range of processes that require consideration under the rubric "international dimensions of democratization." It leaves aside the more intractable regions and periods, and may therefore convey a misleading positive impression of the overall dynamics at work. Even so, the temporal contrast shows how quickly and comprehensively an over-optimistic model of liberal interventionist expansion can be supplanted by a far darker and more diverse international outlook. The comparison between enlarging Europe and the Americas also reveals major differences in the role of regional integration initiatives, in the security components of regime change, and in the conceptions of democracy and democratization prevailing in the two regions. These differences also generate tension and discontent within the Western alliance concerning the most appropriate instruments and strategies for democracy promotion in the transitional regimes it hopes to win over to its cause.

The second section of this chapter concentrates on the contrast between the early 1990s and post-September 11, mainly in the western hemisphere. The third section turns to current contrasts and tensions between Washington and the EU concerning the shared transatlantic commitment to democracy promotion and the world. The final section draws out the theoretical and methodological implications of this survey.

The western hemisphere and democratization since the end of the Cold War

The first Summit of the Americas, convened most appropriately in Miami in December 1994, held out the promise to the peoples of Latin America that henceforth the entire western hemisphere would soon be united around a shared project, which would include the liberalization of trade and investment and a private sector-led process of market integration (not, however, including the labour market) together with mutually reinforcing pro-democratic political reforms including free elections, accountable government, a more vigorous human rights regime, and strengthening of the rule of law. It was recognized that not all these desiderata could be fully achieved in all countries all at once, but the Summit of the Americas process was envisioned as a coherent regional standard by which all actors and institutions could be evaluated, with cumulative reinforcements and incentives to bring everywhere (even Cuba) into the common fold within a decade. The basic assumption was that the US already fulfilled all these requisites, and that by projecting its "soft power" through multiple channels of influence it could extend its constitutional free market model of democracy throughout the Americas. This would reaffirm US values, reinforce US security and international leverage, and be good for business at the same time. A timetable was set, and the Free Trade Area of the Americas (FTAA), open only to those states classified in Washington as democracies, was to be completed by 2005. Looking back from the vantage point of autumn 2006, it seems timely to re-evaluate the strengths and limitations of this project, and to revisit the assumptions on which it rested.

Whatever the solidarity with the US elicited by the terrorist attacks of September 11 and thereafter, Latin Americans have simply not felt the same existential threat, and have been unable to share the Bush administration's discourse. To equate the US with universal freedom and then to subordinate the concerns of bystanders to the logic of a one-dimensional conflict between good and evil has simply not proved marketable in most of the western hemisphere under conditions of open democracy. The White House position was understood as a policy stance that would permit the downgrading of other objectives closer to the interests of the Latin American and Caribbean democracies, and that would block dialogue and joint endeavours in the most promising areas that had been highlighted under the Summits of the Americas timetable. It seemed to require a rewriting of history and the suppression of any sense of co-responsibility for the global challenges that had come to the fore. With distinctive memories of the Cold War (during which a bipolar conflict had provided cover for an episodic disregard of human rights and democratic aspirations in much of the hemisphere), Washington's new Manichaeism recalled the national security regimes of the 1970s. Torture, rendition, disregard for the Geneva conventions, and the selective application of international laws have provided almost daily reminders of this unlovely parallel. Hence, the growing evidence that coercive democratization is proving a failure in the Middle East elicits different responses in different parts of the western hemisphere. For some in the US it may reinforce the sense of existential threat, and the need to heighten security controls. But for the many who were never persuaded that this was a justified response in the first place its ineffectiveness reinforces the argument of principle, that democracy needs to be promoted and protected by other means.

Among the freedoms promised or implied by the Miami Summit process, the easing of controls on international migration was a prospect with great popular appeal throughout the poorer parts of the western hemisphere. This is not usually regarded as an integral component of democracy or democratization according to the standard academic literature (although it is a prominent theme in the rhetoric of US democratic exceptionalism, for example in the "huddled masses" imagery). But if we are to take seriously the international dimensions of democracy and democratization, we can hardly leave out of consideration this crucial issue. There are now signs that the democratization of Haiti is supposed to legitimize the losing of its borders. Once they have been helped to achieve their political rights at home, can the Haitian people then be denied the chance of exit, or even forcibly repatriated, with greater ease than when the international community had it classified as an autocracy, or as a failed state? If democratization paves the way for the ever tighter closure of national frontiers, that carries very different implications for the welfare (and even the freedom) of the average citizen than if it is associated with an international project to liberalize human as well as commercial exchanges from, in the language of the Miami Summit, "Alaska to Tierra del Fuego."

The war on terror, the massified US Department of Homeland Security and prospective changes in US immigration law all convey a strong message about the kind of democracy currently in favour in North America (Canada may be a little different, but it moves in parallel). The protection of a certain kind of democracy through the reinforcement of "control" at the borders can have multiple and far reaching consequences, both for both the balance of power and the nature of rights in all the affected democracies ("receiving" democracies transmit powerful pressures in this area to their "sending" counterparts – and many states in between both send and receive). There are important contrasts here between the EU (with its promise of a single market, a single passport, a single currency, uniting twenty-five or more democracies in a regional integration project) and the regionalism envisaged by the Miami process of 1994. From the perspective of 2006, the EU has proceeded dramatically in one direction (producing many problems and tensions both internal to the Union and also between these twenty-five democracies and the outside world), whereas the much more tentative hopes associated with the plan for liberalizing exchanges across a democratic western hemisphere have not been so fully realized, and could well face further disappointment as frontier controls are tightened.

Only regimes classified as democracies could attend the 1994 Miami Summit or benefit from the prospective FTAA. This is one particularly vivid example of the political conditionality that has long been in operation in Latin America. Only regimes classified as democracies could enjoy the unilateral benefits of the

Caribbean Basin Initiative (CBI), established by the US Congress in 1984. Similarly, from 1996 onwards the Common Market of the South (MERCOSUR) added a democracy clause, used in particular to discourage *golpista* tendencies in Paraguay. Likewise, the Organization of American States (OAS) acquired a "Democratic Charter" that is supposed to be binding on all its members. The EU trade preference regime for the African, Caribbean and Pacific (ACP) states has been modified to include a democratic conditionality component of the Cotonou Treaty – and this was sufficient to prevent the incorporation of Cuba. Outside the Americas this form of democratic conditionality has also been very much in vogue, in particular as the EU expanded first southward (Greece, Spain and Portugal), then into post-communist eastern Europe, and now with Turkey as the key test case for this approach.

Other types of democratic conditionality also exist. It may be functional or sectoral – such as participation in the Inter-American Commission of Human Rights (IACHR), the International Parliamentary Union (IPU) and even, arguably, the Inter-American Press Society (SIP). There are international activities like election observation, justice system reform and the training of congresses, for instance, which are normally included under the rubric of international democracy promotion. For a while in the late 1990s even the US Southern Command was in on the act, training military officials in the protection of human rights.[1]

From a cross-sectional perspective, taking the autumn of 2006 as the baseline, most of these initiatives look tired and perhaps even discredited. On a loose definition, every country in the western hemisphere (except Cuba) is currently classified as a "democracy," has enjoyed that status almost unbroken for one or two decades, and may well continue to receive such classification into the indefinite future. So the earlier preoccupation with "locking in" democratic procedures and creating disincentives to authoritarian regression has lost much of its urgency. But this is not because anxieties over the stability of the democracies of the region have all evaporated – only because the system of classification used by the international community has proved so loose. Major strands of political opinion within key countries (including Mexico and Venezuela) openly challenge the belief that a minimally adequate level of democratic institutionalization can be said to exist there, but so long as periodic elections are held and contested it is almost out of the question that any of the countries officially classified as democracies would be subjected to regional censure as openly undemocratic. If Preval's Haiti qualifies, then on what grounds could Chávez's Venezuela be disqualified? Washington may well argue that Venezuela has abandoned democracy, but Argentina and Brazil will not easily be persuaded to agree, and indeed Venezuela has just been admitted to the MERCOSUR, untroubled by its democratic conditionality. If Colombia is a democracy despite its internally displaced population and kidnappings, then who can object to the inclusion of Guatemala and Guyana? In short, international conditionality tied to regime type only serves now to isolate Castro's Cuba, and seems to have little further capacity to discriminate between good performance and bad. The EU also faces analogous problems (concerning Cyprus, Croatia and Bulgaria, among others) but its conditionality incorporates more leverage.

Latin Americans are well aware of this external context, as well as of the selectivity and distortions that have periodically been in evidence when democratic conditionality has been applied in the western hemisphere. The recent record has been very patchy. There was a success in Peru at the end of Fujimori's term, but the OAS Democracy Charter played no part in the course of Argentine politics after the flight of de la Rúa, nor in Bolivia after Sánchez de Lozada's inelegant exit, not in Venezuela in 2002 (or indeed subsequently). It is irrelevant to the current dispute in Mexico, and is unlikely to help if Ecuador or Nicaragua go off the rails. This might be different if compliance with external standards were very closely aligned with access to/denial of major economic benefits not available elsewhere.[2] But this material foundation for international democratic political conditionality has in general been nullified (at least for the time being) by the disinterest of the US Congress in the FTAA process, by the upsurge in commodity prices and by the rise of Asian political and economic alternatives that leave Washington's traditional mechanisms of guidance by international financial institutions (IFI) stranded.

So, what in 2006 are the dominant assumptions governing the form and content of a good democracy, as disseminated by mainstream Anglo-Saxon media, culture, and example? My suggestion would be that the underlying message serves to promote what O'Donnell and Schmitter termed *democradura* (an assemblage of democratic procedures and structures limited and directed by a society-wide insistence on the need for unity and discipline in the face of imminent danger). This is not the variety of democracy that proved so contagious in Europe at the end of the Cold War; it is also not the Miami Summit picture of what a region-wide convergence on democratic values could produce. If *democradura* has become "the only game in town" it will be hard to disseminate across the Americas, since the "war on terror" simply fails to resonate in most of the democracies of the region. This is partly because it is not very inclusionary (those who fail to display the necessary loyalty and discipline are liable to be marginalized). Moreover, it emphasizes security threats rather than economic opportunities when most Latin American voters fear economic insecurity more than terror attacks. It has limited patience with those who put tolerance, dialogue and respect for divergent viewpoints at the heart of the democratic project, since it requires unity and certainty, and therefore does not welcome too much dissent. Whether or not *democradura* of this kind is the appropriate response to the challenges we all confront is a topic for separate discussion elsewhere. What requires attention here is the simple fact that, in contrast to earlier and more inclusionary variants of democracy discourse, *democradura* is not very contagious.

From the perspective of Latin America in 2006, this version of democracy is liable to be perceived not only as unattractive, but also as unnecessary and unviable. When Chileans turn to their media for enlightenment about terrorism, they see programmes alleging that Eduardo Frei was the victim of a government assassination plot. Uruguayans see the confessions of the self-described "ideological author" of Operation *Condor*. Bolivians see corpses of their lost leaders disinterred. In such a climate, Washington-encouraged visions of *democradura* may even be viewed as threatening to the fragile democratic consensus that had been in the process of emerging in this part of the western hemisphere. And because it fails to capture the public imagination, and to win many new converts to its cause, it leaves a void that can be filled by alternative discourses, based on more locally intelligible and appealing conceptions of democracy.

The international community's stance on the status of democracy in Venezuela provides a striking counterpoint to the initial case of Spain or to the comforting template envisaged by the Miami Summit process. For some, the Chávez government is completely undemocratic; for others it represents the best example of inclusionary transformation with popular support periodically reaffirmed at the polls (*caesarismo democrático*). There is a recall mechanism (not available in most Latin American republics), and Chávez accepted the challenge and (probably) won the recall. He seems likely to secure re-election this December. But Venezuelan society is deeply polarized on this issue. The Fifth Republic does not rest on a very stable foundation of domestic consent.

So what has been the role played by the surrounding regional community of democracies? It is impossible to deal adequately here with this large and controversial question. However, the events of April 2002 certainly provide us with a revealing insight. Whatever criticisms one could direct against Chávez, from a domestic perspective he was unquestionably the duly elected President, and he fell captive to an authoritarian coup. Any doubt about the democratic inclinations of the conspirators should be dispelled by their actions during their brief occupation of the presidency. They not only arrested the President (falsely pretending he had resigned); they also closed the Congress. How did the OAS (fresh from its embrace of a "Democratic Charter" for the Americas) respond? Did the Bush administration oppose the coup? Anyone who watched coverage of this process on CNN at the time would have to acknowledge that the Western media were not precisely forthright in their coverage of this grave setback to democracy in the Americas.

In practice, outside the US and a handful of small Central American republics, it is not possible to silence the assertions of the Boliviarian Alternative by simply reclassifying Chávez as another Castro. There is an open space for those who wish to criticize the existing state of democracy within the western hemisphere using an analysis that is not self-evidently openly antidemocratic, and least in the view of many Latin American voters. There is a high degree of "democratic pluralism" in most of the countries of Latin America and the Caribbean, and within that public space advocates of a "Boliviarian alternative" can operate as freely as those who want to promote *democradura*. A key reason why the international dimension of democratic consent in the Americas is so weak is that neither of these conceptions is currently able to prevail over the other.

Of course, Venezuela's credentials as a democracy are far weaker than those of the US and Canada. The Boliviarian Alternative rests on a small and fragile domestic base, and is likely to have limited staying power or international appeal. If the leading democracies of the hemisphere were to give priority to their shared democratic values and aspirations, and were to act consistently and effectively to demonstrate the superiority of their version, they could in principle achieve a strong reversal of opinion, but at present the climate for this is not propitious. This discussion is limited to a transversal assessment of the structure of international support for democracy in the Americas in the autumn of 2006. From that limited perspective, the level of international consent is low and the dissidents are enjoying an almost entirely free run. For the time being at least, these rival discourses seem to operate on an equal footing in the eyes of many in the western hemisphere.

This section began with a brief reminder of the expectations concerning the advance of democratization throughout the Americas that were generated by the Miami Summit process, launched in 1994. The assumptions underlying that project were quite coherent and interlocking. They reflected a certain fairly agreed idea of what was to count as "democracy" and "democratization." The aim was to reinforce recent encouraging developments in most of the individual republics of the region, articulating a coordinated international strategy that was not directed mainly towards democracy promotion but that did incorporate multiple proposals to "lock in" the type of democracy then in vogue. This international project could reasonably be analyzed according to the four overlapping categories of control, conditionality, contagion and consent that I extracted from the tendencies then observable in the Americas (as well as the EU counterpart practice).

In the mid-1990s there was a surprisingly wide consensus in the Americas about what kind of "democracy" was within reach, and about how and why the many diverse nations of the western hemisphere should come together to support and reinforce it. Looking back from the current vantage point, it is hard to avoid the conclusion that this was in fact a somewhat strained consensus. Beneath the surface a variety of partially overlapping, but also significantly diverging, ideas were in play. There were somewhat varying conceptions of what the ideal of political democracy should contain. There were also substantial differences over how to cope with the inevitable gap between ideals (possibly shared) and "really existing" democratic practices (much more likely to be contested by those who felt they were losing out, or not getting their due share). In addition to these ambiguities over the "what" of democracy, there were already quite evident and keenly felt differences over the "how" (and in particular over the extent to which regional or international procedures and obligations might displace or even supersede purely internal/domestic dynamics). Depending on the vantage point of the observer, the "why?" question was also bound to elicit somewhat different responses. Those just emerging from the insecurity and brutality of authoritarian rule (or perhaps even civil war) might offer rather more urgent and more directly political justifications, whereas those already secure in their own democratic institutions might need more prodding to attach the same priority, and might only be inclined to take up the cause of international democracy promotion if it could be linked to some other desired objectives (enhanced regional security or increased prosperity, for example). The US, as the lead democracy, needed reassurance that a stronger commitment to regional democracy and liberal internationalism, at a minimum, would not threaten its other major foreign policy interests. Given these somewhat discordant regional responses to what/how/why questions, the Summit of the Americas agenda would only progress if it could develop a strong unifying discourse and powerful spokesmen. This the Miami process provided – a unified message backed by the full weight of both the US government and Congress. The message contained a fairly precise promise (the FTAA by 2005), and rested on a pretty explicit basis of teleological argumentation.

Twelve years later, the cracks in this apparent consensus are all too apparent. Here is an illustration list of the kind of practical problems that have arisen from the crumbling of the somewhat artificial regional consensus of the mid-1990s. Is it now permissible to build a democratic regime in the Americas on the foundation of public ownership and control of a nation's natural resources? Is regional convergence around norms of democratic integration compatible with much tighter immigration controls, the possible deportation on a large scale of *indocumentadas*, and the denial of basic healthcare or driving licences to those who are not "citizens"? Or can non-nationals be granted voting rights, perhaps based on transnational reciprocates? Are there circumstances in which it is justified to "torture for freedom," or to wiretap, or to detain without trial? How do projects of "decolonization" and the restoration of allegedly long suppressed "indigenous" rights relate to democracy and democratization? What privileged status (if any) do American democrats accord to the extra-territorial decisions of the US Congress or Supreme Court? If the electorate in a particular Latin American republic, in a free and fair election, decides to rewrite the Constitution so as to abrogate existing laws and institutional commitments, is that an affirmation of democracy or a violation of the rule of law? Does TELESUR (the Venezuelan-Argentine state funded left-wing television station, aiming to compete with CNN and BBC World and other "global" Spanish language television stations) operate within the "freedom of speech" protections that should be upheld in all American democracies, or is it a mouthpiece of anti-democratic subversion to be censored or closed down? If international observers qualify an election outcome as clean, can it ever be justified to disregard their verdict and resort to civil disobedience against what the losers regard as an electoral fraud?

Whereas most – if not all – of these questions could have been answered unambiguously by a mainstream democratic consensus in the mid-1990s, today's responses are likely to be more qualified and divided. It is currently possible to group the options into two alternative poles – *democradura* and illiberal distributive – but neither of these is a stable or all-encompassing discourse. Other variants and combinations are easy to envisage, and may well crystallize as competitive options in coming years.

But, if there is indeed a plurality of democratic conceptions or aspirations in play across the Americas, what dimensions of international support or reinforcement are likely to prove most relevant, and which might turn out to be divisive or counterproductive? And what channels, or procedures, for mobilizing support are most appropriate in this setting? In my view, international control – and also most forms of conditionality – are inappropriate methods of reinforcing regional democratization patterns, and could easily prove counterproductive (or serve to promote non-democratic policy objectives). By contrast, since there is a loose regional consensus in favour of a broadly democratic consensus in the Americas, this is a favourable setting for international democracy promotion by contagion, mutual accommodation and locally-driven consent. The key issue is the legitimacy (or otherwise) of each type of international influence. It is not enough for an initiative to be proclaimed as democracy-promoting; it is not enough for the proclamation to be seriously intended, properly researched and adequately funded. The recipients of the initiative have to accept the truth of all of that, and to share an understanding of the what, how and why with its dispensers.

Finally, therefore, the democratization of the western hemisphere remains an open project, equally capable of regression and of recovery. Despite current difficulties there remains scope to advance in a broad process of democratic dialogue and mutual accommodation, based on the "consent" of all the parties involved, both domestic and international. Consent of this kind will not arise from spontaneous agreement based on consensual values and assumptions, and there is no single consensual model of democracy and democratization, so openness to regional influences and discordant viewpoints tests the extent of pluralism and toleration in all the polities involved, not only those tilting towards illiberal distributivism, but also those single-mindedly geared to "security." So at best it would have to be built up over time, requiring efforts of tolerance and imagination from all sides. In contrast to the assumptions of the Miami Summit process, it would uncover important areas of disagreement and even quite strong clashes of view between rival conception of democracy, alternative understandings of the region's history, and competing models of political participation and of institutional design. Similar tensions and indeed disagreements seem likely to underlie transatlantic efforts at cooperation in the area of democracy promotion, following the shock of September 11, 2001.

Transatlantic discourses on democracy promotion and their discontents

The current "Transatlantic Partnership" can be traced back not just to the creation of NATO, in 1949, but to the Atlantic Charter signed by Churchill and Roosevelt in August 1941. It thus has an unbroken continuity of almost sixty-five years. But, of course, it was the Cold War – and the Marshall Plan – that defined the European component of the Transatlantic Partnership throughout the second half of the twentieth century. And it is the ending of the Cold War that drives the current, and prospective, redefinition of that partnership at the dawn of the twenty-first century.

What this history tells us is that the most fundamental issues of national and collective security, and of the preservation of liberal freedoms, have always been at the heart of the transatlantic partnership, although its national composition has varied. The dismantling of the Berlin Wall not only reunited Germany but also transformed the political landscape of all of Europe, and thereby necessitated a wholesale revision of the partnership. Not only was its geopolitical coverage radically expanded; its internal balance was also redistributed, and the main focus shifted from defence and security to economic cooperation, and to the construction of a liberal international order.

Defence and security issues had always been embedded in a broader framework of economic and political concerns, ultimately traceable to shared liberal democratic value assumptions. That was why the geopolitical coverage and internal power balance could be transformed without destroying the partnership. But for the first half-century of its history physical security lay at the heart of the relationship. There was a self-evident and continuous external threat that could never be disregarded, and that prompted every government involved to preserve the basics of cooperation and surmount whatever divergences might threaten the underlying cohesion of the partnership. Of course Washington's leadership was indispensable here, but the alliance was founded not only on Washington's efforts and resources but also on the willing consent of the other allies.

Looking towards the next half-century, there is little indication of any unified external threat grave enough to restore security cooperation to its formerly preeminent role in the relationship. Despite its current travails in Afghanistan it may be that NATO will remain the decisive military alliance, and it may indeed enlarge its membership and extend its missions to "out of area" operations, perhaps in association with a more independent European Defence Force (EDF). But threats from so-called "rogue states" like Iran and North Korea should be kept in historical perspective. They represent no sustained challenge equivalent to the Warsaw Pact. Other arenas of regional conflict – in the Middle East, for example – may generate more division than unity within what used to be known as the "Western alliance." The Bush administration's "coalitions of the willing" strategy seems unlikely to rekindle past memories of collaboration against shared dangers. In future, therefore, the attractiveness of the transatlantic partnership is likely to depend upon its broader strengths, and on its capacity to tackle new international challenges. Does it still sustain the shared values and cooperative procedures needed to win consent from public opinion across these vast and disparate regions, and to generate shared perceptions of the transatlantic issues at stake with regard not only to the severe problem of global terrorism, but also to the potentially at least as grave dangers associated with, say, economic globalization or joint action to contain global warming? Whatever the immediate stumbling blocks or distractions may be, the future of North American–European relations will be shaped largely by long-term interests and commitments, and by cumulatively relentless structural tendencies.

Let us start with the underlying strengths. Taking both regions together, they contain a very high proportion of the prosperous, technically advanced and securely democratic population of the globe. Both are also in a phase of expansion, reinforcing these attributes in the poorer and more peripheral parts of each region. The combined strength is militarily decisive, in addition to its economic and political solidity. Between them these two partners supply essential underpinnings to an emerging system of global governance, which embraces both the economic and the political dimensions. They share some fundamental historical and cultural common ground, some key institutional characteristics (such as the rule of law, freedom of association and the division of powers) and some consensual liberal values. The Cold War and its aftermath gave them a sense of joint strategic interests. The ending of the Cold War may have led to more airing of divergences, but it would be a mistake to present the rival positions as inflexible, or necessarily counter-posed. Disagreement may be over the *means* of action rather than the ultimate *objective* sought. In addition (as can be seen in both the Balkans and Central America) there can be something of a tacit division of labour, with Washington exercising the discipline and some other allies seeking to induce consent by softer means. Moreover, where multilateral diplomacy seems more likely than a unilateral display of strength to promote a desired security objective, Washington is quite capable of seizing the initiative. To a lesser extent, Europeans are also willing to pursue their security objectives by military means when this is judged absolutely necessary (as illustrated by the current composition of the International Stabilization Force (ISAF) in Afghanistan). In summary, security problems in the Atlantic triangle may have been transformed and perhaps fragmented since the end of the Cold War, but what we are dealing with is a rebalancing of policies and priorities, and the search for new modalities of collective action, rather than the abandonment of security cooperation.

It should not be forgotten that transatlantic security cooperation was founded on a broader base of liberal democratic internationalism. After all, NATO was founded in the late 1940s on explicitly liberal democratic values (although its adherence to such principles during the Cold War was uneven, to say the least). Once the Soviet challenge had abated, the Western alliance came under renewed pressure to uphold its foundational principles. Meanwhile, alternative avenues of regional and transatlantic cooperation had opened up, also based on shared liberal democratic assumptions. The EU was undoubtedly the most substantial and potent of these institutions, and its enlargement to twenty-five members in 2004 (with more to follow) dramatizes its achievements. But, in addition there was also the Council of Europe (CoE), the Organization for Security and Cooperation in Europe (OSCE), and so forth. European party foundations such as the Adenauer, Naumann and Ebert Stifftung played an active role in promoting such values. So in principle there could be an emerging value consensus which links the transatlantic partners (and also the new democracies of Latin America) and which differentiates present and prospective relationships from those of the past (which rested on more traditional assumptions about national sovereignty and the *realpolitik* basis of international alliances). However, this potential value consensus is being severely tested by US unilateralism and by the multiple crises that this has triggered in the Middle East. Before turning to the broad underlying tensions we must therefore examine the specific discontents that have arisen since the American-British operation to use force to overthrow Saddam Hussein's despotic government in Iraq.

After all, since the US-led British supported military occupation of Iraq in 2003, all discussions of "transatlantic cooperation" to promote democracy have been overshadowed by war-induced controversies over its purpose and consequences. Washington and the allies describe their operations in terms of liberation from tyranny. They used force because it was the only way to achieve "regime change," and their actions are benevolent because rather than imposing their own nominees or policies they have enfranchised the Iraqi people to elect its own government, to choose a freer and more plural political system, and in due course to reassume their own sovereignty. The occupation forces will stay until "the job is done," but then they will withdraw, leaving behind a democratic Iraq that should also serve as a beacon for democracy in the Greater Middle East. There could hardly be a more ambitious or coherent agenda for transatlantic cooperation to promote democracy. Consequently, overall assessments of the viability and implications of this broadens discourse will be decisively shaped by the (as yet unfinished) Anglo-American experiment in Iraq.

Objectivity is always difficult to sustain during conditions of ongoing conflict. From the beginning of 2003, if not earlier, a wide array of analysts and opinion formers in the Western democracies (especially in Europe, but also in North America and of course throughout the western hemisphere, including Mexico and Chile) dissented from various aspects of the case for war in Iraq. The UN Security Council never endorsed the operation, and even the supine UK parliament only narrowly backed it in the face of unprecedentedly large popular demonstrations under the slogan "not in our name." So this was never a consensual Western democracy promotion project, and as its consequences have unfolded its parentage has shrunk. Nevertheless, the two prime authors of the Iraqi experiment – President George W. Bush and Prime Minister Tony Blair – both secured re-election after the event, and the UN Security Council also gave it a thin veneer of retrospective authorization. So Iraq provides a valid test of broader claims about the West's role in democracy promotion, even though it is controversial and presumably represents a "limit case."

Three years after the overthrow of Saddam Hussein's oppressive government, the "fog of war" still clouds assessments of this limit case. The US taxpayer is currently spending almost US\$100 billion per year on the Iraqi venture, and also absorbing thirty to fifty military deaths in action per month. Its support coalition has steadily shrunk, and only the UK may remain at Washington's side to the very end of the process. Such unforeseen costs have driven these two advocates of the operation to concentrate resources and invest prestige in this particular project, scaling back their presence in other arenas, and sacrificing room for manoeuvre to promote democracy by other means and in other regions. The need to declare victory (in order to withdraw with honour) has also induced American and British spokesmen to stretch the discourse of democracy promotion to extreme limits, defying common sense in its erroneous description of Iraqi and Afghan realities. Extraordinary contortions are currently being used to deny that the term "civil war" could yet be applicable. These seem likely to prove counterproductive manoeuvres, as public opinion in Europe and even in the US becomes progressively more sceptical of official rhetoric and more willing to crystallize around judgements that diverge from Anglo-American discourse. It would be premature to attempt a final assessment, but on the trends to date it would seem probable that the greatest transatlantic endeavour to promote democracy overseas since the end of the Cold War is likely to provoke widespread anxiety about the extent to which such Western discourse has the potential to deceive and indeed entrap its exponents.[3]

The initial appeal of this Western pro-democracy discourse is easy to rehearse. International cooperation to promote and reinforce democratic government in parts of the world where it is absent or fragile sounds like an unambiguously good idea. And indeed, it has proved a positive reality on many occasions in the recent past. The Polish people, for example, had every right to expect the Western democracies to lend them support in the late 1980s and early 1990s, when (long after their elated allies had themselves enjoyed the benefits of their victory over fascism in 1945) they at last – and largely through their own efforts – enjoyed the opportunity to return to the path from which their country had been so cruelly diverted in the decade following 1939. Once democratized, Poland in turn became a partner in cooperative international efforts to support democracy in like-situated countries (notably the Ukraine and also – less wisely – Iraq) after 2004; similarly, the Chilean people succeeded – largely through their own efforts, but again with some worthwhile external support – to re-democratize after the tragic diversion inflicted on them in the later stages of the Cold War. They too have proved active and enthusiastic (though again not always judicious) in supporting similarly troubled neighbours. There is no need for an exhaustive listing of such examples. The general conclusion is clear. Even if not every instance of well-intentioned international collective action to promote democracy has turned out as well as initially hoped for, these are recurrent and meritorious episodes of foreign policy activism that can be defended both for their nobility of purpose and for their broadly emancipating effects.

Nevertheless, what seems like an unambiguously good idea can prove too good to be true, especially if it is appropriated by Great Powers with other major foreign policy interests to promote, and in particular if it becomes cloaked in such moralism that it becomes exempt from rational debate or critical scrutiny. In that event, governments with dubious credentials as democracy promoters, and scant accountability to the populations they purport to be emancipating, can abuse the discourse of democracy promotion, engaging in adventurism and the manipulation of public opinion, until – as usually happens in a free society – the true purposes and consequences of their activities become impossible to ignore.

Under current conditions, the Western discourse on democracy promotion invites cynicism. It is marred both by incoherence and by illegitimacy. The only truly democratic elections in the Arab world produced majorities for the Islamic

Salvation Front (in Algeria) and from Hamas (in Palestine). In both cases Western democracies withdrew their support from the freely chosen representatives of the people, and tightened their cooperation with those authoritarian rules who felt most threatened by these expressions of popular sovereignty. In Iraq and Afghanistan the mantle of democratic legitimacy has been accorded to authorities that were clearly promoted by the occupying forces, and were selected above all for their acquiescence to foreign military intrusion.

If the incoherence of current Western democracy promotion rhetoric were limited to the familiar reality that other competing priorities must also help shape the foreign policies of all established powers, this might be seen as a corrective to naive moralism rather than as a fundamental flaw. But the confusions surrounding the prevailing discourse are more radical than that. Consider the question of how the transatlantic democracies are supposed to deliberate over, and then commit themselves to, various forms of democracy-promoting joint action. For example, are they to cooperate, to collaborate or to coordinate?

"Cooperation" is a key term here, and it requires some explication. Cooperation is best conceived as voluntary, variable according to the stakes and interests of the respective parties in a particular episode of joint action, and therefore fluctuating, uneven, and perhaps even a little unpredictable in advance (despite any strong value consensus that may provide the underlying rationale for pooled endeavours). There are some significant variants on democracy promotion that may be adequately served by collective discourse and the possibility of intermittent supporting actions of this loosely structured type. A stronger version of transatlantic collective action to promote democracy would involve "coordination" as well as cooperation, and more permanent versions could be established through joint commitment to durable and binding international institutions (such as NATO or the OSCE). The key factors differentiating all such agreements from mere cooperation are two-fold: first, durability through time (and across cases); and second, and above all, the acceptance by all parties to the agreement (including the most powerful) of limits to their freedom of action, imposed by the need to carry the assent of one's partners. Since 2001, the US administration has escalated its discourse of international democracy promotion, but at the same time it has downgraded its commitment to coordination. Its treaty commitments remain in place, of course, but the logic of "coalitions of the willing" and a perpetual war on an undefined energy called "terror" is that NATO, or any other transatlantic partnership, is no more than an option (to be activated when useful) rather than an obligation (to be observed even when this imposes an unwelcome constraint). The doctrine of pre-emptive war runs directly counter to the acceptance of any limits on the dominant states' freedom of action, including the need to secure the assent of alliance partners. Arguably, this conveys the required sense of close and durable joint action in pursuit of a common goal (more so than mere "cooperation") without the sacrifice of US discretionality implied by transatlantic coordination. The discursive difficulty here is that when the Axis powers conquered the bulk of Europe they imparted an unforgettable flavour of subservience to the world "collaborators," and European colonization of the Arab World is also sufficiently recent to discredit the term there as well.

Behind this semantic issue lurks a deeper source of discontent. On what basis is transatlantic joint action to be initiated, executed and monitored? Is all this international democracy promotion to be carried out in a democratic manner and, even if the answer is in principle affirmative, how are such decisions to be taken? From a US perspective, it may suffice to invoke the size of the US electorate, the scale of its financial contribution, and the history of American leadership in this cause. From that viewpoint, the presence of a commitment from Washington could be thought sufficient to trigger a democratic initiative in favour of democracy promotion anywhere in the world, and its absence could be considered a fatal subtraction of support. By contrast, the EU is likely to incline towards a different view, somewhat impertinently imagining itself as a collective actor of roughly equal standing with the US (assuming optimistically that it can generate an agreed position of its own on at least some key international issues). Can there be transatlantic collective action led by Washington and in disregard of majority democratic opinion in Europe? The US view (encapsulated in the "coalition of the willing" formula) is presumably affirmative, but this view threatens the European integration project.

In the absence of a unifying "clear and present danger," transatlantic leaders are liable to find it difficult to harmonize and prioritize their objectives, whether the focus is democracy promotion or other joint ventures. It is proving hard to agree on acceptable burden-sharing formulae, or to empower appropriate international institutions, or to carry their diverse public opinions in all of this. Much fashionable theorizing about "problems of collective action" would benefit from a more practical engagement with the interconnected difficulties arising here. Problems of legitimacy, hegemony and inter-generational equity can all be thrown into sharp relief by an empirically grounded analysis of these challenges. After all, the transatlantic relationship has long been underpinned by a range of sectoral bargains and implicit understandings that are all showing signs of coming unstuck – for example, agricultural protectionism, the fate of peasant farmers, the link between commercial liberalization and labour migration, and co-responsibility for the control of transnational crime. The new "eastern" members of the EU and the "southern" members of the Americas also face long-term processes of technological catch-up; the legitimization of fragile institutions; and the rectification of severe social inequalities – all "problems of development" that have not always been treated with great empathy by the old Atlantic powers, but that will demand a more sensitive treatment if the partnership is to flourish in the future.

Just as the international consensus on democratic values has weakened in the western hemisphere since September 11, 2001, so also has it come under strain at the transatlantic level. In both cases the weight of history may still favour collective action to support liberal internationalism and political democratization, but current security and geopolitical strains are testing the solidarity of the underlying discursive consensus, especially the demand for unity around projects of coercive democratization.

Theoretical and methodological implications

What if the self-styled leading democracy of the "Free World" decides to disregard the views – and the laws – of its allies? What if it proclaims a doctrine of "pre-emptive war," meaning that it declares itself free to use massive force against whatever other nation or external political organization it decides to classify (for good reason or bad) as a major potential to its security? What if it determines in advance of any such conflict that it will not accept as standard the international definition of its obligations under the Geneva Convention? What if it reclassifies the forms of interrogation known in normal parlance as "torture," so that when practiced by its agents or allies these are no longer to be outlawed or condemned? These are not purely hypothetical questions. In September 2006, President Bush acknowledged that the Central Intelligence Agency (CIA) had been authorized to operate secret prisons overseas and that the White House considered it "vital" for this programme to continue. In response, a meeting of EU foreign ministers formally affirmed the European view that "the existence of secret detention facilities where detained persons are kept in a legal vacuum is not in conformity with international humanitarian law and international criminal law." Can a "free world" led in this manner nevertheless be viewed as an investment for international democracy promotion?

Many Europeans and Latin Americans (and some US citizens also) would reply to this last question with an unreflecting "no." But it would be better to reflect with care on the nature of the relationship between means and ends in the field of international democracy promotion. An important strand of US thinking on the question would use realist means to achieve what can be classified as idealist ends. There is both a historical and a theoretical basis for this position. It was not by emphasizing democratic means that the US helped bring democracy to Japan or Germany in 1945. By extension, this historical perspective can be stretched to assert that the US-encouraged coup against constitutionally elected President Allende of Chile in 1973 nevertheless, in some indirect and long-term manner, played its part in bringing about the alternative (preferable?) version of democracy established there after 1989. Arguments of this kind could also be extended to Central America, to the failed coup against Chávez in April 2002, and prospectively to Cuba as well. The intricacies of these historical arguments are complex and varied. Some cases are more plausible than others. But what ties them all together is an underlying conviction that the USA is the secure homeland (the "last best hope") for democracy in the world, so that whatever measures make it more secure will in the end benefit its allies and by extension ultimately turn out to be pro-democratic. Apparently pro-democratic measures (such as those associated with, say, the Carter Administration) that nevertheless weaken the power and influence of the US thereby contribute, in an indirect way, to setting back rather than reinforcing democratization around the world. Whether or not this argument can be substantiated in particular historical cases is not the issue for consideration here. It may be plausible at least *sometimes*. Once one accepts that, then the connection between the pursuit of democratic ends and reliance on democratic means becomes questionable. This brings us to the more interesting and challenging theoretical issue. If such means and ends are not automatically aligned, how far may they vary? Under what conditions, under what restraints, can what types of undemocratic instruments be used by the international democratic community, without nullifying the state or intended purposes of the action?

Like the dichotomy between domestic and international factors, the contrast between means and ends is too neat to capture the full dynamics involved when states engage in democracy promotion. Some means are purely instrumental, but others are value-laden and therefore need to be evaluated not only for their consequences but also for their democratic content. Democracy can be promoted as an end in itself, but it is also typically favoured as a means to other ends (peaceful coexistence, say, or international cooperation). Moreover, in this area the relationship between means and ends is typically indirect, a matter of interpretation (and perhaps of disagreement) rather than a self-evidently causal mechanism. To demonstrate that *this* means produced *that* effect requires consideration of the counterfactual alternatives. It may be argued that the same ends could have been attained by less intrusive means; or it may be claimed that these means impeded the achievement of an outcome that came about for different reasons. In any case, there is a problem of attribution when political leaders claim to be motivated by such a noble purpose as democracy promotion. The possibility cannot be disregarded that they are acting for less worthy motives, and choose to disguise more conventional power political ambitions behind a cloud of rhetoric. So even if the means they choose are transparent, it is necessary to assess whether they may mainly be pursuing aims other than their publicly declared ends. Finally, the following question also needs to be considered: who decides whether the means were appropriate and proportional, and the ends attained? During the course of a democracy promotion episode, voice may preponderantly be exercised by the democracy promoters themselves. However, once their work is completed (assuming they are successful), it is the citizens of the new democracy who will be empowered – and their assessment of the relationship between means and ends may not necessarily coincide with that of their putative benefactors.

These theoretical and methodological complexities can thus be disaggregated into four broad consensus – instrumentality, counterfactuals, attribution of motives, and the evaluation of results. We can conclude by reviewing them in order.

When the subject matter is democracy promotion, a sharp separation between instrumental means and normative ends is problematic. The two can be separated to some extent from a democracy-promotion perspective, and it may in principle be possible to justify the use of undemocratic means (conquest, or other forms of coercion, for instance) if these are the only way to secure an unquestionably democratic outcome. But this only apples under limited conditions: most episodes of externally supported democratization fall into a grey zone where alternative, more consensual, methods of support might produce at least equally desirable results, and where at least part of the impact arises from setting a good example. In such conditions, a purely instrumental model of causation is inappropriate. Some regular instruments of state policy (not just unlawful torture, and assassination, but also more tolerated methods such as disinformation and the use of proxies) are likely to undermine the legitimacy of the prospective new democracies, however effective they may be in overturning its authoritarian predecessor. The means/ends calculus will not deliver on its promise of effectiveness if its terms are too narrowly conceived. Thus, genuine democracy promoters need to consider the longer-term and indirect consequences of their choice of policy instruments, as well as the direct and immediate effects. Results will also be disappointing if they limit their objectives to regime change, without giving careful consideration to the complexities of democratic construction that may follow. Merely convening an election and then declaring "mission accomplished" may not suffice to stabilize a genuinely free and open political system, or to justify the damage and suffering inflicted by an experience of coercive regime change.

Where there is more than one possible method for securing a desired result, and where complex causal sequences are involved, judgements of the effects of any particular policy choice need to weigh up the most plausible counterfactual alternatives. Consider the cases of Algeria and Cuba. In the first, when the Islamic Salvation Front (FIS) achieved an unexpectedly strong showing in the most genuinely competitive elections since Algerian independence, the ruling party chose not to accept the results. Western democracies acquiesced to this authoritarian regression on the grounds that once the FIS had taken power it would suppress all future democratic elections. But there is a plausible alternative view (one that can never be proved because the experience was not undertaken). The West could have tried to hold out for the principle of voter sovereignty. The FIS might have come to see Western democrats as their most reliable and trustworthy allies against a recalcitrant military-dominated regime. Democracy promoters might have established valuable credentials with Islamic moderates, not only in Algeria but throughout the Arab world. This is a question of counterfactual judgement, one with profound implications for how we assess the relationship between means and ends in the field of democracy promotion. Similarly, US policy towards Cuba has been one of consistently imposing and tightening sanctions (unilateral, since Washington's allies do not share its viewpoint) in order to force the Cuban Communist regime to its knees and compel the islanders to embrace a form of democracy dictated by the US Congress. That is the tenor of the Helms-Burton Act, among other measures. It rests on a counterfactual argument that has been challenged by an alternative. The policy of the US has not (so far) delivered the promised results, and Washington's reaction to successive disappointments has always been to argue that tighter and more broadly based sanctions are therefore needed. But critics assert that these sanctions have precisely the opposite effect to what is intended. They provide the Castro regime with a perfect alibi for its policy failings and de-legitimize the democratic opposition, which can always be condemned as instruments of an external subversive plot. According to this alternative view, the most effective way to promote democracy in Cuba would be for the West to lift the sanctions and to offer the islanders support without political conditions. The Cuban regime would thereby lose its most powerful instrument of social control. Again, since the alternative has never been tried, it is a matter of fine judgement which of these two interpretations is the more realistic. The general point that emerges is that means/ends reasoning in the field of democracy promotion often depends heavily on counterfactual judgements that are far from self-evident or consensual.

The cases of Algeria and Cuba can also be used to demonstrate the problem of attribution of motives. Were the Western democracy promoters solely concerned with how best to achieve their stated objectives in these two countries? In the case of Algeria it is not unreasonable to conclude that, on the contrary, the primary concern could have been to protect Europe's energy surplus from North Africa, and to avoid risks of geopolitical instability in this strategic region. The democracy promotion rationale could be (and has been) regarded by many in North Africa as a flimsy excuse. It is not necessary to embrace an overly cynical viewpoint here. All that we need to establish is that the stated motives of the democracy promoters may provide an incomplete – even a misleading – explanation for the drivers of policy in the Western democracies. This opaqueness and possible insincerity will diminish confidence in their reliability, and may therefore increase the likelihood of non-cooperation and resistance. The Cuban case is analogous. Washington policy-makers always insist that their underlying objective is to bring democracy back to the island, but many Cuba-watchers remember the US's equivocal record on this score between 1898 and 1958, and contemporary observers can often explain Washington's policy choices in terms of electoral calculations in the state of Florida. Again, this cloudiness about the motivations of the self-appointed democracy promoters is liable to alter the dynamics of Western activism, and may destabilize their means/ends calculations.

Finally, then, we need to consider who decides whether the means used are appropriate and whether the ends specified are attained. This would not be a difficult issue if the separation between means and ends were clear-cut, if the counterfactual judgements involved were consensual, and if the attribution of motives was unambiguous. But where these favourable conditions are lacking, control over the international discourse of democracy promotion becomes contentious. Some of the long-established democracies (especially those fitting my recent proposed category of "immanence") tend to arrogate to themselves the right to define which means are appropriate, which results can be classified as successes, and which motives for action deserve public recognition. But this is a theoretically and methodologically flawed procedure. In a true community of democratic regimes there would be co-responsibility and multilateral accountability, rather than the self-serving unilateralism that has characterized recent practices. But above all, if democracy promotion achieves its stated goal, it is the citizens of the new democracies themselves whose judgements about the proportionality of the means used, the purity of motivation of the international actors, and availability or otherwise of alternative means to secure the same ends, should carry most conviction. They are the most affected, their freedom would enable them to formulate their own views for the first time, and the self-congratulations of the old established democracies would be subjected to independent verification by those they have claimed to help. We know that the people of Grenada, the Poles and the South Africans have strong views about how international democracy promotion really operated in their cases. The Afghans, the Haitians and the Iraqis also deserve a hearing once their democracies are securely established. It is not just in Washington and London that such questions can be settled.

Notes

1 By contrast, in March 2006 SOUTHCOM Commander General Bantz Craddock spoke of the need for South America's military to address non-conventional new threats "ungoverned spaces, porous borders, corruption, organized crime and narco-terrorism." SOUTHCOM has also warned against threats of "radical populism" and *indigenismo* in Andean countries. The Pentagon is pursuing bilateral policies with each national military counterpart, thereby fragmenting regional cooperation. It is urging local militaries to become more like Central American "constabularies." A law before the US Congress is currently petitioning the OAS to form a multinational political task force, primarily targeting the Argentine, Brazilian and Paraguayan frontier area. Argentina explicitly rejected this "new threats" argument in May 2006, and Brazil protested against the OAS proposal. Instead, Brazilian forces are being deployed there.
2 The Helms–Burton Law presumes that this will prove the case for a post-communist Cuba, but even there, there is room for doubt. Maybe Nicaragua can still be subjected to traditional disciplines, but their coverage has certainly dwindled to a very few residual cases.
3 According to a former Bush administration official quoted in the *Financial Times* (22 April 2006), in March 2006 the State Department set up an Iran Syria Operations Group, reporting to Elizabeth Cheney, the senior US official leading democracy promotion activities in the greater Middle East. The Group "was established to plot a more aggressive democracy promotion strategy" for these two "rogue" states. It is also supposed to coordinate with the Pentagon. The initiative is going ahead not withstanding (according to the report) the fact that "serious Iranian opposition politicians are virtually unanimous in saying that foreign funding of activities designed to promote democracy would be counter-productive," especially "when undertaken by the US and UK occupiers of Iraq." The British input is said to be important because of the Bush administration's lack of experts on Iraq.

Bibliography

Abdenur, Roberto, "A política externa brasileira e o 'Sentimento de Exclusão'," In: Gelson Fonseca Jr. and Sérgio Henrique de Castro (eds), *Temas de Política Eterna Brasileira*, Vol. 1. São Paulo: Paz e Terra, 1994.

Acevedo, Domingo E. and Grossman, Claudio, "The Organisation of American States and the Protection of Democracy," in: Tom Farer (ed.), *Beyond Sovereignty: Collectively Defending Democracy in the Americas*. Baltimore, MD: Johns Hopkins University Press, 1996.

Alfonsín, Raúl, "La integración sudamericana: una cuestión política," *Síntesis FUALI* 9 (24), 2001: 3–7.

Alfonsín, Raúl, *Memoria política. Transición a la democracia*. Buenos Aires: Fondo de Cultura Económica, 2004.

Al-Hasan, Abu and Aal-Mawardi, Ali, *Al-Ah?kām al-Sultāniyya* (1058).

Alípio E. S., *O processo negocial de adesão de Portugal à EFTA 1956–1960*. Unpublished thesis. Lisbon: New University of Lisbon Social Sciences Faculty, 2001.

Almond, Gabriel and Verba, Sidney, *The Civic Culture: Political Attitudes and Democracy in Five Nations*. Princeton, NJ: Princeton University Press, 1963.

Amnesty International, *Torture and Extrajudicial Executions in Urban Brazil*. London: AI, 1990.

Amnesty International, *Brazil Report*. London: AI, 1991.

Amnesty International, *Beyond Despair: An Agenda for Human Rights in Brazil*. London: AI, 1994.

Amnesty International, *The Candelaria Trial: A Small Wedge in the Fortress of Impunity*. London: AI, 1996.

Amorim, Celso, "O Brasil e o Conselho de Segurança da ONU," *Política Externa* 3 (4), 1995: 1–20.

Amorim, Celso, "A reforma da ONU," *Estudos Avançados* (São Paulo) 43, 1996.

Amorim, Celso and Nunes, Luís, "Entre o desequilíbrio unipolar e a multipolaridade: o Conselho de Segurança da ONU no período pós-Guerra Fria," in: Gilberto Dupas and Tullo Vigevani (eds.), *O Brasil e as novas dimensões da segurança internacional*. São Paulo: Alfa Omega, 1999.

Anaya, James S., *Indigenous People in International Law*. Oxford: Oxford University Press, 2000.

Arblaster, Anthony, *Democracy*. Milton Keynes: Open University Press, 1987.

Armero, José María, *Política exterior de España en democracia*. Madrid: Espasa, 1989.

Baptista, Luiz Olavo, "Mercosul: Instituções, linhas mestras, rumos," *O novo multilateralismo. Perspectiva da União Europeia e do Mercosul*, Forum Euro-Latino-Americano. Instituto de Estudos Estratégicos e Internacionais. Lisbon: Principia, 2001.

Barahona de Brito, Alexandra, "A União Europeia e o MERCOSUL: A promoção da democracia e dos direitos humanos," in: Alexandra Barahona de Brito *et al.*, *Além do comércio: As relações entre a União Europeia e o MERCOSUL*. Lisbon: IEEI, 1997.

Barahona de Brito, Alexandra, "Truth, Justice, Memory and Democratisation in the Southern Cone," in: Alexandra Barahona de Brito *et al.* (eds), *The Politics of Memory*. Oxford: Oxford University Press, 2002.

Barahona de Brito, Alexandra, "The Pinochet Case and the Changing Boundaries of Democracy," in: Madeleine Davis (ed.), *The Pinochet Case*. London: ILAS, 2003.

Barahona de Brito, Alexandra, "Direitos humanos, democratização e actores internacionais," *Revista de Estudos Internacionais* 9 (13), 2006.

Barahona de Brito, Alexandra, "Democratization and International Actors: Some Thoughts for the Arab World," forthcoming as a *EuroMesCo Network Publication*, IEEI, Lisbon, 2008.

Barahona de Brito, Alexandra and Panizza, Francisco, "A política doméstica e internacional dos direitos humanos no Brasil: 'Glasnost sem Perestroika'," *Política Internacional*, 17 (2), 1998: 93–130.

Barahona de Brito, Alexandra and Panizza, Francisco, "The Politics of Human Rights in Democratic Brazil: '*A Lei Não Pega*'," *Journal of Democratization* 5 (4), 1998: 20–51.

Barahona de Brito, Alexandra and de Vasconcelos, Álvaro, *Setting Global Rules: A Report of the V Euro-Latin American Forum*. Lisbon: IEEI, 1998.

Barber Benjamin R., "Democracy and Terror in the Era of Jihad and McWorld," in: Ken Booth and Tim Dunne (eds.), *Worlds in Collision: Terror and the Future of Global Order*. Basingstoke: Routledge, 2002.

Barreto, António, "Portugal: Democracy through Europe," in: Jeffrey J. Anderson (ed.), *Regional Integration and Democracy*. New York, NY: Rowman & Littlefeld, 1999.

Benchenane, Mustaph, "Les droits de l'homme en Islam et en Occident," *EuroMeSCo Brief* 9, March 2004 (at: www.euromesco.net).

Bermeo, Nancy, *Ordinary People in Extraordinary Times: The Citizenry and the Breakdown of Democracy*. Princeton, NJ: Princeton University Press, 2003.

Brown, Cynthia (ed.), *With Friends like These: The Americas Watch Report on Human Rights and US Policy in Latin America*. New York, NY: Pantheon Books, 1985.

Brown, Lesley (ed.), *The New Shorter Oxford English Dictionary*. Oxford: Clarendon Press, 1993.

Brumberg, Daniel, "Liberalization versus Democratization: Understanding Arab Political Reforms," *Carnegie Endowment for International Peace Working Paper* 37, 2003.

Brumberg, Daniel and Diamond, Larry, "Introduction," in: Larry Diamond, Marc Plattner and Daniel Brumberg (eds.), *Islam and Democracy in the Middle East*. Baltimore, MD: Johns Hopkins University Press, 2003.

Bruneau, Thomas, "Brazil's Political Transition," in: John Higley and Richard Gunther (eds.), *Elites and Democratic Consolidation in Latin America and Southern Europe*. Cambridge: Cambridge University Press, 1992.

Burgat, François, *Face to Face with Political Islam*. London: IB Tauris, 2003.

Cardoso, Oscar Raúl, Kirschbaum, Ricardo and van der Kooy, Eduardo, *Malvinas, la trama secreta*. Buenos Aires: Editorial Sudamericana-Planeta, 1983.

Carnegie Endowment for International Peace and Herbert-Quandt Stiftung, *Islamist Movements and the Democratic Process in the Arab World: Exploring the Gray Zones*, Carnegie Working Paper 67, March 2006.

Carothers, Thomas, *In the Name of Democracy: US Policy Toward Latin America in the Reagan Years*. Berkeley, CA: University of California Press, 1991.

Carothers, Thomas, *Assessing Democracy Assistance: The Case of Romania.* Washington, DC: Carnegie Endowment Book, 1996.

Carothers, Thomas, *Aiding Democracy Abroad: The Learning Curve.* Washington, DC: Carnegie Endowment for International Peace, 1999.

Carrilho, Maria *et al.*, *Portugal na Segunda Guerra Mundial.* Lisbon: Dom Quixote, 1989.

Casas Pardo, José., Martin Cubas, Joaquín and Flores Juberías, Carlos, "Una selección bibliográfica para el estudio de la transición española," *Cuadernos Constitucionales de la Cátedra Fadrique Furió Ceriol* 18–19 (1997): 205–73.

Castilho, José Manuel Tavares, *A ideia de Europa no Marcelismo 1968–1974.* Lisbon: Edições Afrontamento, 2000.

Chalmers, Douglas, "The Politicised State in Latin America," in: James Malloy (ed.), *Authoritarianism and Corporatism in Latin America.* Pittsburg, PA: Pittsburgh University Press, 1977: 23–46.

Cleary, Edward, *The Struggle for Human Rights In Latin America.* Westport, CT: Praeger Books, 1997.

Colomer, José María, *La transición a la democracia: el modelo español.* Barcelona: Anagrama, 1998.

Correia, Pedro Pazarat, "Descolonização," in: J. M. B. Brito (ed.), *Do Marcelismo ao fim do Império.* Lisbon: Círculo dos Leitores, 1999.

Cotarelo, Ramón, "Visiones de la transición," *Revista del Centro de Estudios Constitucionales* (Madrid), 18, 1994: 9–78.

Dahl, Robert A., *Polyarchy: Participation and Opposition.* New Haven, CT: Yale University Press, 1972.

Davies, Norman, *Europe: A History.* London: Random House, 1997.

del Arenal, Celestino, "Democracia y política exterior: el largo camino hacia el cambio," in: J. Vidal (ed.), *España a debate: La política.* Madrid: Tecnos, 1991.

Delgado, Iva, *Portugal e a Guerra Civil de Espanha.* Lisbon: Publicações Europa-América, 1981.

Diamond, Larry, "Democracy in Latin America: Degrees, Illusions, and Directions for Consolidation," in: Tom Farer (ed.), *Collectively Defending Democracy in the Americas.* Baltimore, MD: Johns Hopkins University Press, 1996.

Diamond, Larry, "Promoting Democracy," *Foreign Policy* 87, 1992: 25–46.

Dicey, Albert Venn, *Introduction to the Study of the Law of the Constitution.* London: Macmillan, 1985.

Dulphy, Anne and Léonard, Yves (eds.), *De la dictature à lá démocratie: voies ibériques.* Brussels: Peter-Lang, 2003.

El-Affendi, Abdelwahab, "The Elusive Reformation," *Journal of Democracy* 14 (2), 2003: 34–39.

Enders, Armelle, *Histoire de l'Afrique Lusophone.* Paris: Editions Chandeigne, 1994.

Escudé, Carlos and Cisneros, Andrés, *Historia general de las relaciones exteriores de la República Argentina.* Buenos Aires: GEL, 2000.

Fagnan, Edmond, *Mawerdi: les statuts gouvernementaux.* Paris: Editions Sycamore, 1982.

Fakhry, Majid, *A History of Islamic Philosophy.* London: Longman, 1983.

Falk, Richard, *Human Rights Horizons: The Pursuit of Justice in a Globalising World.* London: Routledge, 2000.

Fernández-Miranda, P., "Bibliografía sobre la transición política española," *Revista de Derecho Político* (Madrid) 30, 1997.

Ferreira, J. M., "A estratégia para a adesão de Portugal às instituições Europeias," in: M. M. T. Ribeiro, A. M. B. Melo and M. C. L. Porto (eds.), *Portugal e a Construção Europeia*. Coimbra: Almedina, 2003.

Fonseca, Gelson, *A legitimidade e outras questões internacionais*. Rio de Janeiro: Paz Terra, 1999.

Frohmann, Alicia, "Chile: External Actors and the Transition to Democracy," in: Tom Farer (ed.), *Beyond Sovereignty: Collectively Defending Democracy in the Americas*. Baltimore, MD: Johns Hopkins University Press, 1996.

Fundação Alexandre de Gusmão, *A palavra do Brasil nas Nações Unidas 1946–1995*. Rio de Janeiro: FUNAG, 1995.

Fusi, Juan Pablo and Palafox, Jordi, *España 1808–1996 el desafío de la modernidad*. Madrid: Espasa, 1997.

Giddens, Anthony, *The Consequences of Modernity*. Cambridge: Polity Press, 1990.

Gil Calvo, Enrique, "Crítica de la transición," *Claves de la Razón Practica* 107, 2000: 9–19.

Glenny, Misha, *The Fall of Yugoslavia: The Third Balkan War*. New York, NY: Penguin Books, 1996.

Graham, Lawrence, "The Economic and Political Outlook for Eastern Europe," *Alcalde: UT Austin Alumni Magazine* 78 (4), 1990: 7–9.

Griffiths, Richard T. and Lie, Bjarde, "Portugal e a EFTA 1969–1973," in: *Portugal e a Europa 50 anos de integração*. Lisbon: Centro de Informação Jacques Delors, 1995.

Grugel, Jean, *Democratization: A Critical Introduction*. New York, NY: Palgrave, 2002.

Güneş-Ayata, Ayşe, "Pluralism versus Authoritarianism: Political Ideas in Two Islamic Publications," in: Richard Tapper (ed.), *Islam in Modern Turkey: Religion, Politics and Literature in a Secular State*. London: IB Tauris, 1994.

Hafez, Mohammed M., *Why Muslims Rebel: Repression and Resistance in the Islamic World*. Boulder, CO: Lynne Reinner, 2002.

Hagopian, Frances, *Traditional Politics and Regime Change in Brazil*. New York, NY: Cambridge University Press, 1996.

Halliday, Fred, *Two Hours that Shook the World – September 11: Causes and Consequences*. London: Saqi Books, 2002.

Halliday, Fred, *100 Myths about the Middle East*. London: Saqi Books, 2006.

Halper, Stefan and Clarke, Jonathan, *America Alone: The Neo-Conservatives and the Global Order*. Cambridge: Cambridge University Press, 2004.

Hastings, Max and Jenkins, Simons, *The Battle for the Falklands*. New York, NY: Norton, 1983.

Hawthorne, Amy, "Middle Eastern Democracy: Is Civil Society the Answer?" *Carnegie Endowment for International Peace Working Paper* 44, 2004.

Hayek, Fredrich, *New Studies in Philosophy, Politics, Economics and the History of Ideas*. London: Routledge & Kegan-Paul, 1978.

Hegel, Georg Wilhelm Friedrich, *Grundlinien der Philosophie des Rechts*. Berlin, 1821.

Hinnebusch, Raymond, *The International Politics of the Middle East*. Manchester: Manchester University Press, 2003.

Hirschman, Albert, *Exit, Voice and Loyalty: Responses to Decline in Firms, Organizations, and States*. Cambridge, MA: Harvard University Press, 2006.

Hirst, Mónica and Bocco, Héctor E., "Cooperação nuclear e integração Brasil-Argentina," *Contexto Internacional* 5 (9), 1989: 63–78.

Hirst, Mónica and Pinheiro, Letícia, "A política exterior do Brasil," *Revista Brasileira de Política Internacional* 38 (1), 1995: 5–23.

Human Rights Watch, *Anti Terror Campaign Cloaking Human Rights Abuse*. New York, NY: HRW, 2002.

Human Rights Watch, *Opportunism in the Face of Tragedy: Repression in the Name of Anti-Terrorism*. New York, NY: HRW, 2002.

Huntington, Samuel P., *Political Order in Changing Societies*. New Haven, CT: Yale University Press, 1968.

Huntington, Samuel P., *The Third Wave: Democratization in the Late Twentieth Century*. Norman, OH: University of Oklahoma Press, 1991.

Hurrell, Andrew, "The International Dimensions of Democratization in Latin America: The Case of Brazil," in: Laurence Whitehead (ed.), *The International Dimensions of Democratization: Europe and the Americas*. Oxford: Oxford University Press, 2001.

Indyk, Martin, "Back to the Bazaar," *Foreign Affairs* 18 (1), 2002: 87–105.

Inglehart, Ronald, *Modernization and Post-Modernization: Cultural, Economic and Cultural Change in 43 Societies*. Princeton, NJ: Princeton University Press, 1997.

International Crisis Group, "Islamism in North Africa: The Legacies of History," *Briefing*, April 2004.

Joffé, George, "Democracy, Islam and the Culture of Modernisation," *Democratization* 4 (3), 1997: 136–8.

Julia, Santos, "Anomalía, dolor y fracaso de España," *Claves de la Razón Practica* 66, 1996: 10–22.

Keck, Margaret E., and Sikkink, Kathryn, *Activists Beyond Borders: Advocacy Networks in International Politics*. Ithaca, NY: Cornell University Press, 1998.

Kedourie, Elie, *Politics in the Middle East*. Oxford: Oxford University Press, 1992.

Keohane, Robert O. and Nye, Joseph (eds.), *Transnational Relations and World Politics*. Cambridge, MA: Harvard University Press, 1972.

Keppel, Giles, *Jihad: On the Trail of Political Islam*. Cambridge, MA: Harvard University Press, 2002.

Keppel, Giles, *Bad Moon Rising: A Chronicle of the Middle East Today*. London: Saqi, 2003.

Kirchheimer, Otto, "Confining Conditions and Revolutionary Breakthroughs," *American Political Science Review* 59, 1965: 964–74.

Kotb, Sayed, *Social Justice in Islam*. Washington, DC: American Council of Learned Societies, 1953.

Lafer, Celso, "Brazil in a New World," in: Abraham F. Lowenthal and Gregory F. Treverton (eds.), *Latin America in a New World*. Boulder, CO: Westview Press, 1994.

Lafer, Celso, "Relações Brasil-Argentina: alcance e significado de uma parceria estratégica," *Contexto Internacional* 19 (2), 1997: 249–65.

Lafer, Celso, "As novas dimensões do desarmamento: os regimes de controle das armas de destruição em massa e as perspectivas para a eliminação das armas nucleares," in: Gilberto Dupas and Tullo Vigevani (eds.), *O Brasil e as novas dimensões da segurança internacional*. São Paulo: Alfa Omega, 1999.

Lafer, Celso and Fonseca, Gelson, "Questões para a diplomacia no contexto internacional das polaridades indefinidas," in: Gelson Fonseca and Sérgio Henrique Nabuco de Castro (eds.), *Temas de Política Externa Brasileira II*. Rio de Janeiro: Paz e Terra, 1994.

Lambton, Anne K. S., *State and Government in Medieval Islam*. Oxford: Oxford University Press, 1981.

Lamego, José, "A emergência da CPLP e as suas consequêncas," in: J. M. Ferreira (ed.), *Política externa e política de defesa do Portugal democrático*. Lisbon: Edições Colibri, 2001.

Lamounier, Bolívar, "Brazil: The Hyperactive Paralysis Syndrome," in: Jorge I. Domínguez and Abraham R. Lowenthal (eds.), *Constructing Democratic Governance: South America in the 1990s*. Baltimore, MD: Johns Hopkins University Press, 1996.

Langhor, Vickie., "An Exit for Arab Autocracy," *Journal of Democracy* 13 (3), 2002: 116–22.

Leitão, Nicolau Andresen, "O convidado inesperado: Portugal e a fundação da EFTA 1956–1960," *Análise Social* (Lisbon) 171, 285–312.

Léonard, Yves, *Lusophonie dans le monde*. Paris: La Documentation Française, 1988.

Lewis, Bernard, *The Emergence of Modern Turkey*. London: RIIA/Oxford University Press, 1961.

Lewis, Bernard, *What went Wrong? Western Impact and Middle Eastern Response*. London: Phoenix, 2002.

Lewis, Bernard, *The Crisis of Islam: Holy War and Unholy Terror*. London: Weidenfeld & Nicolson, 2003.

Linz, Juan J. *The Breakdown of Democratic Regimes*. Baltimore, MD: Johns Hopkins University Press, 1978.

Linz, Juan J., "La transición española en perspectiva comparada," in: Javier Tusell and Álvaro Soto (eds), *Historia de la transición, 1975–1986*. Madrid: Alianza, 1986.

Linz, Juan J. and Stepan, Alfred, "Crises of Efficacy, Legitimacy, and Democratic State 'Presence:' Brazil," in: Juan J. Linz and Alfred Stepan (eds.), *Problems of Democratic Transition and Consolidation: Southern Europe, South America and Post-Communist Europe*. Baltimore, MD: Johns Hopkins University Press, 1996.

Lópes, Ernani Rodrigues, "O processo de integração de Portugal nas Comunidades Europeias: uma avaliação geral década e meia depois," in: M. M. T. Ribeiro, A. M. B. Melo and M. C. L. Porto (eds.), *Portugal e a Construção Europeia*. Coimbra: Almedina, 2003.

Lópes, José da Silva, *Portugal and EC Membership Evaluated*. London: Pinter Publishers, 1993.

Lusotopie, *Géopolitques des mondes lusophones*, Special Issue of *Lusotopie* (Paris) 1–2, 1994: 5–455.

Macedo, Jorge Braga de, *História diplomática de Portugal: Constantes e linhas de força*. Lisbon: Instituto de Defesa Nacional, 1987.

Machiavelli, Niccolò, *The Prince*. New York, NY: Bantam Classics, 1984.

McMillan, Margaret, *Paris 1919: Six Months That Changed the World*. New York: Random House, 2002.

MacQueen, Norri, *The Portuguese Decolonization: Metropolitan Revolution and the Dissolution of Empire*. London: Longman, 1997.

Magalhães, José Calvet de, "Portugal e os Estados Unidosrelações no domínio da defesa," *Estratégia* (Lisbon) 4, 1988.

Magone, José, M., *The Developing Place of Portugal in the European Union*. New Brunswick, NJ: Transaction Publishers, 2004.

Mahoney, James and Rueschmeyer, Dietrich (eds.), *Comparative Historical Analysis*. Cambridge: Cambridge University Press, 2002.

Mainwaring, Scott, "Brazil: Weak Parties, Feckless Democracy," in: Scott Mainwaring and Timothy R. Scully (eds.), *Building Democratic Institutions: Party Systems in Latin America*. Stanford, CA: Stanford University Press, 1995.

Mair, Stefan, "Germany's Stiftungen and Democracy Assistance: Comparative Advantages, New Challenges," in Peter Burnell (ed.), *Democracy Assistance: International Co-operation for Democratization*. London: Frank Cass, 2000.

Malamud, Andrés, *Presidential Democracies and Regional Integration: An Institutional*

Approach to Mercosur, 1985–2000. Unpublished Ph.D dissertation. Florence: European University Institute, 2003.

Marchueta, Maria Regine, *A CPLP e o seu enquadramento.* Lisbon: Ministérios dos Negócios Estrangeiros, 2003.

Martins, Fernando, "A política externa do Estado Novo, o ultramar e a ONU," *Penélope* (Lisbon) 18, 1998.

Martins, Luciano, "The Liberalisation of Authoritarian Rule in Brazil," in: Guillermo O'Donnell, Philippe Schmitter and Laurence Whitehead (eds.), *Transitions from Authoritarian Rule: Latin America.* Baltimore, MD: Johns Hopkins University Press, 1986.

Méndez, Juan E., O'Donnell, Guillermo and Pinheiro, Paulo Sérgio (eds.), *The (Un) Rule of Law and the Underprivileged in Latin America.* Notre Dame, ID: Notre Dame University Press, 1999.

Mernissi, Fatema, *Islam and Democracy: Fear of the Modern World.* London: Virago, 1993.

Mesa, Roberto, *Democracia y política exterior.* Madrid: Eudema, 1988.

Mesa, Roberto, "La normalización exterior de España," in: Ramón Cotarelo (ed.), *Transición política y consolidación democrática: España, 1975–1986.* Madrid: CIS, 1992.

Mesa, Roberto, "De nuevo la transición," *Sistema* 160, 2001: 3–14.

Milner, Helen V., *Interests, Institutions, and Information.* Princeton, NJ: Princeton University Press, 1997.

Ministério de Justiça, *Programa Nacional de Direitos Humanos.* Brasília: Ministério de Justiça, 1996.

Montgomery-Watt, William, *Islamic Philosophy and Theology.* Edinburgh: University of Edinburgh Press, 1962.

Morphet, Sally, "NGOs and the Environment," in: Peter Willetts (ed.), *The Influence of Non-Governmental Organisation in the UN System: The Conscience of the World.* Washington, DC: Brookings Institution, 1996.

Nelson, Joan M., and Eglinton, Stephanie, "The International Donor Community: Conditioned Aid and the Promotion and Defence of Democracy," in: Tom Farer (ed.), *Beyond Sovereignty: Collectively Defending Democracy in the Americas.* Baltimore, MD: Johns Hopkins University Press, 1996.

Neto, Paulo de Mesquita, "Programa Nacional de Direitos Humanos: continuidade ou mudança no tratamento dos direitos humanos no Brasil," *Revista CEJ* 1 (1), 1997: 82–91.

Netton, Ian R., *Muslim Neo-Platonists: An Introduction to the Thought of the Brethren of Purity.* London: George Allen and Unwin, 1982.

Nisbet, Hugh Barr, *Elements of the Philosophy of Right.* Cambridge: Cambridge University Press, 1991.

Norton, Augustus Richard, "Political Reform in the Middle East," in: L. Guazzone (ed.), *The Middle East in Global Change.* Basingstoke: Macmillan, 1997.

Noyon, Jennifer, *Islam, Politics and Pluralism: Theory and Practice in Turkey, Jordan, Tunisia and Algeria.* London: Royal Institute of International Affairs, August 2002.

O'Donnell, Guillermo, *Modernization and Bureaucratic-Authoritarianism.* Berkeley, CA: Institute of International Studies, University of California, 1972.

O'Donnell, Guillermo, Schmitter, Philippe C. and Whitehead, Laurence (eds.), *Transitions from Authoritarian Rule.* Baltimore, MD: Johns Hopkins University Press, 1987.

Oelsner, Andrea, "Two Sides of the Same Coin: Mutual Perceptions and Security Community in the Case of Argentina and Brazil," in: Finn Laursen (ed.), *Comparative Regional Integration: Theoretical Perspectives.* Aldershot: Ashgate, 2003.

Offe, Claus, "Capitalism by Democratic Design? Democratic Theory Facing the Triple Transition in East Central Europe," *Social Research* 58 (4), 1991: 868–72.

Oliveira, César, *Salazar e a Guerra Civil de Espanha*, Lisbon: O Jornal, 1987.

Paradiso, José, *Debates y trayectorias de la política exterior argentina*. Buenos Aires: GEL, 1993.

Passarelli, Bruno, *El delirio armado. Argentina-Chile: La guerra que evitó el Papa*. Buenos Aires: Sudamericana, 1998.

Peña, Félix, *Momentos y perspectivas: La Argentina en el mundo y en América Latina*. Buenos Aires: Editorial UNTREF, 2003.

Pereira, Bernardo Futcher, "Continuidade na Mudança: As relações entre Portugal e os Estados Unidos," *Política Internacional* (Lisbon) 2, 1990.

Pereira, Juan Carlos, "El factor internacional en la transición española: la influencia del contexto internacional y el papel de las potencias centrales," *Studia Historica. Historia Contemporánea*, 22, 2004: 185–224.

Pereira, Juan Carlos, "Europeización de España, españolización de Europa: el dilema histórico resuelto," *Documentación Social* (Madrid) 111, 1998: 39–58.

Pereira, Juan Carlos, "Transición y política exterior: el nuevo reto de la historiografía española," *Ayer* (Madrid) 42, 2001: 97–123.

Pereira, Juan Carlos, (ed.), *La política exterior de España, 1800–2003*. Barcelona: Ariel, 2003.

Pereira, Juan Carlos and Moreno, Antonio, "Spain's Position with Regard to the European Union: In the Centre or on the Periphery of Europe?" in: António Costa Pinto and Nuno Severiano Teixeira (eds.), *Southern Europe and the Making of the European Union, 1945–1980s*. New York, NY: Columbia University Press, 2002.

Phillips, Ann, "Exporting Democracy: German Political Foundations in Central Eastern Europe," *Democratization* 6 (2), 1999: 70–98.

Pinheiro, Paulo Sérgio, "O passado não esta morto, nem ainda é passado," in: Gilberto Dimenstein (ed.), *Democracia em pedaços: as violações de direitos humanos no Brasil*. São Paulo: Companhia das Letras, 1996.

Pinheiro, Paul Sérgio and Neto, Paulo de Mesquita, "Programa Nacional de Direitos Humanos: Avaliação do primeiro ano e perspectivas," *Estudos Avançados* 11 (30), 1997: 117–34.

Pinto, António Costa, "Portugal e a unificação europeia," *Penélope* (Lisbon) 18, 1998.

Pinto, António Costa, *O fim do império português*. Lisbon: Livros Horizonte, 2001.

Pinto, António Costa, "From Africa to Europe: Portugal and European integration," in: António Costa Pinto and Nuno Severiano Teixeira (eds.), *Southern Europe and the Making of the European Union*. New York, NY: Columbia University Press, 2002.

Pinto, António Costa and Teixeira, Nuno Severiano, "From Atlantic Past to European Destiny," in: Wolfram Kaiser and Jürgen Elvert (eds.), *European Union Enlargement: A Comparative History*. London: Routledge, 2004.

Pravda, Alex, "Introduction," in: Jan Zielonka and Alex Pravda (eds.), *Democratic Consolidation in Eastern Europe: International and Transnational Factors*. Oxford: Oxford University Press, 2001.

Pridham, Geoffrey (ed.), *Encouraging Democracy: the International Context of Regime Transition in Southern Europe*. Leicester: Leicester University Press, 1991.

Pridham, Geoffrey, "The International Dimensions of Democratization," in: Laurence Whitehead (ed.), *The International Dimensions of Democratization: Europe and the Americas*. Oxford: Oxford University Press, 1996.

Pridham, Geoffrey, "EU Enlargement and Consolidating Democracy in Post-Communist States: Formality and Reality," *Journal of Common Market Studies* 40, 2002: 953–73.

Pridham, Geoffrey, *Designing Democracy: EU Enlargement and Regime Change in Post-Communist Europe*. London: Palgrave Macmillan, 2005.

Pridham, Geoffrey, Herring, Eric and Sanford, George, *Building Democracy: The International Dimension of Democratization in Eastern Europe*. Leicester: Leicester University Press, 1997.

Putman, Robert D., *Making Democracy Work: Civic Traditions in Modern Italy*. Princeton, NJ: Princeton University Press, 1993.

Rato, Vasco, "A Aliança Atlântica e a consolidação da democracia," in: J. M. Ferreira (ed.), *Política externa e política de defesa do Portugal democrático*. Lisbon: Edições Colibri, 2001.

Ribeiro, Maria Manuela Tavares, "Le Portugal et le noveau défi européen," in: *Fédérations ou Nations*. Paris: Éditions Sedes, 1999.

Ribeiro, Maria Manuela Tavares, Mello, A. M. B. and Porto, Manuel (eds.), *Portugal e a Construção Europeia*. Coimbra: Almedina, 2003.

Ringrose, David, *España 1700–1900: el mito del fracaso*. Madrid: Alianza, 1997.

Robin, Corey, "Fear: A Genealogy of Morals," *Social Research* 67 (4), 2000: 1085–115.

Rock, David, *Argentina, 1516–1982: From Spanish Colonization to the Falklands War*. London: IB Tauris, 1987.

Rodrigues, Luís Nuno, *Salazar e Kennedy: a crise e uma aliança*. Lisbon: Editorial Notícias, 2002.

Roht-Arriaza, Naomi, "The Role of International Actors in National Accountability Processes," in: Alexandra Barahona de Brito *et al.*, (eds.), *The Politics of Memory: Transitional Justice in Democratising Societies*. Oxford: Oxford University Press, 2001.

Rolo, Fernanda, *Portugal e o Plano Marshall*. Lisbon: Editorial Estampa, 1994.

Roper, Jon, *Democracy and its Critics: Anglo-American Democratic Thought in the Nineteenth Century*. London: Unwin-Hyman, 1989.

Rosas, Fernando, *Portugal entre a paz e a guerra*. Lisbon: Editoral Estampa, 1990.

Rosas, Fernando (ed.), *Portugal e a Guerra Civil de Espanha*. Lisbon: Edições Colibri, 1998.

Rowlands, Ian H., "Environment and Development: The Post-UNCED Agenda," *Millenium* 21 (2), 1992: 209–24.

Roy, Olivier, *The Failure of Political Islam*. London: IB Tauris, 1994.

Roy, Olivier, *Vers un islam européen*. Paris: Éditions Esprit, 1999.

Russell, Roberto, *Política exterior y toma de decisiones en América Latina*. Buenos Aires: GEL, 1990.

Rustow, Dankwart, "Transitions to Democracy," *Comparative Politics* 2 (3), 1970: 337–65.

Rustow, Dankwart, "Transitions to Democracy," in: Lisa Anderson (ed.), *Transition to Democracy*. New York, NY: Columbia University Press, 1999.

Sá, T. M., *Os Americanos na Revolução Portuguesa, 1974–1976*. Lisbon: Notícias Editorial, 2004.

Saikal, Amin, *Islam and the West: Conflict or Cooperation?* London: Macmillan Palgrave, 2003.

Sánchez Cevelló, Josep, *El ultimo imperio occidental: La descolonización portuguesa*. Mérida: UNED, 1998.

Sarsar, Saliba, "Can Democracy Prevail?" *Middle East Quarterly* 7 (1), 2000: 39–48.

Schacht, Jospeh and Bosworth, C. E. (eds.), *The Legacy of Islam*. Oxford: Oxford University Press, 1974.

Schmitter, Philippe C., "An Introduction to Southern European Transitions from Authoritarian Rule: Italy, Greece, Portugal, Spain," in: Guillermo O'Donnell, Philippe C. Schmitter and Laurence Whitehead (eds.), *Transitions from Authoritarian Rule*. Baltimore, MD: Johns Hopkins University Press, 1986.

Schmitter, Philippe C., "O contexto internacional da democratização contemporânea," in: Philippe C. Schmitter, *Portugal: do autoritarismo à democracia*. Lisbon: Imprensa de Ciências Sociais, 1999.

Schmitter, Philippe C., "The Influence of the International Context upon the Choice of National Institutions and Policies in Neo-Democracies," in: Laurence Whitehead (ed.), *The International Dimensions of Democratization: Europe and the Americas*. Oxford: Oxford University Press, 2001.

Schneidman, Witney W., *Engaging Africa: Washington and the Fall of Portugal"s Empire*. Oxford: Oxford University Press, 2004.

Schwedler, Jillian (ed.), *Toward Civil Society in the Middle East? A Primer*. Boulder, CO: Lynne Rienner, 1995.

Scott Palmer, David, "Peru: Collectively Defending Democracy in the Western Hemisphere," in: Tom Farer (ed.), *Beyond Sovereignty: Collectively Defending Democracy in the Americas*. Baltimore, MD: Johns Hopkins University Press, 1996.

Seco Serrano, Carlos, "La transición a la democracia, 1975–1982," in: A. Domínguez Ortiz (ed.), *Historia de España*, Vol. 12. Barcelona: Planeta, 1991.

Silva, A. E. D., "O litígio entre Portugal e a ONU," *Análise Social* (Lisbon) 30, 1995.

Sinova, Justino, "XXV aniversario de un éxito incompleto," *La Aventura de la Historia* 26, 2000: 18–32.

Solingen, Etel, "Toward a Democratic Peace in the Middle East," in: Amin Saikal and Albrecht Schnabel (eds.), *Democratization in the Middle East*: Geneva: United Nations University Press, 2003.

Sourdel, Dominique, *Medieval Islam*. London: Routledge & Kegan-Paul, 1983.

Steinmetz, Sara, *Democratic Transition and Human Rights: Perspectives on US Foreign Policy*. New York, NY: State University of New York Press, 1994.

Stepan, Alfred, *Rethinking Military Politics: Brazil and the Southern Cone*. Princeton, NJ: Princeton University Press, 1988.

Stepan, Alfred (ed.), *Democratising Brazil: Problems of Transition and Consolidation*. New York: Oxford University Press, 1989.

Stone, Glyn, *The Oldest Ally: Britain and Portuguese Connection*. London: Boydell, 1994.

Teixeira, Nuno Severiano, *From Neutrality to Alignment: Portugal and the Foundation of the Atlantic Pact*. Florence: European University Institute, 1991.

Teixeira, Nuno Severiano, "Portugal na NATO 1949–1999," *Nação e Defesa* (Lisbon) 89, 1999.

Teixeira, Nuno Severiano, "Between Africa and Europe: Portuguese Foreign Policy 1890–1986," in: António Costa Pinto (ed.), *Contemporary Portugal*. New York, NY: Columbia University Press, 2003.

Teixeira, Nuno Severiano, "Portugal e as guerras da descolonização," in M. T. Barata and Nuno Severiano Teixeira (eds.), *Nova História Militar*, Vol. 4. Lisbon: Círculo de Leitores, 2004.

Telo, António José, *Portugal na Segunda Guerra*, Vols 1 and 2. Lisbon: Veja, 1991.

Telo, António José, *Portugal e a NATO. O reencontro da tradição atlântica*. Lisbon: Cosmos, 1996.

Telo, António José, "Portugal e a NATO, 1949–1976," *Nação e Defesa* (Lisbon) 89, 1999.

Telo, António José, "A revolução e a posição de Portugal no mundo," in: Fernando Rosas (ed.), *Portugal e a transição para a democrcia*. Lisbon: Edições Colibri, 1999.

Telo, António José, "As relações internacionais da transição," in: J. M. B. Brito (ed.), *Do Marcelismo ao fim do Império*. Lisboa: Círculo dos Leitores, 1999.

Telo, António José, *A neutralidade portuguesa e o ouro nazi*. Lisbon: Quetzal, 2000.

Tocqueville, Alexis de, *Selected Letters on Politics and Society*. Oakland, CA: University of California Press, 1985.

Trindade, Antonio Augusto Cançado, "A protecção internacional dos direitos humanos no limiar do novo século e as perspectivas brasileiras," in: *Temas de Política Externa Brasileira*. Brasília: 168–87.

Tulchin, Joseph S., "Continuity and Change in Argentine Foreign Policy," *Latin American Nations in World Politics*. Boulder, CO: Westview Press, 1996.

United Nations, *Arab Human Development Report 2002*. Geneva: UNDP, 2002.

United Nations, *Arab Human Development Report 2003*. Geneva: UNDP, 2003.

Vakili, Vala, *Debating Religion and Politics in Iran: The Political Thought of Adbolkarim Soroush*. New York, NY: Council of Foreign Relations, 1996.

Weber, Max, "Politik als Beruf," in: Max Weber, *Gesammelte Politische Schriften*. Munich: Duncker and Humblot, 1921.

Weschler, Laurence, *A Miracle a Universe: Settling Accounts With Past Torturers*. New York, NY: Pantheon Books, 1990.

Whitehead, Laurence, "International Aspects of Democratisation," in: Guillermo O'Donnell, Philippe C. Schmitter and Laurence Whitehead (eds.), *Transitions from Authoritarian Rule: Comparative Perspectives*. Baltimore, MD: Johns Hopkins University Press, 1986.

Whitehead, Laurence, "Three International Dimensions of Democratization," in: Laurence Whitehead (ed.), *The International Dimensions of Democratization: Europe and the Americas*. Oxford: Oxford University Press, 1996.

Whitehead, Laurence (ed.), *The International Dimensions of Democratization: Europe and the Americas*. Oxford: Oxford University Press, 2001.

Whitehead, Laurence, *Democratization: Theory and Experience*. Oxford: Oxford University Press, 2002.

Willetts, Peter (ed.), *Pressure Groups in the Global System: The Transnational Relations of Issue-Orientated Non-Governmental Organisations*. London: Pinter, 1982.

Willetts, Peter, *The Influence of Non-Governmental Organizations in the UN System: The Conscience of the World*. Washington, DC: Brookings Institution, 1996.

Wood, Allen W., Geuss, Raymond and Skinner, Quentin (eds.), *Hegel: Elements of the Philosophy of Right* (trans. Hugh Barr Nisbet). Cambridge: Cambridge University Press, 1991.

Wrobel, Paulo S., "Brazil and the NPT: Resistance to Change?" *Security Dialogue* 27 (3), 1996: 337–47.

Youngs, Richard, *Europe and the Middle East: In the Shadow of September 11*. Boulder, CO: Lynne Reinner, 2008 (forthcoming).

Zakaria, Fareed, *The Future of Freedom: Illiberal Democracy at Home and Abroad*. New York, NY: W. W. Norton, 2004.

Index

For Product Safety Concerns and Information please contact our EU
representative GPSR@taylorandfrancis.com
Taylor & Francis Verlag GmbH, Kaufingerstraße 24, 80331 München, Germany

www.ingramcontent.com/pod-product-compliance
Lightning Source LLC
Chambersburg PA
CBHW050429280326
41932CB00013BA/2048